The Lively Experiment Continued

Sidney E. Mead

The Lively Experiment Continued

EDITED BY

Jerald C. Brauer

Y^r petitioners have it much in their hearts
. . . to hold forth a lively experiment, that
a flourishing civill State may stand, yea,
and best be maintain'd . . . with a full
liberty in religious concernm^{ts}

JOHN CLARKE

· MERCER ·

ISBN 0-86554-264-3

Library of Congress Cataloging-in-Publication Data
The lively experiment continued.

    Includes index.
    1. Christianity—United States. 2. Church and state—
United States. 3. Liberty. 4. United States—Politics
and government—1783-1865. 5. Mead, Sidney Earl, 1904–
I. Mead, Sidney Earl, 1904–
II. Brauer, Jerald C.
BR515.L58   1987   277.3   87-2752

Contents

Part III
Exploring the Boundaries
133

Introduction

Almost twenty-five years ago Sidney E. Mead's *The Lively Experiment* appeared in print. It was mainly a carefully reworked series of articles that, over the previous decade, had established Mead as a gifted essayist of extraordinary insight and synthetic ability. Prior to the appearance of the volume, historians of various sorts—religious, literary, political, intellectual, social, and cultural—on the American scene had all learned from Mead's provocative insights. Not only was *The Lively Experiment* an apt designation of the shaping of Christianity in America, it was also an appropriate description of what was taking place in historical studies, particularly historical analyses of religion in America. Mead was in the forefront of that lively experiment.

It is fitting that a volume of essays dedicated to Sidney E. Mead be called *The Lively Experiment Continued* and that even the quotation from John Clarke that graced the frontispiece of Mead's book be here repeated. The lively experiment continues both for the Republic and for those who search for ways to better understand and interpret the meaning and status of that experiment for themselves and their age. That point of departure provides coherence for this volume. Whether the essays center on Mead himself, or probe various dimensions and problems of the national experience on which Mead focused, all explore the lively experiment and continue it.

What is to be said about Sidney E. Mead that will not merely repeat the first three chapters of this volume or simply duplicate previous efforts to salute and explain him? It is not inappropriate to lift up, in a simple summary fashion, what I think are Mead's major contributions, though others would prepare a different list and would order their comments in quite another way. At some point a biographer will do justice to the life and work of Sidney E. Mead by placing him in his context, indicating the full depth of his contributions. Meanwhile, perhaps it will suffice to paint a quick impression of an artist as historian—or vice versa—set against the background of his era.

The first thing that strikes one about Sidney E. Mead the scholar is that he succeeded in doing what few in his profession ever achieve: he broke fresh ground. Sturdy son of the Midwest, he exemplified that pioneer quality that marked his forbears—he went ahead and others followed. This was evident early in Mead's career. He did not stand on his mentor's shoulders; rather, he gratefully accepted the tools and materials William Warren Sweet supplied him, and then went off and built his own house to his own specifications. Many came to admire that house, some to criticize, but all learned from it and incorporated many of his plans and ideas in their own houses.

Sidney E. Mead was in the forefront of those who started to reconceptualize American history, and he led the way for all those who sought a new vision of Christianity in American culture. Nowhere is this more evident than in Mead's concern to be highly self-conscious about methodological problems: what is the nature of history; how can one best study it and write about it; what are its limitations and possibilities; what is church history? This represented a radical departure from his predecessors.[1]

Mead's predecessors took as their starting point the absolute necessity of objectivity and the availability of sufficient resources or raw data. A scholar must be free from all assumptions, prejudices, and commitments except to that of the unbiased truth. The historian should not begin with the self but only with a self emptied of all content that might skew evidence. It was the data, the raw "stuff" of history that, if looked at objectively, would provide the answers as to its significance and meaning. In contrast, Mead, along with some of his contemporaries, started with the self. "Know thyself" was his starting point.

Polonius's advice was Mead's historical dictum: "To thine own self be true / And it must follow, as the night the day / Thou cans't not then be false to any man." One takes the first step in becoming a historian by beginning with those questions that plague one, whether born of simple curiosity or of the most complex search for ultimate meaning. Whether those questions are triggered by the present or the past is not the point. What is important is that they are pressing questions that must be answered. Mead never tired of stating that an answer to an unasked question is meaningless.

Mead could follow that path into history because of his conception of the self. It was neither a tabula rasa nor a self-contained entity; rather, the self

---

[1]For a fuller analysis of Mead's point of view as a historian of Christianity in America, see Jerald C. Brauer, "Changing Perspectives on Religion in America," in *Reinterpretation in American Church History,* ed. Jerald C. Brauer (Chicago: University of Chicago Press, 1968) 8-16.

was a biologically conscious center formed of the rich matrix of a culture of a particular time and special place. Language, customs, mores, habits, social structures and institutions, religion, politics, and the family—all those together shaped and formed the self. The self had no choice in initial selection of these formative influences, yet exercised a degree of freedom in living in and through them.

History arises at that point where the self seeks to explore that rich matrix from which it has arisen and in which it lives, in order to make sense of where it is and where it is going. One cannot answer such questions primarily from one's own resources of self. The self is driven to turn to that complex from which one emerges—the past—in order to find the resources to answer the questions.

But the moment a person confronts the past, a basic historical problem arises. It always concerned Mead that the present, out of which we ask questions, assumes a framework of truth and plausibility that usually is at odds with the past's framework. Early in his career he saw and struggled with that problem and insisted that his students both discover that problem and work to find a method that enables a retrieval of answers that are plausible to one's own age. One must respect the past, one's self, and one's own epoch. For Mead the historian is always a constructive mediator and translator between the past and the present, and the mediator and translator must use intelligible language and propositions of truth.

Where should the questing historian look to find answers? Many places in the past provide clues, hints, and materials from which to create answers. Mead affirmed that religion, for him, was the most fruitful resource to explore because it is the heart and soul of culture. He subscribed to Tillich's belief that religion is the substance of culture, and culture is the form of religion. It is because of this unitary conception of religion and culture that one cannot answer the question whether Mead is a historian, or a theologian, or a philosopher who uses historical materials to philosophize or to theologize. He so defines history and the historian's task that a theological and/or philosophical dimension is integral to them. Neither theology nor philosophy has to be dragged kicking and screaming into historical questions. Mead was not a cryptotheologian nor was he a theologian using history for strictly theological purposes.

Obviously Mead had moved away from his mentor and predecessors to build his own house. He admitted that his generation was more concerned with theological problems and issues, and he properly reflected that concern. Mead

did not in any way denigrate his predecessors; he honestly and self-consciously asked a new set of questions that alone could be meaningful to him
and his peers in a way that the questions of his teachers no longer made sense.
By asking different questions of the past, Mead came up with different answers—answers that proved provocative, evocative, and highly meaningful
up to this day.

In the process of rethinking what he called American church history, or
the history of Christianity in America, or even at times religion in America,
Sidney E. Mead produced the first new conception of the history of Christianity in America since Robert Baird. The simplest way to document this
judgment is to point to the fact that Mead relocated the hinge on which the
history of Christianity in America turns. All previous and most present histories of that subject locate that point either in the founding of New England
or in the early nineteenth century.

Those who opted for New England selected the Puritans as the foundation
for American politics, culture, and society. In this view American history was
but the successive transformations of Puritanism in various reincarnations.
Others affirmed the first quarter of the nineteenth century, within the "National Period," as the crux of American history. Voluntarism and the testing
of the frontier shaped the character of America and everything in American
society, including Christianity. Both interpretations made the coming of religious freedom of fundamental importance but only in a derivative way. Puritanism was understood as the root from which constitutionalism grew, with
religious liberty as the outcome of its inner logic. The frontier became the
testing ground for the possibility of religious liberty.

Mead broke with such interpretations and located the hinge of American
religious history, and hence of the total history, in the revolutionary generation. All of American history moved toward that center and out of that center.
Just as the incarnation that revealed the nature and will of God becomes central for a Christian interpretation of universal history, so for Sidney Mead that
incarnation of religious liberty in the Constitution becomes the center for the
whole of religious history in America. He returned again and again to how
that came about, the forces that produced it, and its consequences for national
and even international life. This is the source for the lively experiment with
which we struggle to this day. Here was born the religion of the Republic.
There emerged in that generation a schizophrenia that has cursed American
denominations and American citizens from that day forward.

By relocating the center of the religious history of America, Mead brought to the fore a host of new issues or reinvested old issues with a fresh perspective. In short, Mead turned the attention of historians to a new set of problems in search of a new set of answers. He would be the first to decry any effort to search simply for the new or to run after fads. He might argue, perhaps, that he did not deal with "new" issues at all: the problems of religious liberty, the numerous denominations, pluralism, the frontier, church and state, the Republic are not new. What was and is new is the kind of questions Mead asked concerning them and the nature of the answers he formulated. It is that which gives an integrity to his work and endows it with durability.

We might focus briefly on some of these central issues that Mead reinterpreted in light of the lively experiment. Early in his career Mead was dissatisfied with the way historians analyzed Christianity in America in terms of categories derived from European experience. Here he was at one with William Warren Sweet; however, Sweet continued the basic error but simply relocated the center of the church in those groups that were never predominant in Europe or Britain—the Methodists and Baptists. Mead argued that the categories of church and sect were meaningless in the American context because under New World conditions there was no church as experienced previously in history. The church in America was a collection of numerous denominations, each claiming to be the true church. The ramifications of Mead's analysis of this problem are still under discussion and will remain a permanent part of historical scholarship. A variety of issues such as pluralism, Christianity and society, and Christianity and culture are all related to it.

Mead employed the frontier concept, but in a way totally different from Sweet, Mode, and his contemporaries. By analyzing the frontier in terms of time as well as space, and by stressing its psychological dimensions, Mead reinterpreted how the frontier functioned in American religious history. Just as the Turner hypothesis probably will never totally disappear from American historiography, so Mead's reformulation of the nature and consequence of the frontier in American Christians' experience will long provoke continuing discussion and analysis. This issue is far from exhausted.

One need only point to the continuing discussion of the religion of the Republic or civil religion to mark Mead's fundamental contribution to American religious historiography. As early as 1956 he had adumbrated "the religion of the democratic society and nation," noted its roots in the Enlightenment, and sketched out some of its beliefs. Additional references were made to this religion of the Republic in other of his essays prior to his major article in 1967. Mead has worked with this basic issue throughout his career; it is the center of the hinge on which Christianity in America turns. It was born in the revolutionary generation, nurtured under the Constitution, and has carried the American people through countless trials. It was distorted by the people yet provided a prophetic resource to correct them. The relation between this faith and that professed within the denominations constitutes, in Mead's judgment, the most critical problem for religious life in America.

Mead's concern with all of these fundamental issues was grounded in his own search for coherence; they did not emerge as abstract problems as he read about and observed American history. He makes clear that his present experience triggered many of the questions that led him to probe the past for plausible answers as to how he and his society got where they are. Sidney Mead lived in denominations—several—that claimed to be the "true" church against all others and asserted the necessity of their particular beliefs for the welfare of society. Yet these denominations were part of a Republic, with which their particular beliefs had little to do; and they existed under the conditions of religious liberty, which they did not really understand, and which equated them, without favor or judgment, with all other religious groups. Mead noted that Lutherans, still one of the most doctrinally committed Protestant groups, believed it absolutely essential to have faith in Jesus Christ for salvation yet believed, at the same time, that many ways were possible to get to God. Mead's question of how we got that way was a departure point for his historical analysis.

At the same time he was aware, both in himself and in his society, that the Republic, even with its bumps, warts, and defects, still functioned as a center of sacrality; moreover, there was a theology underlying it to which all Americans subscribed to a greater or a lesser degree. Where did this come from? What were its origins? How has it functioned in American life? What role does it play today? These were but a few of the questions that impelled Mead to search for answers in the American past and to formulate his conception of the religion of the Republic.

At the heart of that religion is the belief in the absolute necessity of religious freedom, forced by American circumstances, but given theoretical underpinning by the religion of the Enlightenment. The denominations have never been able to provide a theological defense of that reality. That failure has created a major problem for them and for American society. To this day the way religion is related to the political order in America remains a complicated and vexing question. One of Mead's solid contributions is his sophisticated and carefully nuanced analysis of the problem. He rejects the "wall of separation" terminology as misleading and inadequate. A purist with regard to questions of religious liberty and nonestablishment, he has placed the so-called church-state question in a different context. None of the related issues—denominationalism, religion of the Republic, religious liberty, "church-state"—is to be seen in isolation or in simple doctrinaire fashion; all are interrelated in the complex fabric of our past that provides the material out of which our culture is woven. The lively experiment will determine whether that fabric will endure or be shredded in the course of history.

What marks Sidney E. Mead among historians of Christianity in America, including both older and younger contemporaries, is his willingness to incorporate and admit openly his ultimate faith in his work as historian. One may disagree or have reservations about the nature of that faith or the way it is related to his practice of his craft. He hides nothing, and one is not given the uneasy feeling that not all the cards are on the table. Modern historians are agreed that one's ultimate assumptions and commitments inevitably are related to one's effort to reconstruct a usable past, but few are prepared to deal openly and consistently with that fact. Mead always practiced in his profession what he preached in his methodology.

It is little wonder that he selected as an epigraph for *The Lively Experiment* the quotation from John Clarke concerning the possibility of a civil state enduring under the conditions of religious liberty. Frankly it was itself a faith, a belief that that which had never happened in history could occur and continue. That is why it was a "lively experiment," a willingness to risk, an acknowledgment of the necessity of living in hope in the face of an intractable past and dubious future. The founding and history of the Republic was and is grounded in faith and hope and remains to this day only a lively experiment. In fact it is, as Mead called it, a "Tragic Drama."

If one has been born into and shaped by such a drama, then one participates, critically or uncritically, in such a faith. It was Mead's exquisite awareness of the tension between that faith and the faith of Christianity that enabled him to make sense of his life. He rehearsed the religious history of America to be able to affirm and live with *its* past as *his* past so he would be free to live in the present and face a precarious future. In doing so he hoped to sensitize those who share that past so that they too would become free to risk through understanding whence they had come and whither they are going.

Sidney Mead devoted his career to sketching the assumptions, the nature, and the consequences of the "lively experiment" both past and present. It was inevitable that essays prepared in his honor would revolve around that concept. Mead once commented to a group of neophyte, would-be professors that when they list course offerings, they can call them what they wish because if they are good, they will be teaching the same thing in any class. Nobody was more careful in the selection and arrangement of words than Mead. He was stating what he believed and practiced as a historian. There is a center and a ground that provides coherence to all one's research, writing, and teaching in history. If one is good, this will be clear and reflect itself in all that is taught. Whichever of Mead's essays or books one reads, that center clearly shines through. Whether it is *The Lively Experiment, The Nation with the Soul of a Church, The Old Religion in the Brave New World, History and Identity,* or *Love and Learning,* Sidney Mead's basic concerns are absolutely clear.[2]

The initial three essays in this volume concentrate on Mead the historian who stands behind the effort to understand and recount that "lively experiment." The first piece attempts to place him in the context of his preparation and first years of teaching. Only in that way can one understand the educational milieu that formed him, how much he owed to it, and how far he moved beyond it. Mead is one of those rare scholars who has become sufficiently free from his own educational past that he can own it fully in his freedom. Of course, that is what education should be about.

Professor Marty's article treats Sidney Mead as teacher. As one who studied with him—Mead would have nobody study "under" him—and as one who succeeded Mead as professor, Marty is the ideal person to comment on this aspect of Mead's work. What emerges is a picture of one whose teaching methods, set of concerns, and approach to his materials and to his students is itself one long, lively experiment.

The essay does not deal with the classroom itself, though it could have. Instead, Marty's concern is to reveal the basic assumptions that were at work in Sidney Mead as teacher. All can share in these because they are encountered in his writing. Mead wrote as he taught, except the latter was usually the first rough draft of the former. Some professors reflect two different personae in the classroom and in their writing. There is nothing wrong in that as long as there is a continuity of assumptions and concerns. Mead is one of those rare professors who has one persona in the classroom and in writing; hence Marty can legitimately get at Mead as teacher through his writing. What Mead

---

[2]For a full bibliography of the works of Sidney E. Mead, see *Love and Learning,* ed. Mary Lou Doyle (Chico CA: New Horizons Press, 1979) 111-22.

wished to explore with his students in class, he also wished to explore with those students, anywhere in the world, who read him.

Professor Engel undertakes an appreciative and critical analysis of the relation between Mead's fundamental assumptions, his faith, and his retrieval of America's past. Engel is concerned to interpret Mead as he wishes to be interpreted, namely as a man who seeks to make sense of American democratic faith so that he can live in it creatively and critically. To do that, Engel argues, one has to engage in a self-conscious apologetic task on behalf of the Republic and its faith. Because theologians have abandoned their responsibility to do that, Mead took it on by default. Engel endeavors to analyze the way that Mead understands the task, how he proposed solutions to the problem, and wherein his answers require further elaboration. Surely this article is itself a contribution to the continuing "lively experiment."

If the first three essays focus on Mead the historian behind the work, the remainder of the volume shifts its attention to several of the many issues on which Mead concentrated in his work. It is not the persistence of these issues that is striking, for Mead did not discover them; rather, it is the way these issues continue to be discussed as a consequence of his work. Each of the remaining essays reveals the extent to which the issues that were central for Mead remain central today.

The second section of the volume deals with the way the "fair experiment," a phrase used by Jefferson, actually worked out in American history. Religious freedom, liberty, the relations between the religious and civil spheres—all parts of Jefferson's "fair experiment"—bulk large in all of Mead's writings. They are the heart of the "lively experiment" as it is carried on by the Republic. Winthrop Hudson, once a fellow student of Mead at Chicago and for a brief time a fellow professor at the Divinity School, turned his attention to the way colonial concern for liberty, both civil and religious, arose. Hudson is interested in the problem of rhetoric—where and how did these phrases originate? William Penn and the New England pulpits are singled out as two primary sources for the sustenance of the idea of English liberties, which were part of American life prior to the Revolution. When New Englanders confronted Jeffersonian and Enlightenment concepts of liberty at the Continental Congress, they were shocked to discover that they were viewed as oppressive and as not genuinely ready for the "lively experiment."

As Edwin Gaustad observes, Mead's two favorite and most frequently quoted presidents were Lincoln and Jefferson. Mead gave much thought to Jefferson and credited him with being the single most important spokesman for the religion of the Republic. As high priest of that religion, Jefferson was the keenest advocate of liberty during the revolutionary generation. Gaustad turns his attention to an analysis of the dimension of liberty in Jefferson's life and thought; and in so doing he continues the discussion to which Mead devoted so much attention. Jefferson's views of political liberty, religious liberty, liberty and equality, and academic liberty are all investigated as together reflecting a single center. Recalling Mead's development of tragedy in the drama of American history, Gaustad highlights the tragedy inherent in Jefferson's attitude towards blacks, given his view of liberty.

Another aspect of the Republic's history that demonstrates both its tragedy and irony is the American treatment of the native Indians. In his provocative essay William McLoughlin acknowledges his debt to Mead both in building on his work and in embracing his style "to think big." Like Mead, McLoughlin is not content to confine himself to a close-knit exposition of a carefully limited topic or problem. That would be so tempting at this stage of American Indian historiography. McLoughlin, instead, is concerned to sort out the factors that combined to produce and sustain a distinct attitude and pattern in the early Indian-white relations in North America. These very attitudes resemble contemporary attitudes toward the peoples of Central and South America. McLoughlin establishes that this attitude was not grounded simply in the land greed of pioneers constantly moving westward and encroaching on Indian lands. There was also a deliberate policy of the national government to handle Native Americans with disdain at worst or indifference at best. Thus McLoughlin searches for the big pattern in the American past and finds it operative in the Republic to this day.

The third section explores various dimensions of the "lively experiment" at greater depth regarding familiar issues and in new directions regarding untouched issues. Sidney Mead expressed the same curiosity as most fellow American historians with regard to the uniqueness of the American experience. He wrestled with that question throughout his career, from his earliest essays to one of his later volumes, *The Old Religion in the Brave New World*. In a profound sense *The Lively Experiment* was devoted to that problem. Our lack of a past—immediate or long range—marked all Americans as unique in a number of subtle and overt ways. This was something new and different for Europeans. Equally new and strange was the immovable reality of pluralism with which all Americans had to live. Richard Hughes, one of Mead's latter-day students at Iowa, devoted his attention to these two fundamental questions in a chapter on early Mormonism, particularly the work and views of Farley P. Pratt. In a fresh and provocative essay, Hughes demonstrates that early Mormonism is an exemplification of the belief in a radical break with the past and the affirmation of a new aeon that led, logically, to a special view of pluralism hardly in keeping with that of the Founding Fathers.

Two of Mead's more recent students each turn their attention to the ubiquitous question of church-state relations, and both evidence the fact that they learned from Sidney Mead. They too wish to explore and expand the boundaries of the "lively experiment." Ronald Flowers focuses on the contemporary struggle as symbolized by the efforts of the religious right, and he posits the central problem as a conflict concerning the nature and function of the Supreme Court in the argument. This carries one into the difficult discussion of the intentions of the Founding Fathers. With considerable subtlety Professor Flowers works his way through the alternative arguments as embodied both in theories and in concrete court decisions. His conclusion is based solidly on the insights of his mentor, Sidney E. Mead.

Professor Manfra takes a quite different approach in working on the same church-state problem, but her efforts also reflect the influence and concerns of Mead. She engages the problem in terms of the American Catholic episcopacy, but does so in a unique way. She suggests looking at the problem in terms of the contribution of the French-born bishops at work in America. This immediately invokes the influence of French Roman Catholic liberals such as Lamennais. The result is an essay that introduces a whole new perspective into the discussion of the reaction of Roman Catholicism to religious liberty in America.

One of Mead's outstanding early students, Robert T. Handy, has moved into territories seldom explored by scholars working in the United States, and he has boldly employed some of Mead's categories to determine if they are applicable to the Canadian scene. What results is a stimulating and informative essay that sheds considerable light on the development of Christianity in America, and at the same time demonstrates possibilities and dangers of employing Mead's categories in similar but different historical circumstances. This is perhaps the first instance of a comparative use of Mead's interpretative categories, and from the degree of success it achieves, it augurs well for similar efforts in the future.

Sidney Mead himself concludes the volume with an essay that presents as clearly as anything that he has written—or, by his own accounting, could write—the major assumptions and premises on which his work rests. Mead interpreted this essay "as analogous to Becker's 'Everyman His Own Historian.' '' Though he felt ill at ease with the term *American church history,* he entitled his reflections, "Reinterpretation in American Church History." The essay, which originated as an address delivered almost twenty years ago, is, according to Mead, "a summation of what I then thought I was about, done four years before my official retirement, and which I am willing to let stand for better or for worse."[3]

It is doubtful that a new work would have added anything to these earlier reflections. Mead's work shows remarkable consistency throughout his career. From his earliest days he held a few distinct and clearly stated assumptions that undergirded his work, and he never attempted to hide them, nor did he ever deviate from them. Out of that set of assumptions Mead adumbrated the fundamental premises "on which [he] would rest an interpretation of the significance, nature, and place of religion in the United States." History was, for Mead, a highly self-conscious act of faith. So it is appropriate that this essay should conclude the volume we are dedicating to him.

So the "lively experiment" continues both in the life and struggles of the nation and in the scholarly work of historians. Mead's essays were intended not just as formal contributions to historical knowledge because, from his point of view, historical knowledge is never simply or even primarily for the professionals. It is for the people. The historian's search for a usable past implies that it is usable for the present and usable not only for the one who unearths its significance but also for an epoch, and for one's fellow human beings who live in that epoch. Sidney Mead's work has spoken to countless literate people who remain concerned about the Republic. Generations of undergraduates, graduate students, fellow professors, and thousands of laity have read and profited from Mead's insights into the Republic and into the American experience.

The "lively experiment" also continues among historians in their effort to interpret the American past. New insights arise, older insights are reappropriated and fine tuned. The set of issues with which Mead worked—frontier, space, time, destiny, Enlightenment religion, pietistic revivalism, religion of the Republic, religion and the political order (church-state), denominationalism, primitivism, religious freedom—all remain central issues for the interpretation of religion in American culture. The essays in this volume hardly

---

[3]Sidney E. Mead to Jerald C. Brauer, 15 March 1986.

begin to describe Mead's continuing impact on the historiography of religion in America. He remains a formidable presence in that ongoing "lively experiment."

Special thanks are due to Kenneth Sawyer for help in preparing the typescript and for editing, and thanks to Steven Cooley for proofreading both galley and page proofs and to Jon Pahl for preparation of the index.

·● Part I ●·

Sidney Mead as Historian, Teacher, and Theologian

American Religious Studies at the University of Chicago

Jerald C. Brauer

The title of this essay sounds excessively parochial, and in a sense it is; however, it is intended only as an introduction to a much larger issue. One must begin somewhere, and it is appropriate in a volume of essays that honor Sidney E. Mead to analyze, for the first time, the historical tradition out of which he emerged and to which he contributed so much. As the successor to William Warren Sweet, who is referred to as the father of American church history, Sidney E. Mead inherited the major emphases of a long tradition at Chicago and reshaped it in a new direction. The problem is that nobody has bothered to analyze that tradition, and must have assumed that it started with Sweet himself.

In recent years increased attention has been paid to the historiography of American church history. A number of studies have devoted attention to its origins, its developments after the turn of the century, its achievements in the period of William Warren Sweet, and the post-Sweet developments beginning with Sidney Mead and continuing to the present day.[1] These studies shed considerable light on the assumptions and the achieve-

---

[1] Henry W. Bowden, *Church History in the Age of Science; Historiographical Patterns in the United States, 1876-1918* (Chapel Hill: University of North Carolina Press, 1971).

ments of what might be called American religious studies as it emerged out of the study of Christianity in this country. Close attention has been paid to the specific books and articles of the so-called "giants" of the field. However, one thing has been completely overlooked: nobody has checked out what these and other scholars actually taught on a year-by-year basis in their various institutions.

It is time for research into local history with regard to those institutions that pioneered teaching religion in America. A closer study of the records of five key theological programs in American higher education probably would reveal considerable information concerning the way American religious studies developed, why it moved in certain directions, and what proved to be the major turning points in its history. Because the purpose of this volume is to honor Professor Mead and because, for a certain time, the University of Chicago Divinity School was looked upon as the center of such studies, it is appropriate to break into this subject by a careful review of what happened in this one institution.

Similar studies should be made with regard to Harvard University and Divinity School, Yale University and Divinity School, Union Theological Seminary and Columbia University, and Princeton Theological Seminary. Probably a thorough study of the records and catalogues of the vast majority of theological institutions in America would not prove too fruitful because few of them appear to have offered specific courses in American church history except for the history of their own denomination. On the other hand, it would be valuable to check those institutions where men like Philip Schaff and other leaders in the American Society of Church History spent their early careers. The point is that one should go beyond a study of books and articles produced by the outstanding historians of Christianity in America. A careful review of what they taught regularly in the classroom along with what was taught by colleagues provides additional material and insight into the development of this discipline.

The method employed for this brief study is that used in local histories. All of the catalogues and announcements of the University of Chicago from its first year through Sidney E. Mead's early years on the Divinity School faculty were checked to determine exactly what was being taught concerning religious developments in this country. This necessitated a review not only of all the Divinity School offerings but also of materials presented in other parts of the university and in the neighboring theological institutions that moved adjacent to the university campus. There was no way to check class records to determine how many, if any, students actually took these courses. The assumption was made that if a course appeared regularly over a period of four or five years, probably it was attended by a sufficient number of students to make its inclusion in the curriculum worthwhile both from the faculty members' point of view and the institution's as well. Taken together, the materials give a unique picture of how the study of religion in America slowly developed until it became a major effort in one of our leading universities. As a result, certain generalizations can be tentatively offered concerning the development of the discipline, and a fuller appreciation of the background and work of Sidney E. Mead is made possible.

For the sake of clarity, the generalizations that emerged from the study of the material will first be outlined. This will be followed by an analysis and presentation of the data derived from the announcements and catalogues. The first generalization substantiated by the data runs contrary to the assumption held by most contemporary historians of Christianity in America. Most scholars were raised on the belief that William Warren Sweet was responsible for developing American church history into a respectable and responsible discipline. Though there is some truth in that view, it tends to downplay extremely important developments prior to his work. There has always been in the University of Chicago a serious and major effort to study and understand the history of Christianity in America. It will be demonstrated that a substantial number of courses on Christianity in America were taught in the Divinity School and in other parts of the university from its very first days. While Sweet made a major contribution to the discipline, he was not responsible for introducing it to the curriculum in depth or breadth.

A second major conclusion is that teaching the history of Christianity in America was never confined simply to the Divinity School. From the earliest days courses were offered in sociology, in literature, and soon thereafter in the History Department. Contemporary scholars are inclined to think that the study of Christianity in America started in seminaries and divinity schools and became known as American church history; then at a much later date other disciplines within universities picked up those aspects of the study and forged ahead of seminaries and divinity schools in their contributions. Research in the other centers mentioned above probably would illustrate the same fact as that established by the data at the

University of Chicago: the study of religion in America never was a monopoly of divinity faculties.

A third finding that emerged from the data was the demonstration that the study of American church history went through several basic changes both as to its concerns and its methods. Not only do the books and articles of various scholars who taught the history of Christianity in America reveal this fact, so do their courses listed in the catalogues. A review of University of Chicago course offerings indicates a clear shift in those courses taught by newcomers—namely, Peter Mode, William Warren Sweet, and Sidney E. Mead.

A fourth conclusion is that the 1920s marked a special turning point in the development of that discipline, and this was due not only to the work of Sweet but also to a number of other people in the university. It is impossible to say whether a similar development occurred in other institutions. In the case of Chicago, there was a special effort to concentrate at much greater depth and breadth on the study of Christianity in America during the 1920s.

Finally, the data reveals a gradual but perceptible broadening of the base for the study of religion in American culture. Though in its initial days study of religion was not confined to the Divinity School, it cannot be denied that that was its center. Under these circumstances, it was understood and taught as American church history. The early work in sociology as well as in divinity expanded as different facets and dimensions of religion in America were picked up by different parts of the university until there was a broad spectrum of coverage in a number of departments. Though it is Sweet who self-consciously thought of himself as responsible for this movement, probably Peter Mode and Sidney E. Mead actually contributed to broadening that base of study, not just in the university but throughout the scholarly world in America.

From the perspective of the development of the study of religion in America, the material divides itself into three convenient categories. The university opened its doors in 1892; and at its inception, Morgan Park Baptist Union Theological Seminary became the Divinity School of the University of Chicago and was moved onto campus in toto. President Harper had long been identified with that institution as one of its leading professors, and when he left to accept a position at Yale, it was with the understanding that he hoped to return someday and found a great research institution in the Midwest. The basic assumptions, concerns, and methods of the study of Christianity in America were relatively unchanged from 1892 until the appointment of Professor Andrew McLaughlin, chairman of the History Department, as chairman of Church History in the Divinity School in 1908. The arrival of Peter Mode in 1913 also marks the new epoch.

The development of the discipline moves naturally from this second stage until the abrupt dismissal of Peter Mode in 1926, to the arrival of Professor William Warren Sweet in 1927. The Mode era is critical in the development of American church history, and it has been too long ignored or overlooked. Obviously the arrival of Professor Sweet marks the third epoch, and this extends until the early 1940s when Professor Mead first began to teach. Upon Sweet's retirement in 1946, Mead became his successor and remained at the University of Chicago until 1961. Hence the threefold division given here is a natural aspect of the data itself and in no sense is it contrived or forced.

When the university opened in 1892, American church history was not a minor concern of the Divinity School but presented a full complement of courses under the direction of two professors. Eri B. Hulbert, dean of the Divinity School and professor of church history, was the man primarily responsible for teaching American church history. He was assisted by Associate Professor Franklin Johnson, who was both professor of church history and of homiletics. Between the two men, twelve full courses were offered in American church history between 1892 and 1893, and an additional course was taught by Hulbert on the American Baptists.[2]

As one surveys the titles of these various courses, one is astonished by the breadth and the variety offered to the students. This was not denominational church history, though its basic interest was in the English "free church" tradition in America. The offerings were divided into two periods, the colonial era and the national era.

The first course listed for the colonial era was entitled "Columbian Period," and consisted of a review of the total background of colonization and the age of discovery, with special concentration on Columbus and his various trips, the discovery and settling of America by the Spaniards in Mexico and South America, and the English and French in North America. There was even an effort to deal with "the effect of the discovery of America on the Caucasian race; on the Indian; on the African. Its influence

---

[2]*Register of the University of Chicago, 1892-1893* (Chicago: University of Chicago Press, 1893) 146. Hereafter cited as *Register* with proper dates.

in the evangelization of the world and the promotion of free civil institutions."[3] Both this course and another full-quarter course on "Catholic and Protestant Beginnings in North America" were taught by Professor Johnson. Regarding the colonial era, Dean Hulbert taught a full-quarter course on "The Pilgrim Fathers and the Plymouth Colony." It traced the entire history of this group—beginning in England, carrying over to Holland, the journey to America, the settlement of the colony, and its later relation with Puritan settlements. Hulbert also taught a full-quarter course on "The Puritan Fathers and the New England Theocracy," and an additional course on "The Struggle for Religious Liberty in Virginia."[4]

Regarding the national era, Johnson taught courses on "Protestant Christianity in the Revolutionary Period," "The New Life in Protestant Religion in the First Half of the 19th Century," "The Progress of the Evangelical Church in the Last Half of the 19th Century," and "The New England Theology." Three courses on topics of the national period were covered by Dean Hulbert. There was a one-quarter survey course on "The Principal Orthodox Denominations in the United States," "The City Missions in America, Including the Growth, Perils and Need of Modern Cities," and "American Missions, Including the History and Progress of Evangelizing Agencies in the United States." During 1893-1894 Professor Charles Richmond Henderson, who was associate professor of sociology in the Department of Sociology offered, for the first time, American church history courses in the Divinity School. One was entitled "Social Conditions in American Rural Life," and the other was called "Modern Cities and Cooperation of the Benevolent Forces."[5]

In 1894-1895 requirements for students in the Divinity School who wished to major in sociology were clearly outlined in the introduction to the offerings of that department. Among the courses of instruction in the Department of Sociology there were several that obviously centered on American ecclesiastical developments. Henderson taught courses on voluntary associations and institutions of organized Christianity as well as on social conditions in American rural life.[6] In the following year the Divinity

---

[3]*Register, 1893-1894*, 203. For a full description, see *Register, 1894-1895*, 269ff.

[4]*Register, 1893-1894*, 206.

[5]Ibid., 203.

[6]Ibid., 206; cf. also *Register, 1897-1898*, 349.

faculty voted to require all students in Divinity, as of 1 July 1896, to take two majors in the Department of Sociology during their first two years, and among these were courses that clearly specialized in developments on the American scene.

In 1898-1899 a full survey course of Christianity in America was given for the first time by Dean Hulbert entitled "History of American Christianity." The course was described as "an outline survey of the entire field of religious history in America from the beginning of colonization to the present time, Spanish, French and English missions, beginning of permanent settlements in Virginia and New England, development of religious liberty in the Colonial period, the Great Awakening and subsequent decline of religion, Revolutionary period, the second awakening, movements in the present century. An effort will be made to view historically the principal denominations, so far as they are products of American soil or contribute to the sum total of American Christianity."[7] That course was to stay in the curriculum for years to come. In 1897-1898 Professor Northrup, chairman of systematic theology, offered for the first time a course that appeared to be in direct competition with Professor Johnson's church-history course. Northrup's course was an advanced seminar on New England theology. Perhaps Johnson's was an introductory course and Northrup's was an advanced course. In any case, they appeared to be treating the same materials though in different departments of the Divinity School.[8]

Until Dean Hulbert's death in 1907, the offerings in the area of American church history were relatively unchanged except for one major shift in 1903. At that point the Department of Sociology, as it existed in the Divinity School, changed its title to the Department of Ecclesiastical Sociology and continued under Chairman Charles Richmond Henderson with the same list of requirements and courses.[9] One could argue that this is the first major turning point in the teaching of American church history. Though Professor Mode did not join the faculty until 1913, certain major changes occurred as early as 1907-1909. Associate Professor Moncrief was given

---

[7]*Register, 1898-1899*, 352.

[8]*Register, 1897-1898*, 339. "New England theology. Being a study especially of the works of Jonathan Edwards, and an examination of the development of doctrine as carried out by subsequent New England theologians, such as Hopkins, Emmons, Bellamy, together with the reaction under Channing and Bushnell."

[9]*Register, 1903-1904*, 393.

additional responsibilities in American church history beyond those that he already had in the History of Christian Thought and Activity. Along with help from Professor Zenos, who was visiting, Moncrief picked up most of the courses previously taught by Hulbert.

At the same time a distinguished new name appears in the Divinity School catalogue—Professor Andrew McLaughlin, world-renowned historian of colonial America. In 1907-1908 he put together Hulbert's two separate courses on Plymouth and the Massachusetts Bay Colony into a new seminar entitled "Plymouth and Massachusetts Bay" and offered it as an advanced course based on the original documents. In addition, he offered in the History Department course #125 entitled "Early Church Organization in America."[10] In the same year, Professor Gerald Birney Smith of the Department of Systematic Theology taught a new course entitled "The Theological Significance of Leading Units of Thought in the 19th Century, Particularly in France, England, and America."[11] This was not added to take up the slack created by Hulbert's death; rather, it appears to be a new course that remained central to the interests of Smith for many years to come, and continued to be offered from time to time as recorded in the announcements.

By 1908 Professor McLaughlin, already serving as chairman of the Department of History in the university, was appointed chairman of the Department of Church History in the Divinity School. In 1908-1909 the offerings in the area of American church history looked drastically different from the earlier program. Two renowned professors from the History Department now formed the nucleus of offerings in this area. Professor McLaughlin, with his new seminar "Plymouth and Massachusetts Bay" and his "The Beginning of American Church History," was joined by Professor William Dodd who, in 1908, offered a seminar on "The Break-up of the Great Churches, 1840-1860"[12] and added two more courses in 1910, "Church and State in the Old South" and a "Seminar: The Religious Development of the Northwest." These courses, together with a carry-over course in the history of American Christianity, now taught by Moncrief, and "The Principal Orthodox Denominations in the United

[10]*Register, 1907-1908*, 383.

[11]*Register, 1908-1909*, 376.

[12]Ibid., 400.

States," a carry-over course also taught by Moncrief, were joined by a new course temporarily offered by Professor Christie entitled "New England Religious History to the Civil War."[13]

In the April 1908 edition of the *University Record,* Henry Pratt Judson commented, in his president's report, on the appointment of Andrew C. McLaughlin, head of the Department of History in the Faculties of Art, Literature, and Science, as head of the Department of Church History in the Divinity School: "This will make it possible to correlate more closely the history work in these two branches of the University to secure greater unity and greater efficiency."[14] Henceforth many of these courses were colisted in both History and American Church History. This marked a new epoch in the history of the university since from that day forward the work of American Church History was closely related to the work of the History Department. Students and faculty moved in both disciplines and made little or no distinction between them. The university did not await the arrival of Professor William Warren Sweet to achieve this; that honor goes to Professor Andrew McLaughlin of the History Department. His presence made Sweet's work that much easier when he arrived on the scene in 1927. He found an open, accepting, and supportive history department that treated him as a colleague and not as an alien. The same held true with regard to students in both Church History and the History Department.

The middle period from 1908 to 1927 was fundamental in reshaping the way religion in America was studied, taught, and correlated with other parts of the university. The period opens, as I noted, with the appointment of McLaughlin as chairman of Church History, and closes with the dismissal of Professor Peter Mode in 1926. In between, a number of important developments occurred: in 1915 the Chicago Theological Seminary moved adjacent to the university; and that year Professor Winfred E. Garrison was appointed dean of Disciples Divinity House (which had affiliated with the university in 1892) and associate professor of the History of American Christianity.[15] Just as university historians brought instruction and cooperation to the Divinity School, so did the arrival of new historical scholars through neighboring institutions accomplish the same end. Among

---

[13]*Register, 1910-1911,* 389.

[14]*University Record* 12:4 (1908): 147.

[15]*Register, 1919-1920,* 356.

these scholars were Henry H. Walker, Harry Thomas Stock, and William E. Barton at Chicago Theological Seminary, and Professor Francis A. Christie of Meadville Theological School.[16]

However, as early as 1913 Peter G. Mode was appointed as an instructor in Church History and Curtis H. Walker was listed in Church History although he was an assistant professor in the History Department. The only course change in 1913-1914 was Professor Mode's taking over the survey course on the history of American Christianity.[17] All other courses in the American field were identical with those offered in the previous two years. The years 1915-1917 saw the addition of a number of courses by Professor Mode. Once again, American church history courses in the colonial period and in the national period were offered, and for the first time there was a course entitled "Experience of the Church in the Frontier States," also initially taught by Professor Mode.

In 1916-1917 Shirley Jackson Case moved into the field of Church History, which was now designated as the History of Christianity and divided in five parts: general introduction; ancient and medieval periods; British and American; modern European; the history of missions; and a set of cognate courses. The latter were drawn widely from the university, particularly the History Department. Among them was a new course listed as History 52 and entitled "The Social Industrial History of the American Colonies" under Associate Professor Jernegan. Also, Professor McLaughlin's course in the constitutional history of the United States was added because of its emphasis on the church-state problem. Professor William H. Dodd's previous course on church and state in the Old South reappeared.[18]

In 1918 Mode shifted the arrangement of the courses in the American field and taught three separate courses, each one quarter long. The first was entitled "American Christianity in the Seventeenth Century," and the second "American Christianity in the Eighteenth Century," and the third "American Christianity in the Nineteenth Century."[19] This was the initial

---

[16]Walker and Barton were on the Chicago Theological Seminary faculty when the school moved to Hyde Park in 1915, after entering into affiliation with the University of Chicago. Stock joined the Chicago Theological Seminary faculty in 1918. Christie first taught in the summer of 1916.

[17]*Register, 1913-1914*, 330.

[18]*Register, 1915-1916*, 283.

[19]*Register, 1918-1919*, 327.

year-long survey of Christianity in America divided on the basis of the seventeenth, eighteenth, and nineteenth centuries with one quarter devoted to each century. Perhaps it was the first such course in the United States. In 1919-1920 Mode appears to have made a slight shift in his earlier frontier course, since it was now listed as "The Frontier in American Christianity." Obviously he was now fully engaged in preparation for his forthcoming book on the frontierization of Christianity in America.

By 1920-1921 fourteen full courses were offered in the American segment of Church History and cognate courses. In addition to his regular courses already listed, Peter Mode offered a new course entitled "American Christianity from the Revolution to Civil War." Professor Stock of Chicago Theological Seminary offered a course in colonial Christianity, along with "The American Church and Social Reform," "The Religious and Social Development of the Middle West," and "The Expansion of the American Church." H. H. Walker from Chicago Theological Seminary offered a course in congregational history and polity. In addition to the usual courses offered by Professor Jernegan and Professor McLaughlin, Professor William H. Dodd introduced a new course entitled "Religious Forces in the Revolution." There were a large number of offerings in the field of religious education, most of which dealt with developments in America. This set of courses was the largest in the American field to date, and it involved a larger number of professors than ever before.[20]

In 1921-1922 only a few new courses appeared. Among them is Professor Mode's "The Small Sects in America" and "Problems in American Religious History." This is probably based on the materials that he employed in his Source Book and Bibliographical Guide in American Church History, which first appeared in 1921. Assistant Professor Stock from Chicago Theological Seminary offered a new course entitled "Division and Union in the American Church," while Professor Willet from Disciples Divinity House offered a course on the history of the Disciples. Professor Davis of Chicago Theological Seminary taught a new course entitled "The Technique of Missionary Expansion in America" and, as usual, a fair number of courses in religious education dealt with American issues.[21] By 1922 eleven full-quarter courses were offered in the area of

[20]Register, 1920-1921, 323.

[21]Register, 1921-1922, 339-40.

American church history alone, and that particular arrangement of courses continued as basic up to the arrival of Professor William Warren Sweet in 1926.[22] A new course in "Fundamentalism, Modernism, and Christianity" was added in the autumn of 1921. Further, a course at Ryder Divinity School on the history of doctrine among Universalists was listed, as was a new course by Winfred E. Garrison, "The Development of Thought among the Disciples."[23]

Several factors are to be noted in this period. When Shirley Jackson Case assumed the chairmanship of the Department of Church History in 1916, Professor McLaughlin and his colleagues from the History Department continued to list their courses in the Divinity School catalogue, first under the Department of Church History and later under cognate fields related to church history. Slowly, these titles disappeared from the course offerings, though some of them continued to be offered in the History Department. This probably is due as much to the reorganization and new structure of the field as it was to any type of problem or tension between professors or departments. There was still free movement between both professors and students in History and Church History.

So far as the American field is concerned, the work of Professor Mode dominated that activity from approximately 1916 until his dismissal in 1926. In that short time Mode reorganized all of the offerings in American Church History, developed a set of new courses, and wrote two major books. In 1921 the appearance of his *Source Book and Bibliographical Guide to American Church History* marked a milestone in the emergence of that discipline. It was not until the appearance of the Smith, Handy, Loetscher volumes in 1960 that the Mode volume was superseded. It contained an excellent collection of sources that were well balanced and judiciously selected. There were also good introductions as well as a remarkably thoughtful yet concise bibliography. It was an indispensable tool to all scholars in American studies for almost forty years.[24]

In 1923 his second book appeared, *The Frontier Spirit in American Christianity,* a direct outgrowth of the courses he had been teaching since

---

[22]Ibid., 339.

[23]Ibid.

[24]Peter G. Mode, *Source Book and Bibliographical Guide for American Church History* (Menasha WI: George Bantu Co., 1921).

1916 regarding that problem. He was the first to apply the Frederick Jackson Turner hypothesis to the study of Christianity in the American scene. The book was exploratory and introductory, yet within its short scope it succeeded in provoking a number of basic questions that historians wrestled with for the next half century.[25] One could argue that it was a somewhat unimaginative application of the frontier hypothesis to the development of Christianity in America, but that is beside the point. Mode's effort represented the first attempt to understand American religious developments from a fresh perspective. This was his particular way of participating in the assumptions of his fellow church historians in the Chicago school who were busily engaged in developing the socioenvironmental approach that distinguished them. Peter Mode probably stood closer to Shirley Jackson Case on this point than did any of his colleagues.

In the autumn of 1927 William Warren Sweet arrived at the Divinity School to join the faculty of what he called "the largest group of church historians to be found in any University center," and he might have added, "any place in the world."[26] Prior to Sweet's arrival it included Shirley M.M. Jackson Case, W. E. Garrison, John T. McNeill, Matthew Spinka, Wilhelm Pauck, and Charles Lyttle. In addition to responsibility for the history and theology of the Disciples of Christ denomination, Garrison taught the history of Christianity in America with a special concern for post-Civil War developments.

Though he used the term, Sweet did not think of himself as a "church" historian but rather as a historian of religious developments in American culture. He pointed out that he had never had a course in that field, "for American church history as a field of teaching and research was at that time nonexistent" and "few if any such courses [were] offered anywhere."[27] Later he was to discover that courses at the Yale and Harvard Divinity Schools were taught by the deans Luther Weigel and Willard Sperry, who did it as administrators rather than as scholars. This prompted Mead to make the tongue-in-check comment, many years later, that there is "one sound

---

[25]Peter G. Mode, *The Frontier Spirit in American Christianity* (New York: The Macmillan Co., 1923).

[26]W. W. Sweet, "Every Dog Has His Day and I've Had Mine," *Divinity School News* 13:3 (1 August 1946): 4.

[27]Ibid., 5.

. . . justification for having the chief administrator of a seminary teach American Church History. It is that the genius of the American denominations is such that it is probably more readily grasped and articulated by the administrative than the scholarly or rationally ordered mentality." Also, it "will be enlightening because he will communicate to the students an administrative and hence political view of denominational life, which will be practically useful to them as ministers."[28]

Sweet had never taught a course in American church history, and he certainly did not come to Chicago to train preachers. He answered Shirley Jackson Case's call to come to the Divinity School because he was "offered . . . a chance of helping to develop an entirely new field of history," and he was given the support and resources to accomplish the task. Sweet was convinced that there was no other university in the United States where the "experiment could have been inaugurated so successfully." At Chicago he did not have to face "that absurd position" that his subject "could not be treated with sufficient objectivity." Professors William Dodd and Marcus Jernegan had encouraged University of Chicago history students to pursue doctoral dissertations in American religion. Sweet stated that "Professor Dodd's presence at the University had more to do with my coming than any other single factor."[29]

After his arrival Sweet immediately picked up most of the courses taught by Mode, including the one on the church and the early frontier, and added two new courses in his first year. By 1926 he was teaching one course entitled "Slavery and American Churches" and another one entitled "The Great Democratic Churches in America." These two subjects were to remain a center of interest throughout his career.[30] A visiting professor, William Rockwell from Union Theological Seminary, who normally taught at Chicago during the summer term, also helped to fill in after Mode's departure, but only during the year 1926-1927.

By 1927-1928 Sweet was in full control and made a number of basic shifts in course offerings. In place of the earlier course taught by Mode and Rockwell, "American Christianity: the National Period," Sweet substi-

---

[28]Sidney E. Mead, "The Context and Content of American Church History" (mimeographed but unpublished paper) 9.

[29]Ibid., 6.

[30]*Register, 1926-1927*, 269.

tuted a new course (with a new number) entitled "Nationalizing the American Churches, 1775-1800," thereby combining the revolutionary and the constitution-making process in one period. In his second year he added a third course, "The Rise and Development of Negro Churches in the United States,"[31] which was probably the first time that a course of this type was taught in an American institution outside the black educational community. Unfortunately, Sweet did not teach the course often and did not do much writing on the subject, although a number of his students wrote dissertations in that area.

In the late 1920s, in addition to Sweet's work, Arthur Cushman McGiffert, Jr. joined the faculty of Chicago Theological Seminary and developed a series of courses on theology in America beginning with his "Types of American Theology," first offered in 1927-1928.[32] A year earlier Professor Holt of Chicago Theological Seminary and Professor Paul Douglas of the university Economics Department joined in a course that was entitled "Research in Relations between American Religious and Economic Development."[33] In addition, Professors Holt and Kincheloe, who taught social ethics at Chicago Theological Seminary, began to offer a large number of courses involving various aspects of sociology of American religion.[34]

Two professors in the Department of Religious Education in the Divinity School also entered the American field when Professor R. H. Edwards offered "Moral Conditions in American Colleges," and Professor Charles Holman offered "The Church in America." By 1929-1930 Sweet had added an additional five new courses; so he was offering a total of twelve different courses during a two-year period, or six courses each year exclusively in American church history. The new materials included "The Popular Churches in the Early Frontier," "The Makers of American

---

[31]Register, 1927-1928, 253.

[32]Ibid., 254. At that time certain courses and professors from Chicago Theological Seminary were approved for the Divinity School program.

[33]Register, 1926-1927, 266.

[34]Professor Hutchinson offered "Ethical Problems in Chicago. A Social Observation and Discussion Course"; Professor Holt again taught "The Development of the Social Consciousness of the American Church" and "Town and Country Church," concentrating exclusively on the American scene. All of Kincheloe's research and teaching focused on the United States, Register 1927-1928, 255.

Christianity," "America as a Mission Field," "The Era of the Isms," and "Roman Christianity in Colonial Latin America." A. C. McGiffert, Jr. from Chicago Theological Seminary added two new courses, "Development of American Religious Thought" and "Jonathan Edwards."[35]

Sweet continued the same series of courses in 1930-1931, and his colleague from Chicago Theological Seminary, Arthur E. Holt from the Department of Christian Theology and Ethics, continued to offer courses in the development of social consciousness in America, the relation between church and the family in America, and American developments in town and country churches.[36] No other university in America offered such a full, rich, diversified program in American religious studies.

In 1931 there was a major curriculum revision. This marked the first time that "Christianity and the American People" became a segment of a three-course sequence to be taken by all students. Probably for the first time in American higher education, a nondenominational history of Christianity in America was required of all students. In that same year Sweet added a new course titled "Slavery Schisms within the American Churches," which indicated his continuing and growing interest in the whole question of blacks in American Christianity. In addition, he added a new course on Christianity from 1865 to 1914 entitled "The Church in the Age of Big Business,"[37] and in 1932-1933 he offered another new course, "America as a Mission Field," which was similar to the old courses taught by Hulbert and Moncrief.[38] Though 1934-1935 witnessed further major revisions in the total curriculum—one of the Divinity School's favorite pastimes—most of Sweet's work remained, but it now appeared under different titles in several cases.

A. C. McGiffert, Jr. offered a new course entitled "Seminar in 19th Century Religious Thought," and a year later Professor W. E. Garrison taught "Christianity and the Federal Mission, 1830-1930," which was later

---

[35]*Register, 1929-1930*, 253-54.

[36]*University of Chicago Announcements, The Divinity School, 1930-1931*, 30:19:54-55. Hereafter cited as *D. S. Announcements*.

[37]Ibid., 47, 52, 53.

[38]*D. S. Announcements, 1932-1933*, 46.

to become a book.[39] It is important also to note that in this same period, in the early 1930s, Professor Percy Boynton taught in the English Department and educated two of the outstanding scholars in New England Puritanism.[40] Perry Miller and Clarence Faust received their degrees within seven years of each other. Obviously, a good deal of the creative work analyzing religious developments in American colonial life continued to occur outside the Divinity School, though no specific courses taught by Boynton appear to have been New England Puritan literature as such. Professor Sweet did not retire until 1946, but except for one or two things, his set of courses remained unchanged until his retirement.[41]

At the time of his retirement Sweet stood as the premier historian of Christianity in America. He built solidly on the work of his predecessors, though he seldom acknowledged them either in class or in his writing. It is unnecessary to comment further on the interpretive schema that Sweet brought to his studies. This has been well documented in a number of books and articles.[42] Suffice it to say at this point that in addition to those contributions, he focused attention on the serious, scholarly, nondenominational study of Christianity in the American scene.

Sweet was fortunate to move into a situation that had been shaped by McLaughlin, Dodd, and Peter Mode. He did not reject that tradition; instead, he strengthened it so the study of Christianity in America could be viewed as historical study and not as a part of a seminary curriculum. He popularized this view through a large number of books, particularly through

---

[39]*D. S. Announcements, 1934-1935*, 31. In 1936-1937 Garrison took a further step toward his book when he offered "The Church in the Post-War World." Cf. Winifred E. Garrison, *The March of Faith: The Story of Religion in America since 1865* (New York: Harper & Brothers, 1933).

[40]Professor Boynton's courses dealing with American subjects included: "American Literature: the New England Group" (a study of the major New England poets and essayists and of their immediate followers); "Studies in American Literature: Colonial Period"; "Studies in American Literature: The Transcendentalists"; "Colonial American Literature"; "Problems in New England Literature."

[41]In 1939-1940, Sweet offered, for the first time, his course on "Revivalism in America." *D. S. Announcements, 1939-1941*, 31.

[42]Sidney E. Mead, "Professor Sweet's Religion and Culture in America: a Review Article," *Church History* 22 (March 1953). See also James L. Ash, Jr., *Protestantism and the American University: An Intellectual Biography of William Warren Sweet* (Dallas: Southern Methodist University Press, 1982).

several excellent surveys of American Christianity. Perhaps above all, he is important for having insisted on collecting source materials for the university library. In this he had the full support and encouragement of Shirley Case and Dean Mathews.

In addition to building one of the finest collections on American religious studies in America, he also edited a series of volumes pertaining to religion on the American frontier.[43] In his retirement address Sweet, justifiably, pointed with pride to the fact that, partly as a result of his work, materials and concerns had been made available to the general American historian "as will enable him to appreciate adequately the part played by religion in the development of American civilization." Moreover, "the scope of American history has been broadened to include the great civilizing and cultural forces which formerly were almost completely omitted."[44]

Sweet accomplished most of the goals he established for himself when he came to Chicago in 1927. He transcended denominational history and wrote what was accepted as "objective" history by faculty in America's history departments. He provided professors and graduate students with a mountain of material on which they could work. More than thirty graduates received a Ph.D. in American religious history under the tutelage of William Warren Sweet. He did not break with the Baird-Dorchester interpretation of religion in America, but he reformulated and updated their major premises and clothed them in contemporary intellectual assumptions so they made sense to his peers both in history and theology. Sweet made Chicago the center of serious, disciplined graduate study of religion in American culture.

In the highest form of tribute a scholar can pay to his mentor, Sidney E. Mead wrote both a telling critique and a perceptive appreciation of Sweet's work in *Church History*.[45] The article was important not only for its sophisticated analysis of Sweet, but it also marked a turning point in historiography. Mead placed Sweet in the middle of a particular concep-

---

[43]William Warren Sweet, *Religion on the American Frontier*, vol. 1: *The Baptists, 1783-1830* (New York: Henry Holt, 1931); vol. 2: *The Presbyterians, 1783-1840* (New York: Harper, 1936); vol. 3: *The Congregationalists, 1783-1850* (Chicago: University of Chicago Press, 1946); vol. 4: *The Methodists, 1783-1849* (Chicago: University of Chicago Press, 1946).

[44]Sweet, "Every Dog . . . ," 6.

[45]Mead, "Professor Sweet's Religion and Culture," 33-49.

tion of history that dominated Sweet's generation and saluted him as a practitioner par excellence from within that circle. However, Mead pointed out that a new set of assumptions, particularly theological, prevailed in the new generation and so "this generation must try the basic premises which informed the historiography of its fathers in the crucible of its own theological orientation." Thus Sweet could be appreciated and criticized in terms of his performance within his "climate of opinion," but historians must also be willing to press criticism from within their own newly emerged "climate of opinion."[46]

Sidney E. Mead proved to be not only Sweet's most brilliant student but also the scholar who moved the entire discipline in a new direction—the first fresh and new interpretation of the nature of religion in the American context since the Baird-Dorchester-Sweet vision. Mead first joined the Divinity School faculty in 1941; Sweet did not leave until June 1946. Though gracious to his younger colleague, Sweet did not permit him to teach anything that had been offered, past or present, under Sweet's name. Apparently that was typical of professors in those days, particularly those who felt that they had staked out a field of their own. It must not have been easy for a newly minted Ph.D. to teach on the same faculty with his mentor.

A survey of courses offered by Mead in his first four or five years yields strange results because it was difficult for a newly arrived scholar to find interstices in a field blanketed by a senior professor. Though Mead taught jointly with William Clayton Bower (of religious education) a course entitled "The Church and Modern World" in 1943, 1944, and 1945, the new center of his work was revealed in his second quarter in residence, "The History of Christian Thought in America," which he was to teach regularly throughout his tenure in the Divinity School.[47] Sweet never taught a course of that type. Perhaps that is why he wanted Mead on the faculty.

Mead taught a series of new courses never before offered in the Divinity School, "Revivalism and Christian Thought 1830-1860," "Introduction to the Literature of Christianity III—Thomas Hooker to Lyman Abbott," "The History of American Culture, 1815-1860," "American Religious Movements," and "Topics in the Study of American Christianity." In the winter quarter of 1946, Mead taught a course on "Sources and

---

[46]Ibid., 34, 46.

[47]*D. S. Announcements, 1941-1942*, 30.

Methods in American Church History.'' Several of these became permanent in Mead's repertoire and reflected the basis for his reinterpretation of Christianity in America. His course on ''Christian Thought in America'' developed into three parts, one offered each quarter. ''Topics in the Study of American Christianity'' grew from an appraisal of major issues in the development of Christianity in America to explorations of problems on which theses were or could be written. The ''History of American Culture'' was transformed, after Sweet's retirement, into a three-quarter analysis of the development of Christianity in American culture.[48]

Perhaps the course that first reflected most accurately Sidney Mead's new direction was that initial offering on ''Sources and Methods.'' As early as 1946 Mead had broken with the assumptions and presuppositions, the ''climate of opinion,'' of Sweet and his peers. Later that year the shift was documented for the entire historical profession in a work that Mead required all his students to read.[49] It is instructive to note what Mead required of his students in that course both in the way of reading and writing, for it clearly establishes a new direction in the historical study of Christianity both at Chicago and throughout the United States.

The purpose of the course was twofold. Mead wished to introduce students simultaneously to sources for the study of Christianity in America and to the problems of method in employing those sources. To achieve those goals he required a short paper each week throughout the quarter and a larger paper at the conclusion of the quarter. One set of short papers was based on an analytic reading of a series of books that demonstrated a particular ''climate of opinion.'' To that end students read and reported on Walter Lippman, *Preface to Morals;* J. H. Randall, *Making of the Modern Mind;* J. Robinson, *Mind in the Making;* A. O. Lovejoy, *The Great Chain of Being;* A. N. Whitehead, *Adventures of Ideas;* Charles A. Beard, *The Discussion of Human Affairs;* and others. Note how many of these authors are quoted by Mead throughout his writings, from his first articles to his last books.

At the same time students struggled with the question of how one interprets the claims and actions of individuals and movements that operate out of a different ''climate of opinion'' from that of the contemporary his-

---

[48]See *D. S. Announcements* for the years 1942-1948.

[49]J. H. Randall and George Haines, ''Controlling Assumptions in the Practice of American Historians,'' *Theory and Practice in Historical Study* . . . , Bulletin 54, Social Science Research Council, 1946.

torian. Students were introduced to the collection of Peter Force's *Tracts* and required to wrestle with the question of how fifteenth- and sixteenth-century people defended their reasons for colonizing the New World. A difficult task for the new graduate student was to determine what was in the realm of the possible and why it was so for Jonathan Edwards in his *Narrative of Surprising Conversions.* A similar exercise was undertaken with Tom Paine's *Age of Reason.* For my final-quarter paper I worked on the question of "The Origin of the Book of Mormon" by making a careful comparison and analysis of Mormon and non-Mormon historical answers to that question.

During his first five years at the University of Chicago, Sidney E. Mead adumbrated the basic approach and set of issues with which he was to work throughout his career. He was the first historian of Christianity in America to reflect the new "climate of opinion" and to document that in his teaching and writing. At the very beginning of that January 1946 class, Mead announced his basic historical task (derived from Lincoln): that the historian cannot know what to do unless he first knows whence he has come and whither he is tending. Further, argued Mead, this is the problem for every culture and every society, and for every individual within that society; hence the historian, a product of that society, is answering a deeply personal question while answering a historical question about an epoch or an age past.

Mead stood as the heir of Sweet, Case, Dodd, and McLaughlin, but moved church history into a new epoch. For those of us who studied with both Sweet and Mead, it was difficult—if not impossible—to note their connection. Indeed my generation of students was aligned with Mead because he was posing our questions and beginning to find answers that made sense to us. Henceforth historians of religion in America, building on the achievements of their predecessors, moved in a new direction. Mead was a true heir of the long tradition at Chicago. It could be argued that Sweet built on that tradition by bringing it all to a comprehensive summary in a burst of research, writing, and teaching that reflected the consensus of his epoch. Yet Mead built on that tradition and brilliantly carried it through his research, writing, and teaching into a vital, fresh, and new perspective.

·● 2 ●·

The Historian as Teacher

Martin E. Marty

The writing career of Sidney E. Mead resembles that of Cotton Mather in an important respect. On one hand, in *The Lively Experiment* and subsequent books[1] he has been writing his *Magnalia Christi Americana*, telling "the *Wonders* of the CHRISTIAN RELIGION, flying from the Deprivations of *Europe*, to the *American Strand*."[2] His interpretation is widely regarded as the most influential of his generation. On the other hand he has been busy with *Bonifacius*, "Essays to Do Good," always remembering with his

---

[1]*The Lively Experiment* (New York: Harper & Row, 1965) is a collection of nine essays that appeared between 1954 and 1956 in various journals. Mead's other books are:

Nathaniel William Taylor, 1786-1858: A Connecticut Liberal (Chicago: University of Chicago Press, 1942). [A revision of his doctoral dissertation.]

The Nation with the Soul of a Church (New York: Harper & Row, 1975).

The Old Religion in the Brave New World: Reflections on the Relation between Christendom and the Republic (Berkeley: University of California Press, 1977).

Love and Learning, ed. Mary Lou Doyle (Chico CA: New Horizons Press, 1978).

History and Identity (Missoula MT: Scholars Press, 1979). [AAR Studies in Religion, no. 19.]

His teaching career has been spent at the University of Chicago (1941-1960), at the Southern California School of Theology at Claremont (1960-1964), and the University of Iowa (1964-1973).

[2]Portions of Mather's book are reprinted in Perry Miller and Thomas W. Johnson, eds., *The Puritans: A Sourcebook of Their Writings* (New York: Harper & Row, Torchbooks edition, 1963) 1:162ff. See esp. 163.

predecessor especially that "the SCHOOLMASTER has manifold *opportunities* to *do good.*"[3]

Few observers would have noticed the Mather-Mead resemblance or have been bold enough to point out the comparisons had not Mead himself done so. Tongue tucked lightly in cheek, he once described how and why he had felt so free to comment on subjects reasonably remote from conventional historians' purviews. The two elements in his program, he declared, were united. On one occasion he spoke of one of his "essays to do good" as making a contribution to the kind of self-understanding that is "the peculiar province of historical interpretations to provide."[4]

His "essays to do good" have revealed Mead to be preeminently the historian as teacher, a rather surprising role for a well-known writer-historian. It is not unusual for a gifted teacher in the historical profession to segregate pedagogical topics and to write articles or books on the art of teaching history or to reflect on historical method.[5] Much rarer are the instances in which a historian almost never isolates and fully develops the theme, but whose whole literary corpus displays a concern for students and suggests that the teacher has been learning from the classroom. The present essay, which at least intends to "do good," will trace the teaching theme through Mead's writings. I shall avoid comment on the oral tradition, which is less accessible for public examination, and shall make no comment on his general approach to history unless it bears directly on his stance as a teacher.

---

[3]*Bonifacius: An Essay upon the Good* has been reprinted in *The John Harvard Library,* ed. David Levin (Cambridge MA: The Belknap Press of Harvard University Press, 1966); see 83.

[4]"The Rise of the Evangelical Concept of the Ministry in America (1607-1850)," in H. R. Niebuhr and D. D. Williams, eds., *The Ministry in Historical Perspectives* (New York: Harper & Brothers, 1956) 207, 237.

[5]It should be noted that in this essay I am shunning the temptation to engage in personal reminiscences of the classroom experience, though those who have been Mead's graduate students share warm appreciation of that setting and are prepared to illustrate the present set of topics with anecdotes. I would like to thank Mr. Paul Carnahan for his extensive bibliographical assistance as this essay was being prepared. The kind of literature to which I have reference here is typified by Allan Nevins, *The Gateway to History* (Chicago: Quadrangle, 1963); Page Smith, *The Historian and History* (New York: Knopf, 1964); G. R. Elton, *The Practice of History* (London: Crowell, 1967); G. Kitson Clark, *The Critical Historian* (New York: Basic Books, 1967).

I
The Pilgrim Picture:
Five Features

Sidney Mead has *almost never* isolated the teaching theme, but at least one apparently modest exception exists in the form of a homily addressed to a community of theological students and professors. Only seven pages long and deceptively simple in plot, it could easily be overlooked. The main lines of his understanding of the teacher's role were set forth there, however. He conjured the picture of the teacher as Pilgrim, and spoke of the Pilgrim's alienation. To this he added the confession that he had been ready to trust his feelings and that he needed to work in the context of a community. With St. Paul as his reference, he half-playfully located the teacher between "inspired preachers" and "wonder-workers," reminding his hearers that the teacher was neither of these.

He then outlined the five elements in teaching, elements that were to reappear throughout his essays. "This, then, is my teacher—a Pilgrim called to *be* something, to *know* something thoroughly, to *communicate* what he knows, to *awaken* and *inspire,* and to *judge.*" First, he is to *be* in community; then, he is to *know* by seeing something "in the longest perspective and with all its implications." The historian especially is to *communicate* knowledge of the particulars of his subject matter "in the perspective of their universal and lasting significance." At this point, with John Cotton, he parted company with the positivistic historians who "take the easy way of communicating only a series of the particular facts of [their] subject matter." Cotton has said that "the study and knowledge of the passing away of one generation after another sheweth us [only] our mortality and misery, and thereby yieldeth us grief and vexation, but no relief, if we rest there."

Fourth, so far as *awakening* and *inspiring* are concerned, "the teacher is saddened when the student imitates *him,* for he is not called unduly to influence students." As *judge,* finally, the historian rates the competence of students, but then prays, "God give me the courage to flunk my best friend tomorrow if necessary—and courage sincerely to weep with him afterward—and the ability to communicate to him why it was necessary so that he may become a constructive participant in the action." Professor Mead's pilgrimage may have taken him far from the context in which he spoke all those words, but the motifs remained consistent whenever he later spoke of teaching or of the historian as teacher.[6]

II
A Student's Historian

From time to time Mead has been called "a historian's historian," which is probably a way of saying that he developed his craft highly but was not read widely by the general public. But he clearly has not seen himself as responsible first of all to his collegial and professional peers. His fellow pilgrims are students, whether in his discipline or in others. During the widely advertised student revolution of the 1960s, some professors were accused of having been tempted to cater to students in a pathetic quest to cross generation gaps, become relevant, relive lost youth, or because they shunned the rigors of their disciplines. Mead cannot be accused of having been a convert to such a course, nor had he been affectatiously cultivating a "Mr. Chips" image. The influence of students on him and his whole view of history shows up too frequently in incidental and accidental ways to permit such interpretations.

Sometimes he could be polemical on this point: "I agree with David Riesman that American education began to go astray when professors ceased to teach and write for students and began to teach and write for their peers in their respective disciplines."[7] He could also be confessional:

> I was a historian of the historians, trained in all of the techniques of the craft, and if not the chief of sinners in this respect, it was not because I lacked zeal. It was the students, who are not always such sources of blinding light, who met me on the historians' Damascus Road and began to turn me about. They made me think about what I was doing, and pressed me to expose my assumptions and premises—which being a modest scholar I was very reluctant to do. What the students began in me, my colleagues on the faculty pushed me to complete. Not that I have arrived.[8]

Such an attitude implies considerable confidence in students. In one graduate-

---

[6]"Teaching as an Aspect of Our Vocation as Christians," *Divinity School News* 17 (1 February 1950): 1-6.

[7]"Character and Continuity," *Criterion* 9 (Winter 1970): 26.

[8]"Historical Studies and the Ministry—Address for Summer Convocation," *Chicago Lutheran Theological Seminary Record* 58 (Autumn 1953): 34.

school orientation address he spoke in the name of the whole school but may only have been accurately describing his own assumptions in detail.

> The student is looked upon as an individual, a person, who comes here with all the attributes of more or less mature personality—including a faith he actually lives by, a sense of direction, and a more or less coherent and integrated set of ideas about himself and the cosmos in which he lives and moves and has his being. . . . He must begin where he is. There is no other place to begin.[9]

At the same time Mead did not indulge the student or accept the mystique associated with the noble savagery or the innocence of the student's "beginning where he is." A kind of game or even a war between faculty and students, particularly in the field of history, has to be waged:

> In history as elsewhere, nothing is as useless as the answer to an unasked question. This suggests . . . that the reason why some courses in history seem dull to the students is that they are not interested in the questions the Professor is answering. Half the job of teaching history is in getting the students interested in the questions the Professor deems important.[10]

Given that creative contest in which students and faculty in effect awaken and inspire curiosity and questions in each other, it is understandable that, for Mead, the professor who has raised himself above teaching and elevated himself to "pure research" is not likely to know what questions to ask and will soon be one of the "desiccated, book-wormish antiquarians several years removed from the world of today."[11]

Curiously, our "historian as teacher" has spent much more time discussing teaching in general than he has the teaching of history. But whenever he has pondered the meaning of his own discipline, he has credited students with having sharpened the questions that were basic to it. When he underwent metamorphosis from graduate student to faculty member, he first wondered at the munificent salary he was paid for "doing what I liked to do," and asked why society paid him at all. This was "the question of the purpose of teaching American religious history, formulated in the con-

---

[9]"Church History in the Federated Theological Schools," *Divinity School News* 20 (1 February 1953): 7.

[10]"Church History Explained," *Church History* 32 (March 1963): 19.

[11]"The Laborers Are Few," *Divinity School News* 12 (1 November 1945): 2.

text of a functionalist approach. It meant, 'What does the teaching of such history have to contribute to the functioning of our society?' "

III
Two Types of Students

He had said then that he could evade the depths of that question while teaching graduate students in theological schools and history departments, but in 1964 he began to encounter undergraduates who "came in large numbers, from every area of the university and from every social, economic, and religious background that our pluralistic society affords." He could no longer assume, as he had done with graduate students, that all students possessed an interest in the discipline of history. Much of his reflection in later years turned on the difference between questions posed by graduate history majors and undergraduates with their infinite variety.[12]

The distinction between the two types of students was very important to Mead, and his pilgrimage makes little sense unless one separates his discussions of both. Of course, they have some things in common, and in neither case will they learn anything unless and until their conventional rituals and patterns of security are interrupted:

> The tension between the individual and his community comes when a routine breaks down for one reason or another, and only then does self-consciousness come into play. Self-consciousness is thus always associated with tension, more or less painful. This is why students always suffer when they are really being educated. By and large, the more they gripe the more they are learning—or consciously refusing to learn. Deliver me from a school where everybody is happy and serene.[13]

Mead has frequently contrasted the contexts of undergraduates with those of graduate theological students who are not specialists in religious history. He did not consider either to be naturally curious about history and has been careful not to oversell his specialty in their presence. "I would claim only as Carl Becker said that 'history is an indispensable even though not the highest form of intellectual endeavor.' A professor, as any child,

---

[12]"History and Identity," *Journal of Religion* 51 (January 1971): 1-2.

[13]"The Task of the Church Historian," *Chronicle* 12 (July 1949): 135.

if he is to avoid neurosis, needs the feeling of security that comes from a sense of being at least needed even if not wanted.''[14]

In the context of graduate theological school, Mead devoted much less attention to commenting on his own history students than on the theologians or would-be theologians whom he came eventually to view with considerable distaste and who have almost always been viewed in negative contrast to his later-discovered undergraduate students.

In the case of Protestants, the theologians shared the "general estrangement of Protestant Christianity from the dominant intellectual currents of the modern age."[15] Though they were involved with religion, they regularly tried to distance themselves from the messy life of those religious institutions with which Mead himself has long had a love-hate relation. But as a historian he argued that a relation of some sort was necessary, while many of them pretended every kind of tie away. Reviewing his years in graduate theological education, he complained:

> I suppose that through most of Christian history one primary and perennial task of the theologian was to examine, explain, and defend the premises of the intellectual structure explanatory of the modes of thinking and acting that characterized the church-community of which he was an actively participating and responsible member. In this situation the nature of his responsibilities and the purpose of his school were reasonably clear. But few theologians today are practicing and responsible churchmen. Most appear to belong to the highly abstract and conveniently "invisible" church whose fulfillments are "beyond history" and not of this world. Hence, they tend to be at best tolerant, at worst contemptuous of the actual institutional incarnations of this church in our denominations and congregations. Therefore, much of their written work is addressed only to their fellow denizens of the self-made ghetto in which they live, and is almost totally unrelated to the experienced order of the mill run of pastors and church members.[16]

He had by then been freed from these community-disdaining theologues and placed among undergraduates, who provided him with a new context for his historical work.

---

[14]"The Federated Theological Schools," 3; "The Task of the Church Historian," 142 n. 25.

[15]"The Evangelical Concept of the Ministry," 237.

[16]"Reinterpretation in American Church History," in Jerald C. Brauer, ed., *Reinterpretation in American Church History* (Chicago: University of Chicago Press, 1968) 175-76.

Mead relished collegians' variety, their pluralism, the extremes of sec-
ularity and religiosity they manifested. They were capable of helping him
raise a better range of questions than theological students had been able to
do. "I am more interested in addressing the modern so-called 'secular man,'
and I think it is very important and strategic for the church historian to do
so." He outlined theological reasons for reaching to "secular man," but
he also believed that Western society would have to recover a sense of its
religious roots or it would be lost. With John Baillie he argued that there
is an "underlying 'Christian-ness' of western civilization" that today's man
has to be taught about his continuity with his Christian past. Written and
oral history exists in part to stimulate this sense of continuity.[17] Among
undergraduates this teaching can best be effected. In them

> one meets a cross section of our society in all its pluralistic complexity and
> stubborn actuality, ranging from rampant profanity to hidebound sectarian-
> ism. I fell in love with the undergraduates and I am probably somewhat starry-
> eyed where they are concerned. . . . The teacher of undergraduates . . . con-
> fronts in them the fact of pluralism in our society, which means that he cannot
> assume any common religious orientation or common understanding of the
> terms and concepts traditionally used in discussing matters pertaining to re-
> ligion. Because these terms and concepts are still the stock-in-trade of almost
> all seminary education, such education is in danger of becoming a positive
> barrier to discussing religion with, or presenting the claims of religion to, this
> generation. The traditional language has become obsolete as an instrument
> for talking about present religious experience.[18]

Mead has stressed the contrast between types of students with almost wea-
rying frequency and with the passion one expects from a latter-day convert. "I have . . . moved across the spectrum from 'sacred' to 'profane'
history of religion in America—a movement signified by passage through
theological schools into a State University. And there among the profane
(i.e., outside religion's temple) professors I discovered not only a realistic
interest *in* religion, but attitudes and acts worthy of religion itself."[19]

---

[17]"The Task of the Church Historian," 138-40.

[18]"In Quest of America's Religion," *Christian Century* 87 (17 June 1970): 754.

[19]"Character and Continuity," 27.

IV
The Historian and Self-Understanding

Since Mead has not been the kind of man to engage in crusades for their own sake, it is profitable to ask what he has thought the study of religious history in a culture is supposed to accomplish and, therefore, why he has found it more profitable to work in "profane" settings. Were someone to have approached Mead with the simplicity and directness of Marc Bloch's son and ask, "What is the use of history?" Mead would not have been at a loss to provide an answer. In his world, however, the question has been posed less elegantly by the students. Study history? "Why the hell should I?" He has provided two sets of answers, but devotes by far the most attention to the first, which has to do with the location of the individual in society. A person studies history for self-understanding or, as he has chosen to put it in later essays, for finding one's identity.

A teacher cannot coerce attention to historical study, whether with the brass-edged ruler of the old elementary school or with the covert coercion of graduate-school grading and financial-award systems. Instead, he or she must communicate "the sense that what one has to offer is relevant to the student's living of *his* life. This, indeed, seems to me to be a primary purpose in teaching." "We are all egotists." "What is there in it *for me?*" Concerning the question of history's usefulness,

> the most simple form of the answer is "Self-understanding—that is what there is in it for you." Or, as one student wrote me, "you reaffirmed my feeling that no amount of knowledge is worth two cents unless it somehow increases self-knowledge."
> Whatever else it may be, a sense of identity is a matter of self-knowledge—or of understanding one's self.

The self does not exist in a vacuum but in community. Hence, history must be taught and learned. This has been the consistent motif in Mead's career.

He has always credited R. G. Collingwood for this accent, though he may well have simply been on a parallel track with the British idealist historian and may not really have needed Collingwood for anything more than confirmation of his independently developed view. Back in 1949 he was already answering the question, "What is history *for?*" by reference to Collingwood's general statement of the answer—"that history is 'for' human self-knowledge." Here he quotes Collingwood: "It is generally thought to be of importance to man that he should know himself: where knowing himself means knowing not his merely personal peculiarities, the things that distinguish him from other men, but his nature as man."[20] Such self-knowledge is the basis of human freedom. In the case of Christians, church history helps free them from a narrowly tradition-bound life and, by "bringing into the consciousness of the 'traditionless' the buried sense of continuity with the Christian past, can make them obviously 'Christian.' "

Mead enjoyed telling the story of a student who had come to him to announce that he could see no reason for studying history. "Why?" The answer: "I think you will understand what I mean better if I tell you about my past life." His teacher responded, "Fine—but if you meant to argue yourself out of taking the courses you have just lost the argument."

The community that provided identity has been progressively enlarged in Mead's vision. In 1953 he had been most concerned with the Christian past. But the principle of the larger community was there already then: "Each individual is the repository of all his past. History is the study of the past that has formed him. Hence the study of history is the study of one's self—and in this sense the purpose of the study is self-knowledge." In that passage he illustrated his point by cozy references to Midwest American Methodists, Baptists, and Presbyterians. By 1970 he needed cosmic space and geological time:

> We find a stable identity only through an imaginative grasp that we are one with all of life in time and space, and, recognizing that there is no marked boundary between what we call organic and inorganic, that human life *is* the planet become conscious of itself. . . . The purpose of the study of history should be to orient the individual to this great community.[21]

This is not the place to debate the point as to whether stable identity can be found by many people against such a vast and vague backdrop. At the time Mead was speaking, a counterview predominated as people sought identity in particular ethnic, racial, religious, generational, or intentional subcommunities. Still, the paragraph does illustrate something of Mead's own universalistic grasp.

---

[20]R. G. Collingwood, *The Idea of History* (New York: Oxford University Press, 1956) 10.

[21]"History and Identity," 3; "The Task of the Church Historian," 131, 128; "The Federated Theological Schools," 8; "History and Identity," 14.

V
Ancillary Uses of History

The other uses of history that Mead has mentioned enhance or are ancillary to the quest for self-understanding. The teacher exists first to raise questions and offer problems.

> I discovered that the *primary* duty of the teacher, at least the teacher of graduate students, is not to give the students answers, but to raise questions for them, and to raise them in such fashion that they will be uneasy and unhappy until they try to answer them. What students really need is someone to induce them to do the thinking they can do if they try.[22]

Rephrased, "the primary purpose of teaching" is communication. "Therefore the question has become for me: How does one communicate to those of the coming generation an understanding of the place and significance of 'religion in American history' . . . and its relevance to them?"[23]

Mead has seen this task to be the opening of vistas. In expressing gratitude for predecessors who had stressed a method that they called "social-historical," he issued a cautionary word about keeping any method in its proper place and letting it serve as a means, not an end, of study and instruction. To the good teachers "the method was merely their modern picture window through which they viewed the magnificent panorama of men and women as human as they were, calling themselves 'Christians,' and stumbling forward into an ever unpredictably and often terrifying future."[24] Today too many professors have concentrated on teaching about windows and their students have seldom seen vistas.

> When, for example, the professors began to talk about "dialogue," I practically gave up all hope for any further meaningful communication. For once "dialogue" is made a concept to be analyzed it becomes the final object for concentrated study—an end, not a means. This represents the old academic tendency to forget the view while studying the window frame and texture of the glass.

Perhaps this preoccupation has kept Mead from devoting much attention to the "how to" of teaching history and has led him to concentrate instead

---

[22]"Historical Studies and the Ministry," 34-35.

[23]"In Quest of America's Religion," 754.

[24]"Character and Continuity," 26.

on the substance and intention of such teaching. After raising problems, seeking to communicate, and opening vistas, the teacher still has to be preoccupied with the problem of complexity. In Mead's case, this preoccupation has occasioned some ambivalence. All of life seems to be a drive toward clarity and simplicity, yet Mead has mistrusted historians who have found too much of each. Religious history "is a fearfully baffling field to anyone whose disciplined drive to achieve clarity is balanced by an equally strong aversion to oversimplification. A. N. Whitehead's phrase makes an appropriate motto for the historian of religion in America: 'Seek simplicity and distrust it.' "[25]

Mead has summarized this whole half of his understanding in a passage that shows why simplicity is difficult to attain, since identity is to be located in the complete set of interactions between the individual and community, a nexus that implies matters of infinite complexity.

> I agree that self-identity is rooted in a sense of solidarity with the ideas and ideals of a historical community . . . [that] man is the creature as well as the creator of his culture. . . . It seems to me to follow that the study of the history of the religion of one's culture is perhaps the most direct and efficacious route to self-understanding, and that insofar as the historian is immersed in his culture (as I am in mine) his history of the religion of his culture is his "internal history and his approach will be autobiographical."[26]

VI
The Historian
and Historical Tendency

The other major use of history in Mead's approach stresses the social side of history and allows for a measure of projection toward action. This he calls his "Whither Tending" motif, one that came to be so common that a canny associate of his, no historian herself, regularly referred to one whole family of his addresses by that name.[27] If Collingwood had been his mentor so far as the self-understanding idea was concerned, Abraham Lincoln provided the "epitome of the nature and purposes of all history which [Mead thinks] all historians would accept":

---

[25]*The Lively Experiment*, xi.

[26]"In Quest of America's Religion," 753.

[27]"Tending: Whether or Whither," *Journal of the Liberal Ministry* 6 (Winter 1966): 1.

Lincoln was right—definition of ''what to do and how to do it'' waits upon
a decision regarding ''where we are and whither we are tending.'' . . .
Lincoln was right when he told the pompous ministers who waited upon
him that he believed he should not expect ''a direct revelation'' of ''where
we are and whither we are tending,'' but that he must depend upon a ''study
of the plain physical facts of the case.'' This is to say that the only possible
answer to the question ''where we are and whither we are tending,'' on
any level, as well as the answer to ''what to do and how to do it'' are arrived at through the interpretation of human experience. There is no shortcut answer to either question. Both come only through hard and careful
mental effort.

And Lincoln was right . . . when, having implied that the answer to
the question ''where we are and whither we are tending'' is an interpretation based upon the analysis of historical events, he proceeded in that
speech to an acute historical analysis of the situation which made the answer to the lesser questions—''what to do and how to do it'' obvious and
imperative.[28]

''History, in brief, is an analysis of the past in order that we may understand the present and guide our conduct into the future.'' That approach
had become central for Mead by 1949 and he has not wavered from it since.

When one can successfully intervene in a person's or a society's collective
thought processes has been a subject of concern to Mead. People are not always receptive to such intervention by historians. They can be reached especially at times of crisis, when the structures of routine have been interrupted
or can be disrupted. Once again the essay of 1949 is helpful. Man has preserved, says Mead, ''the results of his self-conscious understanding—profitable ways of doing things, ways of thinking, tools—in a 'cumulative tradition'
of habits, and institutions which are super-individual and, so far as any one
individual is concerned, practically immortal.''

The common function of these continuing structures is to preserve the answers to questions regarding ''what to do and how to do it'' that have proved
profitable. They are preserved by being reduced to routines—that is, to a
level below self-consciousness and choice—and hence are analogous to the
instincts of other creatures. They differ radically from the instincts in that
they are always subject to change by intelligence.

If a community's ''structures of routine'' were perfectly static and sta-
bilized, the individual would never need to rise to a self-conscious level

[28] ''The Task of the Church Historian,'' 127-28.

and "hence need never become peculiarly human." Tension between the individual and his community comes when a routine breaks down; *then* self-consciousness enters, and so does historical inquiry. "Hence, as Theodore Parker once suggested, by and large one is about as bound by his past as he is ignorant of his history." The good and the evil are preserved by the structures of routine, so the historian-teacher is to help students appreciate the former and to be free of the latter.[29]

With the goals of self-understanding and the realization of "whither we are tending" as steps toward both the appreciation of tradition and liberation from the dead hand of the past, Mead has never bothered to comment extensively on other uses of history. His students have heard little support of the regnant positivists' program, the one against which J. H. Plumb railed with his assertion that "ninety per cent, perhaps, [of the professional historians] have the view that the subject they practise is meaningless in any ultimate sense."[30] They see little social purpose for it as a coordinator of human endeavor or human thought. For Mead there has been little entertainment of the suggestions that history is merely "an intellectual pastime, with little rhyme and less reason." There is not even a "history for history's sake," no simple esthetic delight in the historian's comprehension of the subject. Obviously Mead has not used history to help students predict the future, or to provide them with laws of history. He has never lapsed back into the old pedagogical theories about the value of history in the training of mental processes.

Again and again Mead has confessed that he had been haunted by the question about historical work suggested by Charles A. Beard: "The historian would be a strange creature if he never asked himself why he regarded these matters as worthy of his labor and love, or why society provides a living for him during his excursions and explorations."[31] His own conscientious answers as to why these were worthy matters always had to do with the help he could give students or readers as they tried to come to terms with their own identities and to discern cultural tendency as a step toward some sort of action or intervention in history.

---

[29]Ibid., 135-37; a parallel article is "An Address to Unitarians," *Proceedings of the Unitarian Historical Association* 12 (1958): 12-22.

[30]J. H. Plumb, "The Historian's Dilemma," in J. H. Plumb, ed., *Crisis in the Humanities* (Harmondsworth, Middlesex: Penguin, 1964) 24ff.

[31]"The Task of the Church Historian," 135, or "Church History Explained," 17.

VII
The Academic Contexts
for the Historian

Sidney Mead has been a contextual thinker, a creature of and partial creator of the communities of which he has been a part. In his larger historical work he has been preoccupied first with national community and, more recently, with man's cosmic connections. But when he has written in the role of historian-as-teacher, he has concentrated almost entirely on the academic setting. He and his students did not live in a vacuum there either; they were both set back and advanced by their colleagues and the surrounding institutions.

Like any good Pilgrim, Mead has seen himself prevented from making simple progress because the academic world is in range of the City of Destruction, the Slough of Despond, the Valley of Humiliation, the Valley of the Shadow of Death, Vanity Fair, and the Doubting Castle. He makes so much of the obstacles that his course of life has sometimes sounded less like that of *Pilgrim's Progress* and more like the *Perils of Pauline*. He has seldom elaborated on why academia is so stultifying and capable of creating conditions of bondage. Sometimes he has hinted that a kind of doctrine of original sin is operative everywhere there except among his fellow suffering undergraduates. His analysis is not particularly profound, but it antedates, has outlived, and is as far ranging as anything dreamed up by the student counterculturalists of the late 1960s; and it comes with better credentials from him than from them. The analysis deserves some attention since it makes up so much a part of his perceived world.

His approach was well summarized in the title of an address from 1958, "Learning versus the School." In it he quoted Whitehead:

> Unless we are careful, we shall conventionalize knowledge. Our literary criticism will suppress initiative. Our historical criticism will conventionalize our ideas of the springs of human conduct. . . . In such ways the universities, with their scheme of orthodoxies, will stifle the progress of the race, unless by some fortunate stirrings of humanity they are in time remodeled or swept away.[32]

He has spoken regularly of his "pilgrimage through the American edu-

---

[32]"Learning versus the School," *Unitarian Register* 157 (1958): 30.

cational establishment," of his "coming of age in Academic Samoa."[33]
Justly proud of his ability to use his hands, he sometimes has seemed edgy
about having had a place in the academy.

> The highest compliment I have received since becoming a professor came
> from an electrician. After appraising some of my carpentering, and find-
> ing out that I was a teacher, he said—with just a hint of resentment—"Why
> you could go to work for a living!" So I could. And sometimes I suspect
> that some of my learned colleagues think I should. But I won't.[34]

In "Learning versus the School," he identified himself with Robert Maynard Hutchins's "tilt with the aimless windmills of the American universities." His standard complaint has always begun with comment on the
complexity and anomie of the university, especially on its graduate level,
with its "pompous and formal red tape—including the grading system—
all so carefully nurtured and directed in long committee and faculty meetings." With James Harvey Robinson he had said, "I have participated in
many oral examinations, God forgive me!" "Not learned enough really to
be contemptuous of learning," he decided that such talk was not really becoming to him, so he concentrated chiefly on the bureaucratic aspects of
the complex university system. "We must believe in learning with a consuming passion, and love the university as the seat of learning in our culture. But we must not love, or even readily believe in, the complex
bureaucratic machinery of the university, necessary as it may be." The task
of running the machinery too easily becomes all-consuming, and teacher
and student are then lost.[35]

Beyond bureaucracy, the most irritating and debilitating problem for
the good teacher is the departmentalized, self-segregated, overdefined, and
self-defensive pattern of university education. In a reminiscent lecture delivered to his former colleagues in graduate theological education, Mead
particularly attacked this issue. Our modes of education are "cluttered up
with unorganized snippets of accumulated information, and the only thing
the snippets have in common is that they are all entertained in the same
head." Scholars resort to too many footnotes; the "knowledge explosion"

---

[33]"Character and Continuity," 25.

[34]"Love and Learning," *Christian Register* (June 1957): 12.

[35]"Learning versus the School," 30-31.

results in overpublication; teachers bring their students a "total commu-nications overload" and "blow their intellectual fuses." Students' sys-tems become clogged.

They are exposed to conflicting perspectives of experts, who make no at-tempt to help them see patterns of coherence and integrity in whole programs. Seminaries have been especially culpable, for they often turned out to be uni-versities in microcosm, broken down into rigid and autonomous fields.

Professors seem to be competing or are unaware of each other across disciplinary lines or even within them.

> A faculty often appears to be merely a gathering of highly independent en-trepreneurs, each paid to operate his own private concession stand in a "plant" maintained by a board of trustees with funds the president can persuade or coerce "the constituency" to contribute. Each belongs to his own national association of the manufacturers of knowledge in his spe-cialty, in whose meetings he finds consolation with those who speak his dialect and refuge from his immediate colleagues who do not. The student is left on his own.

Faculty meetings have come to be made up of political-interest groups, with each member tending to bargain rather than to contribute to a dia-logue. "The outcome is seldom a rationally coherent and understandable program." But faculty members try to convince students and themselves that their effort does represent a rational program. What do students learn? Little except "that at least the institution that most directly impinges upon their lives at the moment is not subject to rational understanding, and that there is not necessarily any relation between the ideas academics expound, and the institutions academics run."[36] Mead has agreed with Robert Hutchins's definition of the university as an "agglomeration of entities connected only by a central heating system," or Clark Kerr's, which saw a university faculty as a group of "independent entrepreneurs held to-gether by a common grievance over parking." Semiautonomous depart-ments were the villains.[37]

Mead's colleagues seemed offensive when they gathered for meetings. A former dean under whom he had taught had once wholly won Mead's heart when he had told "a group of entering students that only periodic

---

[36]"Reinterpretation in American Church History," 171-77.

[37]"Church History Explained," 18.

visits to the monkey cages at the zoo enabled him to live through faculty meetings during the year.''[38] As for administration: if Paul had located ''teachers'' between ''inspired prophets'' and ''wonder-workers,'' he had placed administration—the real villainy in Mead's world—''next to the last . . . just before 'ecstatic speaking.' '' ''Was this a subtle way of suggesting that being an administrator hovers perilously on the verge of effervescent incoherence?''[39] ''Those who have tried to escape the routine often have become faddish innovators and attention-getters, and thus have also been diverted from the task of teaching. Such professors are often so concerned about their 'revelance' that they tend to climb onto any passing bandwagon that promises them a moment of recognition.''[40]

Through this whole criticism Mead has offered little advice concerning ''the way out,'' but he has helped the students survive with counsel that they should be as innocent as doves and as guileful as serpents. Students too often have yielded to the temptation to rush through the first open door to stringent criticism, ''before they have gained a reputation for knowing what they are talking about.'' Hence, however right their criticisms may be, these will not be heeded. It is wisdom on the part of a student instead ''to exhibit enough conformity to the rules and regulations of the bureaucracy of the university to enable him to stay in it, and enough facility in getting grades to establish himself as a citizen worthy to be heard.''[41]

Despite consistently voiced criticisms, Mead has loved the academy and gladly devoted his career to teaching there.[42] In part, he has been free of this setting because he has not reposed all his hopes in it. With Emerson, Mead believes that ''everyman is my schoolmaster in some respect. The secret of growth is to recognize this and learn what he has to teach me.''[43] Sometimes a tone of irony has given Mead distance and perspective. He regularly enjoyed himself by indulging in self-derisive comment on the injunction each faculty member implicitly had received to refer at least once per public lecture to the fact that theirs was the world's greatest university.

---

[38]''Character and Continuity,'' 2.

[39]''Teaching as . . . Our Vocation as Christians,'' 5.

[40]''Character and Continuity,'' 26.

[41]''Learning versus the School,'' 31.

[42]''Character and Continuity,'' 25; ''Love and Learning,'' 13.

[43]''The Task of the Church Historian,'' 31.

The university has played a positive part in Mead's work, for he has been a contextual or perspectival thinker. "I have often advised students to study their teachers as well as the subject content of their courses. For one cannot understand a person's interpretation of a subject until and unless one understands the perspective from which he views it."[44] That perspective is shaped in no small measure by the academic community. People "live mentally in furnished apartments—furnished that is by the culture born to them through their community."[45] This provides them with a worldview necessary for historical communication.

In such contexts Mead has been ready to send cards of thanks to those who shaped his career as historian-teacher. His predecessors have been noted most of all. Told that he had inherited the mantle of one of his teachers and former deans, he "immediately conjured up the image of throwing a circus tent over a Volkswagen."[46] He could subject his immediate predecessor, William Warren Sweet, to intense criticism,[47] but Mead could also say:

> I gratefully acknowledge him as the Master who tutored me both when I was his student and his colleague. . . . Like all good Masters he expected his students to accept his work critically and go beyond him if they could.

---

[44]In "Reinterpretation in American Church History," 192, Mead said: "After a reviewer of my work said that I had been greatly influenced by A. N. Whitehead, I began seriously to read Whitehead's works, and found . . . an overall view of historical development that greatly enlightened my understanding of what I was trying to do." As I reread Mead in the light of numbers of years, rereading on my part the works of José Ortega y Gasset, it occurred to me again and again that Mead's work—while not necessarily influenced by Ortega—parallels many Ortegan themes; now I commend to him for serious reading those aspects of Ortega's work introduced by Julian Marias, *José Ortega y Gasset: Circumstance and Vocation* (Norman: University of Oklahoma Press, 1970); Robert McClintock, *Man and His Circumstances: Ortega as Educator* (New York: Teachers College Press, 1971); "Ortega y Gasset," in Karl J. Weintraub, *Visions of Culture* (Chicago: University of Chicago Press, 1966). In all of these Ortega's concepts of the worldview, *creencias,* identity and "shipwreck," circumstantiality, and perspectivalism are discussed with references to both Ortega's translated and untranslated work. See Mead's "Reinterpretation in American Church History," 171.

[45]"The Task of the Church Historian," 133, 132.

[46]"Character and Continuity," 25; "Reinterpretation in American Church History," 192.

[47]"Professor Sweet's Religion and Culture in America," *Church History* 22 (March 1953): 33ff.; *The Lively Experiment*, xi.

In due time I expressed my growing independence from his basic interpretations in a critical evaluation of his work—an effort which he acknowledged with appreciation.

Ties to the past were paralleled for Mead by recognition of the aid his
larger circle of colleagues could give a teacher-historian in a community
of scholars. He paid tribute to these others in his major book.

> The community of congenial souls in which the professor lives and moves
> and has his being transcends by far the collegiate fellowship of his partic-
> ular academic household, and because his indebtedness is coextensive with
> that community, it cannot adequately be expressed. He is the beneficiary
> even of those with whom he differs. Indeed, he may owe more to one who
> has etched his faults with acid than to the ninety-nine who have merely
> said, ''I enjoyed your article.''[48]

A university should be a community of scholars, of people thinking; but
Mead has not believed that an American university—or even a theological
school—can readily be developed into one, however ''right'' it is that it
should be so. People have to work in and transcend their contexts. The
greatest aid to that task in the academy comes from students, who also serve
parabolically. ''One loves an institution both as it is and, for what it could
be. This, I think, is the way we love people; certainly it is the only way we
can love students. From this stance it is highly irrational to suppose that a
person or an institution must be rational in our way, and to judge him or it
solely on that basis.''[49] While we are on the subject of ambivalence, it
should be noted that Mead had a ''nothing personal'' angle in his comment
on administrators; he dedicated his major book to his three deans, quoting
Hutchins once more: ''Yet if I were asked what single thing American education needed most, I should reply that it needed such men.''[50] These
qualifying remarks may not quite have prepared Mead the Pilgrim to see
the Palace Beautiful, the Delectable Mountains, or the Celestial City on
the academic horizon, but not all has been bleak for him and his students.
    Like many a Pilgrim, Mead had seen himself as ''on the boundary,''
as a man on the margin, and he seems to have been directing his students

---

[48]*The Lively Experiment*, xii.

[49]''Reinterpretation in American Church History,'' 182.

[50]*The Lively Experiment*, dedication page.

to see the creative potential of such a location. He has stood between pietism and the Enlightenment, between religious and secular communities, between theological settings and a profane world, between seminary and university, between graduate and undergraduate:

> As American Church Historian, I sometimes feel that I stand in a "no man's land" between seminary and university, between church-history and secular-history; or again, that I stand one foot in each, with the gap between them ever widening. I have found that when I am addressing a group of "secular" historians I apparently sound to them like a "Christian," and when addressing a group of self-consciously Christian churchmen I apparently sound to them like a secular historian. Of course, in a mixed group I merely sound confused—which is probably closer to the truth of the matter.[51]

Behind the irony and self-deprecation is Mead's consistent interest in teaching people to live in, with, and through institutions without giving their whole hearts to them. He has spoken, not entirely critically, of "sanctified duplicity," which is known as being "politically realistic."[52]

VIII
Neglected Themes

If there has been a void in Mead's comprehensive approach to the life of the historian as teacher, it has appeared in his failure ever to devote extensive attention to the topic of being a historian who teaches historians. Much of his career and his impact have been directed to training Ph.D.s who would continue to teach religious history. But the majority of his students have usually been undergraduates or graduate theological students. His criticisms of the "Ph.D. world" have been regular and conventional; the "Ph.D. world" is "myth-enveloped"; he agreed with Deans who, in 1957, found "many a man less mature, less self-poised and less confident after two years in a graduate school than he was as an inspirited college senior." "Too many men emerge from the ordeal spiritually dried up."[53]

---

[51]"A Historian's View of the Church and Theological Education in America," Bulletin 24 (June 1960), the 22d Biennial Meeting of the A.A.T.S., Union Theological Seminary, Richmond VA, 14-17 June 1960, 120-21.

[52]"Some Current Forms of Infidelity: An Address to 'Liberal Theologs,' " *Christianity and Society* 20 (Summer 1955): 15.

[53]"Learning versus the School," 30.

Mead has offered a few hints as to how he would alter the circumstances or outlook of the history graduate student. His ideal historian ''is a creative artist. To him written history is a drama . . . and all the world is a stage.'' He needs imagination,[54] which means ''the complex ability intellectually to conceive and emotionally to entertain the possibility of what A. N. Whitehead called the 'vast alternatives' to one's cultural and hence personal ideals, and to the current specific notions about the limits of what is possible, and the means available.''[55] Imagination is linked to expertise. ''An 'expert' in this sense, is one who has met certain conditions—that is, one who is trained to observe and record the 'meaning' of certain kinds of events—and hence one who has to begin with certain potential capabilities making it possible for him to benefit from such training.''[56] Mead's essays have hardly been devoted at all to discussing the technical skills that will help produce the expert. He has shown little interest in the topics of research, suspicion, appraisal, evidence summoning, organizing, expounding, or propagating material; his own students have been expected to pick up these elsewhere. It would be picayune to fault Mead for having failed to deal with these topics, since he has been most venturesome and more generous than most historians in discussing teaching in general.

In the end Mead has not discussed teaching teachers how to teach history because his real interests in his Bonifacius-type work, if not also in his Magnalia, have been in some senses theological. Whether his community be seminary or university, nation or church or cosmos, he has always been trying to provide some sort of interpretation of life in the face of a transcendent reality. ''In the final analysis the church historian is an evangelist''[57] more than a prophet, more appreciative of his religious community and culture than critical of it. Simple anti-institutionalism on the part of religionists or historians produces loud and fantastically individualistic burps, reminding Mead of ''Henry David Thoreau's cynical suspicion that what really bugs every reformer is the pain in his own digestive tract.''[58] At other times he has seen the church historian as a kind of chap-

---

[54]''American History as a Tragic Drama,'' *Journal of Religion* 52 (October 1972): 342.

[55]''Reinterpretation of American Church History,'' 187.

[56]''The Task of the Church Historian,'' 130.

[57]Ibid., 140.

[58]Ibid., 184.

lain to culture, responding, as it were, to the doctor in the hospital corridor, after the doctor has asked what a chaplain is doing there: "I was sent here by the Christian Church which invented Hospitals in the first place, founded this one, and is still supporting it. Since you are living off that Church in more ways than you know, I am here to ask what *you* are doing here!" Translation: "I am here to teach you a little church history as it ought to be taught."[59]

Mead's concept of the church may have broadened or become more attenuated since he wrote that in 1953. He may sound less triumphalist and more disappointed about the church in culture, and he may now look for responsible community in larger concentrics proceeding out from that church; but he is no less assertive about the role the historian can play in providing self-understanding and a sense of "whither we are tending" in culture and community. If he as a historian-teacher has trained pilgrims, evangelists, and chaplains in such contexts, it is little wonder that he has left the "how-to" details of graduate historical teaching and writing techniques to be developed by others.

[59]"Historical Studies and the Ministry," 38.

The Theology of the Republic

J. Ronald Engel

> The fanaticism of all parties must be allowed to burn down to ashes, like a fire out of control. If it survives, it will be only because it will have humanized itself, reduced its dogmas to harmless metaphors, and sunk down a tap-root to feed it, into the dark damp depths of mother earth. The economy of nature includes all particular movements, combines and transforms them all, but never diverts its wider processes to render them obedient to the prescriptions of human rhetoric. Things have their day, and their beauties in that day. It would be preposterous to expect any one civilization to last forever.
>
> —*George Santayana,*
> "My Host the World"

Sidney E. Mead is both historian and seer of the American democratic faith. For several decades his essays have given to students of American history what Ralph Barton Perry's *Puritanism and Democracy* and Ralph Gabriel's *The Course of American Democratic Thought* gave to earlier generations. They have provided grounds for belief in the enduring greatness of the Enlightenment ideal of the Republic in spite of the events of the twentieth century. Even when liberal hopes for a new dispensation of liberty and equality gave way late in the 1960s to bitterness and defeat, Mead's finely crafted retrieval of the "Republic of our agrarian dream," the "time when wise men hoped," performed a redemptive function. He is one of a very few who has had the literary capacity to link his contemporaries with the immortals of the revolutionary age and the deathless vision they beheld.

Of equal significance has been his spirited insistence that a democratic society requires democratic religion. In debate with sociologists and historians such as Will Herberg, Martin Marty, and Winthrop Hudson, who sought a transcendent source of judgment of American cultural religion in a renewal of the prophetic biblical heritage, Mead argued that there is an authentic prophetic heritage resident in the American founding and that this heritage holds any and all denominational traditions accountable. It is the responsibility of the churches to articulate, each in its own way, grounds for affirming the Enlightenment heritage of religious and political freedom.

While Mead has been justly celebrated for his contributions to the ''recovery'' of American religious history as a foundation for understanding American culture, his constructive role as theological apologist for the ''religion of the Republic'' has largely gone unrecognized and uncriticized. It does not matter that the role was assumed reluctantly or—as Mead might insist—by default because of the failure of professional theologians to shoulder their proper responsibility. The fact stands that through and beyond his historiography he has developed a theological perspective on the meaning and outcome of the American experiment that has exercised considerable influence within and beyond the historical disciplines while simultaneously qualifying the scope and character of his own historical investigations. There is need for a delineation of Mead's ''theology of the Republic,'' its relation to his writing of history, and an evaluation of its adequacy.

Although Mead does not always discriminate between them, there are four distinct subject matters in his discussion of the religion of the Republic. The first is the founding documents and legal institutions that established novel practices of political and religious freedom and equality in the United States and launched the ''lively experiment.'' The second is the constellation of symbols, ideals, and principles that motivated and expressed these novel practices and that, for our purposes, can be most precisely called the ''religion of the Republic.'' For Mead these symbols, ideals, and principles are by no means limited to American society; although they took specific form here, they are in fact universal truths with roots in Judeo-Christian mythology and Greek philosophy. The third subject matter is the various theological and philosophical rationalizations of these practices and principles publicly espoused in the first century of the American Republic—what may be called collectively the "theologies of the Republic." The fourth is Mead's own theological interpretation of these practices, principles, and rationalizations, written from the vantage point of the middle-to-late twentieth century. His theology is superimposed upon the preceding history and conditions almost everything that he says about it.

To prove that Mead's work taken as a whole expresses a theology that may be described as close to the worldview of Greek tragedy, and that is inadequate to the actual history of the "lively experiment," will be the main task of this essay. Two things need to be explained at the outset, however: first, how, in pursuing such an interpretation, I am not doing violence to his intentions as historian; and second, the definition of the tragic vision, on the basis of which I am characterizing the unacknowledged presuppositions of his theology.

I
Christian and Greek Presuppositions

Mead has tried to be quite self-conscious about the valuative dimensions of his historiography. In a series of articles published between 1949 and 1968, he developed his conception of the proper methodology for American church history.[1] He argues that there are several theological affirmations at the core of his methodology, and these are biblically grounded:

(1) God is the free and transcendent Creator and Governor of the world. He is not bound by any social, cultural, or ecclesiastical forms or doctrines. Rather, the creation is contingent upon Him. He is always more than His creation can know or grasp: ultimately, He is mystery. It follows that any statement about God must be tentative and subject to correction, poetically intuited, and of high generality.

(2) God is also at work within the world. He has the courage to become flesh and identify Himself with the destiny of His creation. As participant within the world, He gives to history a transcendent meaning in and through which He can be known by human beings. "Hence the study of the his-

[1]See "The Task of the Church Historian," *Chronicle* 12 (July 1949): 127-43; "Professor Sweet's Religion and Culture in America," *Church History* 22 (March 1953): 33-49; "On the Meaning of History," *Christian Century* 78 (15 November 1961): 1361-64; "Church History Explained," *Church History* 32 (March 1963): 17-31; "Reinterpretation in American Church History," in *Reinterpretation in American Church History,* ed. Jerald C. Brauer (Chicago: University of Chicago Press, 1968) 169-94.

tory-that-happens is always somehow the study of the works of God in history—and by his works we shall know Him, though now we see only through a glass darkly.''[2]

(3) The end of human consciousness is understanding the transcendent movement of history. The freedom of persons to affirm this meaning as an article of explicit faith is the purpose for which the universe was created. The church historian has the vocation of helping his fellow human beings reach such understanding. His task is to tell the story of God's redeeming activity in the history-that-happens. In this respect, ''church history is a continuous meditation on the meaning of the incarnation.''[3]

Mead also observes that the writing of American religious history is a *constructive* theological enterprise. The church historian is a ''speculative historian''—an ''evangelist.'' This is because the basis of the historian's interpretation of facts is his own particular conception of the ''culmination of the story'' of God's redemptive work in history. ''The historian's selection of what to emphasize in the past depends upon his conception of the end and culmination of the story he wishes to tell—which story is itself selected from a practically infinite number of possible stories.''[4] The selection of *a* story depends upon the historian's decision of what constitutes the norm of human experience in history—depends, in other words, upon his ontology, or his particular view of the character of God's participation in the world. Every written history is at least implicitly a reasoned defense of the faith of the historian: ''This means that the basic differences between historians . . . are theological and/or philosophical and cannot be resolved by historical methods.''[5] Mead's history of America is therefore a testament to *his* faith.

What Mead does not acknowledge in these methodological excursions is the degree to which his writing of history—including both his interpretation of the biblical faith and his conception of the culmination of the story of God's redemptive work in history—is filtered through a tragic worldview. This is hardly surprising. A tragic view of life pervaded the cultural milieu in which he lived and wrote. Mid-twentieth-century American in-

[2]''Church History Explained,'' 29.

[3]Ibid.

[4]Ibid., 22.

[5]Ibid., 23.

tellectuals teaching in divinity schools were well tutored by neo-orthodox theologians and existentialists in neglected tragic dimensions of human experience. The move to incorporate Greek tragedy into Christian theology was part of the quest for a philosophy that would explain the disorders of the age. Yet, as we shall see, Mead's peculiar version of the tragic vision is uniquely his own and reveals an underlying sympathy with Enlightenment modes of thought that also went well beyond the biblical presuppositions that he chose to highlight in his methodology.

What is the Greek tragic vision? For the purposes of the following analysis, it shall be assumed to consist of four key elements in Edmond LaB. Cherbonnier's explication of the idea: (1) that "truth resides in the Whole"; (2) that the relation of the whole to its parts, or God to the world, is properly expressed as that of the infinite to the finite, or the absolute to the relative; (3) that hubris, the "absolutizing of the relative," is the principal cause of humanity's doom; and (4) that human failure is not finally a matter of human choice, but is somehow grounded in human nature as such, and that consequently humanity's doom is inevitable. At the center of the tragic vision, according to Cherbonnier, is a double perspective that holds in tension simultaneously both the standpoint of the infinite whole (in which all things are unified and which is beyond good and evil) and the standpoint of the finite parts (composed of incompatible and yet equally valid forces).[6]

II
Mead's Tragic Vision

The superimposition of a tragic world view on top of theocentric biblical faith and Enlightenment rationalism enables Mead to make many of the crucial turns in argument that characterize his distinctive interpretation of the meaning and history of the religion of the Republic: the essential continuity of biblical and Enlightenment thought, the truth in the relativist view that all roads lead to God, the tragic failure of sectarianism, the failure of the denominations to take responsibility for their own charter of liberty, the diminished power of the Republican ideal after the Civil War.

---

[6]Edmond LaB. Cherbonnier, "Biblical Faith and the Idea of Tragedy," in *The Tragic Vision and the Christian Faith,* ed. Nathan A. Scott, Jr. (New York: Association Press, 1957) 23-55.

To use Hegel's words, the first axiom in the tragic vision is "the truth is in the whole." From this first principle, according to Cherbonnier, everything else follows.

I contend that the heart of Mead's constructive position is the adoption of this axiom, its exemplification in his idealist philosophy of culture and his evolutionary ontology, and its development in terms of several interlocking ways of viewing the whole/part relationship: infinite/finite, genus/species, universal/particular.

Mead adopts the first axiom of the tragic world view in two primary ways. The first is his critical methodological assumption that there is a unified cultural "substance" at the base of every society. In Western society this means that the biblical "archetypal motivational myth . . . of God's spirit hovering over the dark and formless void" is shared by all members of Western civilization even when it is not acknowledged as such.[7] The notion of a Creator God is a "metaphysical intuition" that has informed Western civilization as a whole from its biblical beginnings. It follows that secularization is best understood as a forgetfulness of the source and character of this apprehension—a forgetfulness of one's true antecedents and "true self."[8]

Since biblical Christianity is the unifying and authentic truth that resides in Western civilization as a whole, each society within Western civilization is normatively accountable to it. It follows that the "religious substance" of American culture is biblical in character: "The presuppositions of our American culture have to do with a Judeo-Christian view of the existence and nature of God; the nature and structure of the universe; and the nature and destiny of man."[9] It is this biblical substance, in effect only a "new configuration of old ideas," that Mead calls the "religion of the Republic."[10]

The assumption that there is a unitary spiritual truth embodied in the whole of American culture is conceptualized by Mead in a variety of ways. For example, he frequently evokes Tillich's version of the Hegelian dic-

---

[7]*The Old Religion in the Brave New World* (Berkeley: University of California Press, 1977) 13.

[8]"The Task of the Church Historian," 139.

[9]*The Nation with the Soul of a Church* (New York: Harper & Row, 1975) 94.

[10]*Old Religion in the Brave New World*, 28.

tum: "Religion is the substance of culture, culture is the form of religion." In *The Old World Religion in the Brave New World* he cites Robert Bellah, Ruth Benedict, and Robin Williams in support of the sociological axiom that every coherent society is built upon shared religious understandings. It is on this basis, too, that he can readily affirm Chesterton's observation that the United States is a "nation with the soul of a church."

It should be noted how well this axiom also confirms the Enlightenment belief in a preestablished harmony behind or beneath all apparent contradictions.[11] The first principle of the Enlightenment was universalism: the belief that whatever is true in matters of faith and morals must be true for all persons and verifiable by all persons. Whether by an appeal to the "consensus gentium" or the single "pure light of nature" in each individual's mind or heart, the Enlightenment rationalists sought to move beyond the unique and changing to the common and permanent—to the truth that resides in the whole. When Mead set out in 1953 to write an "American church history that is to rise above denominationalism," he articulated an Enlightenment perspective on the priority of the whole over its parts.[12]

But Mead has another way of invoking the truth residing in the whole, one drawn much more from nineteenth-century evolutionary naturalism than from Enlightenment thought. This is his claim that the whole that alone can provide a true and salvific religious identity for humankind is one that embodies *immensity, permanence, and universality* in space and time. Mead finds such wholes in inclusive natural communities that persist through time and gather into their membership all who share a common biological origin and destiny. The greater the size and permanence of the community in space, and especially time, the greater the truth that it embodies, and the greater the opportunity for the individual to develop a stable and saving identity. "The larger, the more massive, inclusive and persistent in time, is the 'community' to which one relates—in brief, the more it transcends all the vicissitudes of man's day-by-day experiences,

---

[11]See A. O. Lovejoy, "The Parallel of Deism and Classicism," in *Essays in the History of Ideas* (New York: G. P. Putnam & Sons, 1968) 78-98. Mead's thought closely follows the elements of uniformitarianism, rationalistic individualism, cosmopolitanism, and intellectual equalitarianism that Lovejoy identifies as typifying Enlightenment thought.

[12]"Professor Sweet's Religion and Culture," 46.

the stronger and more stable will be his sense of personal identity."[13] For most of Mead's writing, the whole that includes all antinomies and yet itself knows no differences, discord, good or evil is the inclusive community of humanity itself.

But what is the meaning of community or the whole/part relationship here? In the first chapter of *The Nation with the Soul of a Church,* Mead establishes the dialectic of the infinite and the finite as definitive for the relation between the divine (whole) and the human (part). The first principle to which "every religion points" is that "no man is God": "This is what I understand to be the functional meaning of God in human experience. Whatever God may be—if indeed being is applicable to God—a concept of the infinite seems to be necessary if we are to state the all-important fact about man: that he is finite."[14] For Mead the human recognition of mortality is the crux of the religious quest: "To know where we are and whither tending religiously is not easy. Even a modicum of confidence that we are following a charted course to some destination other than dusty death, rests upon an unstable foundation of knowledge, faith, and desire."[15]

The quest of the divine is a quest for transcendence, or as Mead frequently refers to it, a quest for identity, by identification with something that surpasses the individual's brief span of existence. By faithful identification with that which is truly infinite, human beings overcome the despair of their mortality and learn to make peace with their transient particularity.

A second conception of the divine/human, whole/part relationship is the biological family/genus/species/individual hierarchical relationship. Indeed, so basic is this taxonomic model to Mead's thought that, in most basic respects, his account of the relation of the religion of the Republic to other forms of religion, past and present, may be perceived as the simple outworking of the model's structure. Thus, "If we presume to talk about 'religion' in our pluralistic society we must realize that the word points to

---

[13]"History and Identity," *Journal of Religion* 51 (1971): 10.

[14]*Nation with the Soul of a Church,* 9. Cf. Mead's definition of religion: "Religion . . . has to do on the one hand with the vastness and possibly infinite openness of the universe that our knowledge enables us to sense; it has to do on the other hand with the exquisitely intimate that we know in our individual being; and with the relation between them." In *Love and Learning* (Chico CA: New Horizons Press, 1978) 105.

[15]"The Lost Dimension and the Age of Longing," *Criterion* 4 (Autumn 1965): 9.

a numerous family in which there are hundreds of genera (the world's religions) and thousands of species and sub-species (e.g. denominations) each with its own protective institutional shell."[16] According to this reading, true religion (for Western culture, Christianity; for American culture, the religion of the Republic) points to the most encompassing entity for which it is itself only a genus.

It is now possible to spell out Mead's full theological schema. This can be done in terms of the double perspective that typifies the tragic worldview. The first perspective is that of the whole, which for Mead is manifest in unifying ideas and large and enduring communities: infinite, generic, universal. The second perspective is that of the parts, which is manifest in diversified, finite species or particulars. The relation between human beings and God, as the relation between the religion of the Republic and the "religion of the denominations," is the relation between the first and second of these two perspectives. Any drama that ensues from this starting point is inevitably a tragic one.

III
Mead's Tragic Drama

The consequences of Mead's tragic theology for his interpretation of the meaning and outcome of the religion of the Republic are evident in his dramatic interpretation of Western history. Mead divides his history into three successive acts, each more universal than the one preceding: Judeo-Christian, American, and Global. Each of the three acts begins with the promise of a new birth of holistic faith—a new intuition of the true meaning of the infinite community of which human beings are finite parts. The first two have ended in the tragedy of hubris and flawed human limitations. Although the third act has yet to reach its denouement, Mead anticipates a tragic conclusion.

There are two principles of the religion of the Republic that Mead traces through the course of the historical drama: individual freedom and equality. Each of these is interpreted in terms of the tragic double perspective. Because of limitations of space, I can only briefly note Mead's treatment of the first, freedom. The second, equality, will be the focus of a more extended summary.

---

[16]*Old Religion in the Brave New World*, 64.

The principle of individual freedom is variously described by Mead as the principle of "persuasion," moral autonomy, the right of private judgment, government by "consent of the governed" or by "reflection and choice." It is a principle that lies at the root of Western civilization. According to Whitehead, it is the sublime intuition of Plato manifest in the life of Jesus. For Mead it was also revealed in the Hebrew myth of the Garden of Eden when human beings first acquired moral independence and were forced to distinguish good and evil. Its reappearance in the religion of the Republic of the United States was predicated upon the prior assumption of the "finite limitation of the creature, man, *in every respect.*"[17] The American founders saw that, given the reality of human limitations, the notion of freedom inevitably followed. Since human beings could never have final knowledge, they could only reach opinions, and opinions were inherently matters of persuasion.

In the essay "American History as Tragic Drama," Mead spells out the historical fate of the "creative idea of the potential capacity of mankind to be 'free.' "[18] The tragic heroes of his drama are "the people" (the many finite particulars), and he finds that the idea of freedom (the truth in the whole) no longer speaks to them with power. Mead argues that the tragic outcome of the era when "wise men hoped" was clear by the end of the Civil War. By then most Americans sensed what the ninety-six communitarian experiments launched prior to 1860 had already discovered, that somehow human beings were incapable of achieving a social embodiment of the ideal of liberty. American history is best understood as a tragic drama because the "catastrophic end of the action is . . . a result of the free working out of flaws in the individual's character," because of "some flaw inherent in the nature of the medium itself—in other words, a flaw in the available human material, in 'the people.' "[19]

Americans became aware of their finitude as a moral category, that is, recognized the insufficiency of their capacities as finite creatures to embody their master ideal. As a consequence the ideal itself lost power, and the United States entered a period of long and slow decline.

---

[17]Ibid., 84.

[18]*History and Identity* (Missoula MT: Scholar's Press, 1979) 40.

[19]Ibid., 35, 40.

The drama of humanity's evolving awareness of the meaning of equality also begins in the Garden of Eden when Adam, having eaten of the tree of knowledge of past and future, knew that *as an individual* "he shall surely die." But at the same time, the Serpent (who in Mead's interpretation becomes the agent of God) assures Adam that *as a member of mankind* "he shall not surely die." Individual men, in their finitude, as "unique self-conscious creatures," live out their lives in the constant knowledge of their dissolution. In this they believe the Creator. As participants in the community of "mankind," however, they have hope of survival beyond death ("the substance of things hoped for, the evidence of things not seen"[20]).

Christ, whose death was swallowed up in victory, again revealed the hope of this kind of generic survival that Mead calls "Christian optimism." It follows that the ideal of the Church that took his name bears the cosmopolitan notion of a "single, organic, society which transcended and included all earlier distinctions" of humankind.[21] Tragedy ensued, however, when the Church took as its criterion of membership not universalistic Christology but the boundaries of absolutist nation-states.

The American religion of the Republic inherited the fundamental principle of Christian salvation and enshrined it as the premise of its New World revolutionary creed: "All men are created equal," that is, all men are equally finite before the infinite God. But the American founders carried the principle to a greater level of generality by analogizing the relationship between *individuals* and the species *humanity* with the relationship between particular *religions* and the universal religious identity that embraces and transcends them all: " 'A particular religion' is analogous to the particular individual who shall 'surely die,' while 'the religious' is the generic entity that 'shall not surely die' and may indeed 'overcome.' "[22] Thus every species of religion can contemplate its death while the genus in which it participates will survive.

---

[20]"Prospects for the Church in America," in *The Future of the American Church*, ed. Philip J. Hefner (Philadelphia: Fortress Press, 1968) 1-29.

[21]*Nation with the Soul of a Church*, 49.

[22]"Prospects for the Church in America," 5. Cf. "but now, in our pluralistic societies since the eighteenth century, the word 'religion' points to a genus in which there are thousands of different species, each with its own peculiar protective institutional shell." In *Nation with the Soul of a Church*, 115-16.

This ontology is the basis of Mead's claim that the religion of the Republic is theonomous, standing in opposition to idolatrous tendencies. All persons and all religions are equally finite and correct one another. The fundamental principle is the same in its Christian and New World embodiments. In Christianity, ''The sin of sins is the refusal to accept one's finite state and be truly man.''[23] The fundamental conviction of the religion of the Republic is ''remember, you too are mortal.''[24] The critical difference between Christianity and Enlightenment faith is that in the latter the metaphor of generic inclusiveness achieves a higher culmination by embracing all religions, as well as all races and nations, as equally finite parts of one humanity.

Because the United States embodied the principles of the religion of the Republic in its founding legal agreements, it has led the other institutions of our society in embodying the universal communal ideal.[25] America became an intermediate class, somewhere between the discrete individual and the species collectivity, the whole of humanity, which it was dedicated to exemplify. In this context the hope of denominationalism was that each individual religion brought to these shores would transcend itself and seek, before it died, to disclose how in the depths of its particular form resided the ideal of one humanity. Philip Schaff's hope of ''something wholly new'' was the potential emergence of a collective faith of higher universality than even that to which Christianity aspired.

Abraham Lincoln stands as the ''spiritual center of American history'' because he, above all others, in Mead's view, understood and affirmed this particular theological interpretation of the Republic. The infinite nature of

---

[23]''On the Meaning of History,'' 1363.

[24]*Nation with the Soul of a Church*, 10. See also 119: ''The obverse side of the Enlightenment's high doctrine of the Creator and Governor of the universe was the finite limitation of the creature in *every* respect.''

[25]Two of the essays included in *Nation with the Soul of a Church*, ''Neither Church nor State: Reflections on James Madison's 'Line of Separation,' '' and ''Religion, Constitutional Federalism, Rights, and the Court,'' are devoted to showing how constitutionally this is true. At the root of Mead's approach to the reading of the Constitution, however, is his own presupposition ''that the 'bonds of affection' which bind all the heterogeneous people together in such a union must somehow be more cosmopolitan, more universal, more general, than the 'bonds of affection' which bind a particular group of these people together in a particular voluntary association, even though it be called a church.'' In *Nation with the Soul of a Church*, 39.

God ("the Almighty has his own purposes") along with the finite and er-
ring nature of persons ("if, after endeavoring to do my best in the light
which he affords me, I find my efforts fail") were the twin perspectives
that Lincoln eloquently articulated and the foundation on which he sought
to save the Union. Operationally, this meant humility in the face of all relationships between persons ("with malice toward none; with charity for
all"). For Lincoln, it was the *whole* Union—the *whole* people, the United
States as the representative of humankind ("the last, best hope of earth"),
not any part to the exclusion or advantage of any other—that embodied the
will of God on earth.[26]

It is against this background that Mead tells his story of the tragic outcome of the ideal of religious equality in America. Within Protestantism,
the dominant right-wing Reformation denominations especially have failed
to see their specific religious forms as subspecies of an inclusive democratic faith, and themselves as equally partial embodiments of the inclusive democratic community. Indeed, they and their fellow denominations
of every creed now constitute the very antithesis of the kind of religious
community Mead's theology prescribes: "Any one 'church' in our society
is too small, too circumscribed in time and space, too droopy in its thinking, too competitive, too involved in its own survival, to offer a plausible
claim even to point to the transcendent community necessary for the
achievement of . . . identity."[27]

By rejecting the religion of the Republic, by claiming that they uniquely
represent infinite Deity, by—in a word—falling prey to the hubris of "sectarianism," the American churches have betrayed their spiritual trust. They
have committed the sin of Christian sins because they have refused to accept their finitude. They have absolutized the relative. Intellectually, this
sin has expressed itself in their failure to contribute to a theology of the
Republic. Still, it is in the realm of faith and works that their apostasy has
had its gravest consequences. They have created a society divided against
itself because it is divided into two religions—the "religion of the Republic" and the "religion of the (sectarian) denominations."

Mead brings down the curtain on the second act of his tragic drama with
the conclusion that by virtue of the American experiment "on behalf of all

---

[26]*The Lively Experiment* (New York: Harper & Row, 1963) 72-89.

[27]"History and Identity," 8.

humanity,'' humankind found itself as a species incapable of effectively
entertaining the Republican principles of freedom and equality, specifically that "no man is God." Not only the denominations, then, but humankind itself is shown to be incurably sectarian! It is a short step from
here to Mead's despair over the future of the human species and his oc-
casional characterization of humanity as a "planetary disease."[28]

If during the last decade Mead could still write convincingly of the ideals of the religion of the Republic, it is because this faith embodied what
ought to be true of humanity: "Truth resides in the whole." Yet in finite
historical existence we have learned that ontological truth cannot be realized. Those persons who live by it in spite of that knowledge are the tragic
heroes of the faith.[29]

However, in 1945 a change in the meaning of human finitude occurred
with the appearance of the atom bomb. This event, compounded by the
destructive consequences of additional technological feats since, has un-
dercut the Enlightenment faith in humanity as the transcendent community
of identity—even as an unrealizable tragic ideal. For Mead, Bertrand Russell and his religion of "the whole human race as one cooperative unity"
was an example of Enlightenment faith carried into the twentieth century,
but now "it should be obvious that Russell's community, although it included the 'whole human race,' is not inclusive enough or secure enough
to guarantee one a stable and secure identity."[30]

The third act in the drama of the religion of the Republic is beginning
for Mead as persons look beyond the human species to "Nature and Nature's God" for their transcendent community of identity. Only the natural
universe, the "mythology of modern man," has enough immensity, universality, and permanence in time and space to manifest the infinite. Loren
Eiseley supersedes Jefferson, Lincoln, and Augustine as a religious seer:

> The modern's analogy to the traditional "city of God," wherein "nei-
> ther moth nor rust doth corrupt, and where thieves do not break through or

[28]Mead quotes Loren Eiseley to this effect in "Not in Our Stars but Ourselves," address
delivered at the Meadville/Lombard Theological School 125th Anniversary Commence-
ment, 9 June 1970, Chicago IL.

[29]An important influence upon Mead has been Ross Lockridge's novel *Raintree County*
(Boston: Houghton Mifflin, 1948), which portrays the loss of the dream of the American
Republic.

[30]"History and Identity," 11.

steal'' (Matt. 6:20), is reared on the presupposition of unbroken continuity in the universe through billions of years, and must include not only all "living" things but all "inorganic" matter as well. . . . Finally, I am trying to suggest that the modern man can find a stable identity only in the context of unimaginable time, as he senses a mystical unity with all of life on its "immense journey."[31]

Yet this too is most likely only a prelude to a tragedy that is global in scope. Mead closes *The Nation with the Soul of a Church* with a brief epilogue that begins: "I have written these pieces with the chilling realization that we live today under the shadow of man's power to destroy all life on this planet. . . . I agree with Arthur Goldberg that probably man now has less than a fifty percent chance of survival."[32]

IV
The Judgments of History

Perhaps the greatest tribute that can be paid to Sidney Mead is to say that he has assumed the theological responsibility appropriate to a historian in the American Republic. In the words of David Noble, "Just as the historian is the citizen who is most responsible for describing our covenant, he is also the one most responsible for defending it—he is our most important secular theologian."[33] Most notably, Mead has performed this function from *within* the discipline of religious history.

But his theological contributions are not unambiguous. Mead aimed to provide an ontology for Enlightenment faith that underscores its theonomous center as opposed to an alleged Christian exclusivism and parochialism. By formal criteria this aim has been achieved, and Mead's theology has proven apologetically effective (if not always persuasive) in current debate. There is serious question, however, as to the adequacy of his tragic vision for illumining the principles of the Republic and for doing justice to the actual course of American history.

The difficulty is that both Mead's history and theology of the Republic are inadequate to the actual experience of the Republic. This is true in sev-

---

[31]Ibid., 11.

[32]*Nation with the Soul of a Church,* 127.

[33]David W. Noble, *Historians against History* (Minneapolis: University of Minnesota Press, 1965) 3.

eral respects. In the first, Mead's own historical retrieve is not adequately represented in his theology.

As a historian, Mead has repeatedly pointed to the positive pluralist character of Enlightenment faith. "Multiplicity," he wrote in *The Lively Experiment*, "is of the essence of democracy and must be maintained."[34] In *The Nation with the Soul of a Church* he observed that the viewpoint of the Founding Fathers was "synergistic" rather than "syncretistic."[35] Yet, in his own theology, by adopting the double perspective of infinite and finite, he fails *logically* to do justice to the differing perceptions of the transcendent in the historically various and particular. Individual religious differences become swallowed up in the infinite whole or lost among an infinite number of equally finite parts.

There are no categorical grounds in Mead's theology, as distinguished from his history, for the value of pluralism as a source of divine transcendence in human community. Nor is there room for the possibility that there may be differences in the capacities of various particulars to serve as bearers of a universal vision.

Yet the story that Mead has frequently told about the struggle for religious freedom in the course of the Revolution, and the reaction of orthodoxy to infidelity afterwards, is not a story about equally true or false opinions, but a story of struggle between *some* who affirmed the universal vision of the religion of the Republic and *some* who did not. By Mead's own reckoning, some Christian leaders, such as Lyman Beecher, became advocates of Republican principles, and others, such as Horace Bushnell, did not. It is a story, in other words, of partisanship.

By assuming the tragic worldview, Mead confounds rather than resolves the problem that the founders bequeathed to later generations. If, for example, we examine closely Mead's account of Benjamin Franklin's faith—that the same essential universal is "encapsulated" in the variety of unique particulars—then we must acknowledge that the early American theologians of the Republic maintained their *practical* respect for finite empirical diversity and their *theoretical* proclivity for universality at the cost of a sharp distinction between the "forms" (multiple and unique) and

---

[34]*Lively Experiment*, 83.

[35]*Nation with the Soul of a Church*, 59.

the "content" (single and uniform) of religion.[36] The religion of the Re-public has been plagued by this bifurcation ever since. It is still present, as Mead notes, in the contradictory assertion, made by many Christians, that all religions lead to the same God and that belief in Jesus Christ is abso-lutely essential for salvation. It is also present in the perplexity of those who choose the democratic faith because of a real commitment to plural-ism and universalism and discover that the choice has no particular content but is merely the common core of all faiths.

Mead can hardly be faulted for failing to provide a solution to the long-standing and difficult philosophical issue of the one and the many. What may be suggested, however, is that in his zeal for a theonomous univer-salism he has adopted an ontology that, when tested against his own his-torical testimony, obscures the fact that the religion of the Republic has never been a common religion but only a particular religion seeking to be common. *That* historical reality would seem to find far more adequate theological treatment in a biblical theology that affirms life's incurably partisan qualities and God's active struggle for allegiance among willfully good and bad human beings. The discrepancy between what is and what should be is not, in the first place, a metaphysical but rather a moral dis-tinction. And it is one that is still quite alive in the choices concerning free-dom and equality that face the citizen of the Republic today.

A second way in which Mead's theology is inadequate is that it has ap-parently blocked him from attending to the full story of the religion of the Republic in American history. In addition to eighteenth-century rational-ism, Mead has developed in his writings only three other major historical versions of the religion of the Republic: romantic transcendentalism ("that one mind, one will, pervades everything and is bodied forth in particu-lars"),[37] evangelical Protestantism ("that 'the church'—the body of Christ—was . . . the symbol of the unity of all believers in the 'idea and purpose' of God"),[38] and Lincoln's faith in the ultimate wisdom of "the people." But this means he has omitted entirely from the purview of both

---

[36]"Here, then, was a radical conceptual separation of the substance or essence of reli-gion from its tangible forms, the socially devised vehicles, of religion." In *Nation with the Soul of a Church*, 120.

[37]*Lively Experiment*, 94.

[38]"Prospects for the Church in America," 14.

his history and theology the development of democratic faith in the century following the Civil War.

Yet such ground offers rich soil, as Ralph Gabriel's portrayal of Whitman's "religion of humanity" suggests.[39] Certainly there has been no more influential protagonist of the religion of the Republic than John Dewey, whose condemnation of the churches' attempt to "claim a monopoly in a common world" (1893) and whose distinction between the "religious" and the "religions" (1934) constitute the proximate historical background to Mead's own work.[40] If I were to posit the cause of Mead's neglect, it would be this: the worldview of Dewey and other early-twentieth-century naturalistic humanists was reputedly so uncritically optimistic regarding the outcome of American democracy that it was perceived as an obstacle by Mead, who wanted to prove the theonomous character of democratic faith and its capacity to do justice to the tragic aspects of contemporary existence. This stereotype of American pragmatism regrettably robbed Mead of important philosophical resources within the Enlightenment tradition. In particular, it robbed him of the help of an evolutionary theology that was frankly pluralistic and that in its functionalism sought to maintain an inclusive vision of humanity without a split between form and content.

There is one further respect in which Mead's theology is not adequate to the American experience. Mead's interpretation of American history has from the beginning run on the axes of time and space. In the first chapter of *The Lively Experiment,* Mead argued that space—unlimited space—was the determinative influence upon the immigrants to the New World: "He who would understand America must understand that through all the formative years, space has overshadowed time—has taken precedence over time in the formation of all the ideals most cherished by the American mind and spirit.''[41] Most basic of the ideals that the vast space gave to the new American was the definition of freedom as unconfined movement in space, as separation from habit, custom, and tradition, as the possibility of an autonomous moral existence. The turning point in American religious and

---

[39]See Ralph Gabriel, *The Course of American Democratic Thought,* 183ff.

[40]See John Dewey, "Christianity and Democracy," in *The Early Works,* 1882-1898, ed. Jo Ann Boydston, 5 vols. (Carbondale: Southern Illinois University Press, 1969-1972) 4:3-10; and *A Common Faith* (New Haven: Yale University Press, 1934).

[41]*Lively Experiment,* 11-12.

political history came when the unlimited space ran out. It was then that the brute necessity of persons living together in a common place led to what the frontier islands of American Christendom had never really accepted: religious toleration. As a result, the frontier idea of freedom was shown to be "askew and inadequate."

Mead had an answer to that problem in 1954: "While space on this earth is obviously limited, time is less so and may indeed be infinite."[42] Mead's most recent evolutionary theology of the Republic, initiating the third act in his tragic drama of Western civilization, may be seen as an extended development of that early insight. Unfortunately, his preoccupation with duration through time has entailed a gradual attenuation of the worldly, ethical dimension of human experience. The content of the transcendent community of identity, as Mead has conceived it, has changed from the people as the "moral structure . . . on which all inequalities and injustices break" to the people as "unbroken biological continuity . . . not good or evil," to "life itself." The religious importance of concrete, practical human interaction with space disappears from view.

However, space is not so easily discarded from our experience. It is both the stage of our earthly drama and the sacrament we daily share. Apart from the diverse qualities of nature in their spatial spread, "life itself" is unimaginable. The fact that today these qualities are diminishing under the impact of urbanization, and that choices must be made about them within the finite limits of this earth, cannot be avoided by a faith in life itself, no matter how poetically portrayed. It is time to consider again the American experience of space.

What Mead's profound grasp of the contemporary human condition calls for—what his penetrating retrieval of American religious history leads us to seek, yet what his theology fails to provide—is an ecological perspective on human history and destiny in which the variety that is our common humanity takes its place within the variety of all natural creation. Here every individual and every species would be potentially both an end in itself and a synergistic means to the flourishing of a common world. I submit that it is to some such vision of a "Republic of the World" that Mead's theology of the democratic faith must move if it is to do justice to the full American experience of the tragedy and hope of our shared existence.

---

[42]Ibid., 13.

· ● Part II ● ·

Mr. Jefferson's "Fair Experiment" in Practice

·● 4 ●·

"Liberty, Both Civil and Religious"

Winthrop S. Hudson

Sidney E. Mead, in one of his earliest and most perceptive essays, "American Protestantism during the Revolutionary Epoch" (*Church History*, 1953), noted that "the Revolutionary Epoch is the hinge upon which the history of Christianity in America really turns."

> During this period, forces and tendencies long gathering during the colonial era culminated in new expressions which came to such dominance that a fresh direction was given to the thought patterns and institutional life of the churches. The symbolic center of these new expressions is found in the declarations for religious freedom and the separation of church and state.

The intention of this essay is to explore one aspect of the gathering force in the colonial era that made the new direction by the new nation and its churches almost inevitable.

A curious feature of the American Revolution was the conviction of the colonists (in other words, those who supported the war) that by defending their own rights as Englishmen, they were at the same time engaged in a struggle to preserve the liberties of Great Britain. Bernard Bailyn's analysis of the pamphlet literature of the decades preceding the Revolution has made it clear that "the fear of a comprehensive conspiracy against liberty throughout the English-speaking world" stood at the center of the revolutionary movement. Himself believing in such a plot, Jonathan

Mayhew contended that by defending their own rights, the colonists may have "the great felicity and honor" to "keep Britain herself from ruin."[1]

While the immediate aim of the conspiracy was thought to be the reduction of the colonists to docility, the colonists were convinced that the ultimate aim was the destruction of the rights and privileges of all Englishmen. Thus it was no parochial struggle in which the colonists were engaged. First the colonies were to be reduced and then Britain herself. John Adams later recalled that Oxenbridge Thacher reflected common opinion when he spoke of the determination of the British government

> to new-model the colonies from the foundation, to annul all their charters, to constitute them royal governments, to raise revenue in America by parliamentary taxation, to apply that revenue to pay the salaries to governors, judges, and all other crown officers, . . . and further establish bishops and the whole system of the Church of England, tithes and all, throughout British America. This system, he said, if it were suffered to prevail, would extinguish the flame of liberty all over the world, that America would be employed as an engine to batter down all the miserable remains of liberty in Great Britain and Ireland, where only any semblance of it was left in the world.

As for Adams himself, he was convinced that "temporal and ecclesiastical tyranny" were ever conjoined; so in 1765, in an essay on feudal and canon law, he had issued a peremptory summons: "Let the pulpit resound with the doctrines and sentiments of religious liberty," for there is "a direct and formal design on foot to enslave all America."[2] The preachers did respond to the peremptory summons. The slogan they used to summarize the colonial concern was brief and to the point—"liberty, both civil and religious." This was to be the rallying cry of the revolutionary cause, the rallying cry of preachers, pamphleteers, and stump-speakers alike—"liberty, both civil and religious."

The story thus far is familiar enough, but there are two points that are puzzling and deserve attention. The first point actually is more neglected than puzzling. How was such a lively sense of the colonists' rights as Englishmen maintained in the American wilderness? How was an awareness of their legacy as Englishmen preserved and not allowed to grow dim?

---

[1]Bernard Bailyn, *The Ideological Origins of the American Revolution* (Cambridge: Belknap Press of Harvard University Press, 1967) ix, 140.

[2]*Works of John Adams,* edited by C. F. Adams (Boston, 1850-1856) 3:450-51, 462, 464, x, 286.

The second point is more mystifying than the first. How did the concern for religious liberty become linked to the concern for civil liberty in the rallying cry of the American Revolution? What is the explanation for the widespread acceptance of religious liberty as a commonplace aspect of the colonists' heritage? The puzzling feature of "liberty, both civil and religious" as a shorthand summary of the rights for which they fought is that it appeared everywhere and was constantly reiterated by everyone as a concise statement of the revolutionary cause.

Before proceeding to deal with these two questions, it is important to note that "liberty, both civil and religious" was but one of a series of slogans or catchwords that, taken together, constituted the American self-image. Among the figures of speech that were utilized to express the American sense of vocation were such phrases as "a city set on a hill," "the eyes of the world are upon you," "an example to the nations," "an asylum for the oppressed," "the guardians of liberty," "the last hope of earth" (the latter slogan became more luminous when Abraham Lincoln expanded it to "the last best hope of earth").

Each of the slogans has a long history. Most American political rhetoric dates from the earliest years of the colonial period when the colonists, particularly in New England, quickly developed a language and vocabulary—almost a litany—to convey their sense of identity and vocation. The figures of speech took on a sort of independent life of their own, accumulating powerful emotional connotations and becoming touchstones that identified America's role and mission in the life of the world.

One such phrase, which conveyed a commonly accepted image of America, was the simple designation of America as an "asylum for the oppressed." John Winthrop and William Penn, among others, used the phrase in their accounts of the colonies, and for more than three hundred years it remained a central feature of the American self-image: an image that was partly eroded as the nation became preoccupied with the problem of immigration, but an image that still retained sufficient compelling power in the emotions of the American people to precipitate a minor crisis for the Nixon administration.

"The eyes of the world are upon you" has been equally commonplace as a rhetorical expression to delineate America's understanding of its vocation as an "experiment" or an "example" to the nations. From John Winthrop through Andrew Jackson to Woodrow Wilson, this exhortation has constantly recurred in patriotic oratory to remind the American people that they have been engaged in no parochial venture, that a cosmopolitan role important to all mankind has been assigned to them, and that by exhibiting before the eyes of the world the prosperity and happiness of a free society, their very example will provoke reform and revolution among enslaved peoples everywhere until the whole world is free. In this sense, as "guardians" and "exemplars" of liberty, the American people constituted, in Abraham Lincoln's words, "the last best hope of earth." If the American experiment should fail, little hope would remain for the rest of mankind.

It also is important to note that the literary images of commonly accepted political rhetoric, so long as they retained some degree of vitality and did not become purely conventional and devoid of emotional content, operated in three ways. They served, first of all, as symbolic expressions of an ideology to which people, consciously or unconsciously, committed themselves and found it difficult to abandon. The rhetoric thus became a type of ideological constraint holding them firm to a specific role in or understanding of the national vocation. Ideological constraint also was exercised in the sense that the various symbolic expressions, watchwords, slogans, and phrases of the commonly accepted rhetoric had to be capable of harmonization, of being brought together in the service of a single, consistent ideology. Unless this could be done, it would be necessary to abandon some of the rhetoric, for a people cannot long maintain a split image embracing incompatible elements. The third and last feature of commonly accepted rhetoric is that it exerts constant pressure for practice to be brought into conformity with profession. For a time—occasionally for a considerable period of time—shelter from the discrepancy between profession and practice can be found in an apologetic based on supposedly practical considerations. Ultimately, however, the apologetic has to give way or the ideology be surrendered. In many cases, when the issue is forced, the rationalization is found to be weaker than the ideology, and the apologetic is abandoned more easily than the ideology. This presupposes, of course, that the ideology—inculcated in the patriotic rhetoric of schoolbooks, political orations and sermons, as well as in the communal memory of family life—has retained a degree of vitality and emotional power.

With these reflections on the coercive power of political rhetoric in mind, let us return to the rallying cry of the Revolution, "liberty, both Civil and Religious," and consider the two points that I previously invoked.

First, how was a lively sense of the colonists' rights as Englishmen maintained in the American wilderness? How does one explain the widespread familiarity with both the details and presumed historical rootage of English liberties, privileges, and rights?

In early New England where charters gave the colonists almost complete independence, Scripture was more cherished as a basis for modeling a new government than anything else. It was only when Massachusetts Bay was seriously threatened with the loss of its charter and then after the charter had been revoked that New Englanders began to give attention to their rights as Englishmen and to rehearse them in their election sermons. And it was not until the Revolution of 1689 in Massachusetts that they expounded their rights as Englishmen in systematic fashion.[3]

There were several sources, including communal memory, for New Englanders to draw upon for their knowledge of the rights of Englishmen; but these sources were limited. For the most part they were limited to tracts and treatises published during the English Civil War.[4] Commonly overlooked, however, is William Penn's contribution in helping colonists remember their rights as Englishmen. At a critical juncture he gave them an easily available source that spelled out the detailed specifications of the rights and privileges of all freeborn Englishmen. John Locke's *Two Treatises on Government*, published in 1690, may have quickly reached New England; however, it was published too late for the Massachusetts Revolution of 1689, and it was of little use for the immediate purpose at hand since the portion of the manuscript dealing with English precedents and the English constitution had been torn

---

[3]Their rights as Englishmen were rehearsed within the context of a communal memory nurtured by historical accounts written as continuations of Foxe's "Book of Martyrs" and by references and allusions to experiences of their forbears in the weekly sermons and lectures of the preachers. Practical politics may have been learned at the town meeting, but it was the long memory of past events that gave meaning and significance to present crises. So familiar were common folk with past crises that pointed up a present moral that Ezra Stiles could refer to "half a dozen bishops on this continent and a long string of &c. &c." in perfect confidence that the reader would recognize the allusion to the "Et cetera Oath" that had troubled the consciences of Englishmen more than a century before.

[4]An important Civil War publication was the printing, by order of the House of Commons, of parts 2, 3, and 4 of Sir Edward Coke's *Institutes of the Laws of England*, the manuscript of which had been seized and suppressed in 1634. While small tracts and treatises had considerable circulation in New England, one wonders how many copies of these large folio volumes made their way across the Atlantic. Certainly they were not widely available.

out and destroyed. Algernon Sidney's *Discourses Concerning Government* also was of no help, not being published until 1698. William Penn, though, had been concerned with the rights and liberties of every freeborn Englishman for almost thirty years, and he had been writing and publishing with regularity throughout these three decades.

In 1677, when Penn drafted his "Laws, Concessions, and Agreements" for the province of West Jersey, he stated that his central purpose was to make known to the inhabitants of the province "such liberties as were guaranteed by law for the good government of a people, in accord with . . . 'the primitive, ancient, and fundamental laws of the people of England,' " and by making them known to enable the inhabitants to preserve such liberties in the New World.[5] Penn took equal care in drafting his charters of "liberties" and "privileges" for the province of Pennsylvania. These charters were supplemented by Penn with a little book, printed in Philadelphia in 1687, entitled *The Excellent Privilege of Liberty and Property, Being the Birthright of Freeborn Subjects of England,* to which was appended a copy of the second Frame of Government. Once again, as he observed in the preface, Penn's purpose in publishing this small booklet was to acquaint the settlers of his infant domain with their "inestimable inheritance" as freeborn Englishmen and to help them understand "how to preserve" their inheritance "from unjust and unreasonable men." The Magna Charta, the Petition of Right, the *Habeas Corpus* Act, and other pertinent documents were printed in full, and supplemented with commentaries, heavily larded with citations from Edward Coke's *Institutes of the Laws of England* that made plain the colonists' rights as Englishmen. Penn noted that law books were scarce in America and that few colonists "have leisure from their plantations to read large volumes." Consequently he expressed the hope that the printing of these basic documents, with accompanying explanations of "what is their native right and inheritance," would be of "use and service" in raising up "noble resolutions in all the freeholders in these new colonies not to give away anything of liberty and property that at present they do (or by right as loyal English subjects ought to) enjoy." Heed "the good example of our ancestors," he exhorted them, "and understand that it is easy to part with or give away great privileges but [they are] hard to be regained if once lost."

---

[5]Bailyn, *Ideological Origins,* 195-96.

It is important to note that, at a time when John Locke had scarcely cast off Hobbesian political views, Penn was insisting that no one can "take away the Liberty and Property of any (which are natural rights) without breaking the law of nature."[6] Nor was this concern for the rights of Englishmen an incidental and transient preoccupation. It dated from Penn's own arrest in 1670 for preaching (that is, creating a tumult) in the streets, an event that provided the occasion for his publishing *The People's Ancient and Just Liberties Asserted in the Trial of William Penn and William Mead* (1670). During the 1670s Penn wrote and published six more tracts or treatises explicating "the ancient and undoubted rights of Englishmen," including a treatise, *England's Great Interest in the Choice of This New Parliament* (1679), written to advance the candidacy of his close friend, Algernon Sidney. Penn's concern for the rights of Englishmen did not abate thereafter: thirty years later, in 1709, Penn edited and published Bulstrode Whitelocke's capsule account of English history in order, as Penn put it, "to make it easy for every Englishman to know his own country, its settlement, constitution, customs, and laws . . . , that we may have a true idea of their legal power and our legal liberty."[7] Thus Penn's interest was consistent and continuous over a period of forty years.

Of all the compositions that can be assigned with reasonable assurance to William Penn, none was of more importance than his *English Liberties; or, The Freeborn Subject's Inheritance,* first published in 1682 and destined through repeated editions to have a long and influential history in both England and America.[8] This small handbook was designed to help Protestant Dissenters manage their defense when hailed into court. More specifically, its purpose was to help them maintain their "liberties, both civil and religious." The first section was the compilation of documents and commentaries that he later published in Philadelphia in 1687. This section was followed by a discussion of the role and powers of Parliament, reproduced verbatim from his 1679 treatise written to advance Algernon Sid-

---

[6]*The People's Ancient and Just Liberties Asserted in the Trial of William Penn and William Mead* (London, 1670) 48.

[7]*Memorials of the English Affairs from the Supposed Expedition of Brute to This Island to the End of the Reign of King James I, Published from His Original Manuscript . . . by William Penn* (London, 1709) vi.

[8]For assignment of authorship, see Winthrop S. Hudson, "William Penn's *English Liberties*: Tract for Several Times," *William and Mary Quarterly* 3rd ser., 26:578-85.

ney's candidacy for a seat in Parliament. A third section set forth "the laws against conventicles and Protestant Dissenters," with suggestions as to how legal technicalities could be invoked to escape conviction or win release. Finally, there was a section devoted to instructing ordinary people in the principles and procedures of jury trials.

New editions of *English Liberties* were published in 1691 and 1692, but the 1700 edition was a new book in purpose and design. The Act of Toleration having been promulgated, the section presenting "all the laws against conventicles and Protestant Dissenters" was deleted and two new sections added. The title page summarized the additions as follows.

> II. OF JUSTICES OF THE PEACE: their oath, office, and power, . . . with several law cases alphabetically digested for ease and brevity, and warrants proper thereto placed exact after each case. . . . as also directions for drovers, badgers, butchers, tool-keepers, and clerks of the market, etc.
>
> III. THE CORONER AND CONSTABLE'S DUTY, relating to dead bodies, murder, manslaughter, felo-de-se (suicide); arrests, escapes, and conservation of the peace.

By this substitution *English Liberties* became a general legal handbook for almost everyone. Its use was facilitated by the inclusion of a "Table of some of the most material contents," which quickly directed the user to the information he was seeking. But basically, as the Epistle Dedicatory affirmed, the book remained "an abbreviation of the laws, rights, and privileges" of Englishmen that "every man and woman become heirs to so soon as they are born into the world"—the consequence being that "all the nations of the world" can but "wonder and admire the blessed freedom of Englishmen" while at the same time they "condole their own nativities, being born under the tyrannic yoke of arbitrary princes."

The great utility of *English Liberties* was its size, being small enough to slip into one's pocket. The publisher of the 1700 edition noted that members of Parliament had large legal tomes (for instance, the works of Coke, Fitzherbert, and Lambarde) at hand, but few others had ready access to information concerning their legal rights and constitutional liberties. The dependence upon such a small compendium was even more true in America where, as Penn had noted, law books were unusually scarce. The continued usefulness of the book both in England and in America is attested by the fact that a new London edition in 1719 was followed almost immediately by the first American edition published in Boston in 1721 (still another American edition was published in Providence in 1774). Meanwhile Edward and Charles Dilly, who were active in exporting books to America, had brought out an updated version entitled *British Liberties; or, The Freeborn Subject's Inheritance, Containing the Laws That Form the Basis of Those Liberties with Observations* (1766).

There are several important features to note in connection with the initial 1682 edition of *English Liberties:* the unusually large number of copies printed, the arrangement for widespread distribution, and especially its availability in New England (and presumably elsewhere in the colonies) prior to the Revolution of 1689 in Massachusetts.[9] It was printed by George Larkin "to be sold by most booksellers" with separate imprints for John How and Benjamin Harris. All three publishers of this edition—Larkin, How, and Harris—were zealous partisans who specialized in providing books and tracts to serve the Dissenting and Whig interests. Benjamin Harris fled London and set up shop in Boston in 1686, gaining fame posthumously as the publisher both of the first newspaper in America and of the *New England Primer,* an adaptation of *The Protestant Tutor* that he had previously compiled and published in England. A surviving reference, however, indicates that in 1686 he was chiefly known in New England as one of the three publishers of *English Liberties.*[10] There is also a suggestion that John How visited Boston at about the same time. In any event, Harris was in Boston at the time of the Revolution of 1689 and had close connections with leading political and religious figures.

One would expect that *English Liberties* would have been widely used in the area of greatest Quaker influence, which was New Jersey, Pennsylvania, and Delaware. Although no attempt has been made to document this reasonable supposition, some confirmation that *English Liberties* was not unknown in the Delaware and Chesapeake area may be inferred from the fact that Daniel Dunlavy, Sr. made use of it when he drafted his *Right of the Inhabitants of Maryland to the Benefit of English Laws* (Annapolis, 1728).

At the very least, it would seem clear that this 250-page pocket-size handbook, first prepared in 1682 and widely circulated in seven subsequent editions, had more to do with acquainting the colonists with a detailed knowledge of their rights as Englishmen and in forming the mind-

---

[9]Ibid., 583-84.

[10]Harris maintained his interest in *English Liberties,* recognizing it as an unusually marketable item, for it was he who published the revised 1700 edition after his return to England.

set of the American Revolution than larger but less accessible tomes. It is
not unlikely, for example, that many of the citations of Coke's *Institutes*
were derivative, being culled from the commentaries provided by Penn's
English Liberties.

More mystifying than the colonists' intimate and detailed knowledge
of the specifics of their civil rights and privileges as Englishmen was their
widespread acceptance of religious liberty as a commonplace aspect of their
heritage. This is the second puzzling point that deserves some attention.

John Adams's summons to "let the pulpit resound with the doctrines
and sentiments of religious liberty" would surely not have been a puzzling
rallying cry for participants in the Revolution from Pennsylvania, New
Jersey, Delaware, and New York, places where an extensive religious
freedom prevailed and was cherished. Nor would it have been surprising
as a summons to dissenting Presbyterians and Baptists in the Southern colonies who were firm opponents of the Anglican establishment. Moreover,
the slogan "liberty, both civil and religious" would not have seemed
strange on the lips of Rhode Islanders. It was the universal watchword of
the Revolution, and New Englanders of Massachusetts and Connecticut,
with their established churches, were as insistent as anyone else that they
were fighting for "liberty, both civil and ecclesiastical." The puzzle is
further compounded by the fact that the slogan itself, so far as the colonies
are concerned, seems to have been derived from New England. What we
have, quite obviously, is a phrase that through the years had been given
broader meanings and broader applications and that was susceptible to further redefinition in the future.

According to William Bradford, the Plymouth contingent in New England initially had sought refuge in "the Low Countries where they heard
there was freedom of religion for all men." Then because the twelve-year
truce with the Spaniards was about to expire, they had sought a place of
"less danger" and more secure "liberty" amid the acknowledged hazards
of the New World. A similar desire for liberty to "bring into familiar and
constant practice" that which previously they had been able to "maintain
as truth in profession only" was the motivating desire of the "great mi-
gration" that began with the Winthrop fleet. The freedom that they sought,
however, was freedom for themselves. The right to dissent was circumscribed; and this limitation stood in marked contrast to the broad toleration
that was granted in such havens for dissent as Rhode Island, Maryland,
and Pennsylvania. New Jersey, under Quaker influence, early extended a

welcome to people representing a broad spectrum of differing religious views. New York, in more halting fashion, moved in this direction as a result of inherited diversity and pressures exerted first by the Dutch Reformed and then by the Presbyterians. The adjustment of New England Congregationalists, on the other hand, was long and torturous.

Early New England Congregationalists saw no reason why their attempt to fashion a new Zion in the American wilderness should be compromised by dissidence. Others, they contended, had full liberty to stay away. They reminded those who differed from them that they had equal freedom to establish settlements of their own in unoccupied areas of America. Banishment became an established policy, but John Cotton explained that, in view of the "large and fruitful" country "round about," banishment was not so much "a confinement as an enlargement." As a result of this type of thinking, Nathaniel Morton, in his *New England's Memorial* (1669), found nothing incongruous in concluding his report of the year 1657 by rejoicing that "we sit under our vines and fig trees in peace, enjoying both civil and religious liberties."

The attempt to suppress dissent in Massachusetts was never wholly successful. A degree of indulgence was granted, as in the case of Henry Dunster. More important, the policy of banishment created new settlements from which the contagion of dissent filtered back into the older settlements. Moreover, all New Englanders had been taught from childhood that faith was a gift of grace and that forced worship was an abomination to the Lord. Augmenting the problem of suppressing dissent was the fact that every orthodox New Englander made at least a formal acknowledgment of his own fallibility and of the possibility that the Lord may have "more light yet to break forth out of his Holy Word." It is not surprising, therefore, that Congregationalism was forever spawning its own dissidents—men and women who defended themselves by appealing to the truth that had been made known to them from "the written Word of God." Nor were Congregationalist consciences eased by the constant needling from fellow Congregationalists in England who sought to persuade them to adopt more liberal views and a more liberal policy.

These several factors created a degree of uneasiness regarding efforts to preserve the facade of uniformity in their new Zion. However, what most immediately effected a new stance in Massachusetts was the prospect of the colony's charter being revoked. This would cost the colony its relatively independent status. The defense of the charter demanded a vigorous assertion of the colonists' liberties, both civil and ecclesiastical. The election sermons exhibit the shift that began to take place. John Oxenbridge's sermon of 1671 was an impassioned plea "not to part with any of our liberties," with a reminder to his audience that "your civil and your religious liberties are so coupled" that "if the one be lost, the other cannot be kept." The sermon concluded with a rhetorical question and a rhetorical answer: If you "neglect your golden liberties, what will England say of you?" The answer will be "that you are not new English but no English men." Two years later Urian Oakes was equally intent on alerting the magistrates to guard against any attempt to "undermine and rob us of our liberties, civil and religious, to the enslaving of the people and their children after them." The sermons, to be sure, exhibit the tortuousness involved in asserting one's own liberties without granting too much to others. Still, it must be remembered that not even Roger Williams or John Locke advocated an unlimited religious freedom.[11]

After the charter was revoked and the English Act of Toleration (1689) was adopted, New England Congregationalists utilized the Act of Toleration as their chief defense of their own liberties, and an effort was made to develop a united form of sorts with Baptists to provide a broader base to counter Anglican pretensions and Anglican intrusions into New England religious affairs. Still later the aggressive designs of Anglican missionaries, backed by their prestige as representatives of the established faith of the governing authorities, pushed the Congregationalists to defend their own rights even more strongly on the basis of rights that belonged to all. By 1736 the entire story of the New England settlement had been recast, with Thomas Prince—in the dedication to his *Chronological History of New England*—reporting that "the worthy fathers" of these plantations had "left their own and their fathers' houses" out of "their great concern" that "liberty, both civil and ecclesiastical, might be continued to their successors." A quarter century later, in 1760, Ezra Stiles spoke of "the grand errand" of our fathers into America, an errand that must "never be forgotten."

> The right of conscience and private judgement is unalienable; and it is truly the interest of all mankind to unite themselves into one body for the liberty, free exercise, and unmolested enjoyment of this right. . . . And

---

[11]For a discussion of this limitation, see Winthrop S. Hudson, "John Locke: Heir of Puritan Political Theorists," in George L. Hunt, *Calvinism and the Political Order* (Philadelphia, 1965) 121-24.

being possessed of the precious jewel of religious liberty, a jewel of unestimable worth, let us prize it highly and esteem it too dear to be parted with on any terms lest we be again entangled with that yoke of bondage which our fathers could not, would not, and God grant that we may never, submit to bear.[12]

In a similar vein, Amos Adams in 1768 contended that "liberty is the *fundamental* principle of our establishment."[13]

Believing themselves firmly committed to the principle and practice of religious liberty,[14] the Massachusetts delegates to the Continental Congress in 1774 were astonished, disconcerted, and aggrieved to be accused of maintaining an oppressive establishment of religion. John Adams indignantly replied that the Massachusetts establishment was "the most mild and equitable establishment of religion in the world," so mild indeed that it could scarcely be called an establishment.[15]

The Massachusetts leaders in general tended to regard Massachusetts practice as a most perfect system of liberty, for each town was perfectly free in the determination of its own affairs, thus obviating the possibility of any centralized engine of ecclesiastical tyranny. The congregational form of polity itself was a sure and safe guarantee of universal liberty. Futhermore, when new towns were formed, as in New Hampshire, it was not unusual for Baptists, Presbyterians, and even Quakers to constitute themselves the town church, with all the rights and privileges appertaining thereunto. Moreover, within the towns, dissenters were free to organize, pick their own minister and officers, and, having secured a certificate from others of their own denomination, to receive exemption from all "ministerial taxes." The depiction of the religious liberty then prevailing was somewhat ideal-

---

[12]Carl Bridenbaugh, *Miter and Sceptre: Transatlantic Faiths, Ideas, Personalities, and Politics, 1689-1775* (New York: Oxford University Press, 1962) 3.

[13]*Religious Liberty an Invaluable Blessing* (Boston, 1768) 39.

[14]When the Continental Congress convened on 5 September 1774, a communication was received from Massachusetts outlining how important it was for the colonies to unite as a means of recovering "their just rights and liberties, civil and religious." Twelve days later the Congress was reminded by the Suffolk (MA) Resolves of the "indispensable duty which we owe to God, our country, ourselves, and posterity . . . to remain, defend, and preserve those civil and religious rights for which many of our fathers fought, bled, and died, and to hand them down entire to future generations."

[15]Bailyn, *Ideological Origins,* 248.

ized, for there were gaps both in theory and in practice. Still, the important point is that New Englanders, no less than inhabitants of other colonies, were firmly committed to a verbal acceptance of the principle of religious liberty and had no hesitancy in adopting "liberty, both civil and religious" as the slogan of the American Revolution. In so doing, however, they were subjecting themselves to an ideological constraint that was to have further and more drastic consequences for both their theory and practice.

For most of the colonies, the slogan "liberty, both civil and religious" provided no real problem. Where Anglican establishments existed, with the exception of Virginia, they quickly toppled. In North Carolina a paper establishment ceased to exist even before hostilities had begun. The toppling of the establishment in Virginia was not so easily or quickly accomplished, but the result was foreordained by the compulsive power of the slogan to which Virginians had so readily committed themselves in the revolutionary struggle. It was difficult to harmonize Patrick Henry's "give me liberty or give me death" with continuing restraints and disabilities.

In Massachusetts, Connecticut, and New Hampshire the situation was a bit different. Over the course of three-quarters of a century the leadership had evolved its own apologetic that permitted them to believe that practice matched profession—that they had in actuality worked out if not the most perfect, at least the most practical, mild, and generous form of religious liberty. The apologetic, however, was not convincing to New England's sectarian dissenters—Baptists, Episcopalians, Quakers, Methodists, "New Light" Congregationalists, and other enthusiasts. And in the end the lingering quasiestablishments of New England had to match profession with practice and fall in line with the understanding of "liberty, both civil and religious" that prevailed throughout the rest of the country.

·● 5 ●·

On Jeffersonian Liberty

Edwin S. Gaustad

Sidney Mead is a man of steady loyalties: to wife, to profession, to philosophers and presidents. His presidential loyalties are conspicuously two: Thomas Jefferson and Abraham Lincoln. His fascination with these great oaks, known to his students years before, became evident to a wider world in separate articles published in 1954 and to a still-wider world in book form in 1963 (*The Lively Experiment*, Harper & Row). But for two decades more, this teacher (how he has made that appellation noble again!) has continued to remind us of and elaborate on the insights of the Jeffersonian and Lincolnian minds. If Lincoln is the "spiritual center of American history," Jefferson most clearly adumbrated the Enlightenment religion that Mead considers the mainstay of what he designated "the religion of the Republic." Here I return not to that specific theme, but to the broader dedication to liberty that was so much a part of Jefferson and that became, therefore, so much a part of the nation's fabric and the nation's struggle for its own soul.

In our orgy of bicentennials that began in 1976 and will continue for a few years more, the name of Thomas Jefferson is repeatedly invoked, his hovering presence repeatedly felt—with good and sufficient reason. For more than half a century his voice, even more his pen, guided and goaded a nation along its somewhat unsteady path. A politician of considerable skill, an intellectual of incredible scope, Jefferson cannot be captured in a single phrase or fully revealed in a single sketch. If, however, there is one key that unlocks more of his complexity than any other, I believe it is his dedication to and articulation of the concept of liberty. Four facets of his libertarian career will be considered: political liberty, religious liberty, liberty versus equality, and academic liberty.

Political liberty. From the perspective of chronology as well as of impact, Jefferson's pursuit of political liberty deserves first notice. It was such pursuit that first placed him on the public stage, and it was such pursuit that fixed him there year after year, decade after decade. He longed for family, farm, and home, but for more than thirty years he saw little of them. In the summer of 1774, having just turned thirty-one years of age, Jefferson wielded that ever-more-powerful pen on behalf of the "natural and legal rights" of all British Americans. Britain had "invaded" those rights by closing down the port of Boston, and from his own Albermarle County in Virginia Jefferson presented resolves on behalf of the freeholders to the effect that Boston's difficulty was a "common cause": "We will ever be ready to join with our fellow subjects . . . in exerting all those rightful powers, which God has given us." We affirm those rights, and are prepared to defend those rights "when, where and by whomsoever invaded."[1]

In a more formal and forceful way, Jefferson argued for rights and liberties appropriate to free English citizens in his first publication: *A Summary View of the Rights of British America* (1774). Here Jefferson proclaimed that nothing could persuade the colonists that "they hold their political existence at the will of a British Parliament." Rhetorically he asked: "Shall these [colonial] governments be dissolved, their property annihilated, and their people reduced to a state of nature, at the imperious breath of a body of men whom they never saw, in whom they never confided, and over whom they have no powers of punishment or removal?" To answer that question in the affirmative, one must abandon all principles of common sense as well as all common feelings of human nature. And to answer that question in the affirmative is to bow down before not one, but one hundred sixty tyrants otherwise known as Members of Parliament. "Instead of being a free people, as we have hitherto supposed," we would suddenly become slaves. We speak frankly, even when addressing His Royal Majesty, because this is the way that free people are inclined to speak. "Let those flatter, who fear: it is not an American art." And then in a line deservedly set to music by Randall Thompson, Jefferson wrote: "The God

---

[1]Julian P. Boyd, ed., *The Papers of Thomas Jefferson* (Princeton, 1950–) 1:117.

who gave us life gave us liberty at the same time: the hand of force may destroy, but cannot disjoin them."[2]

All of this (written in July 1774) failed to bend either Parliament or the king. It did, however, along with many rapidly moving events, stiffen the resolve of those British Americans scattered up and down the Atlantic seacoast. A year later Jefferson wrote to a friend: "As our enemies have found we can reason like men, so now let us show them we can fight like men also."[3] A month later Jefferson addressed a fellow Virginian who, having decided that his loyalty lay with Britain and not the colonies, was leaving for England. Writing in friendship yet with unwavering determination, Jefferson indicated that he too would welcome reconciliation, but not at the expense "of our just rights." He confessed that he was one of those who rather than submit to an imperious Parliament "would lend my hand to sink the whole island in the ocean."[4] Tempers and rhetoric were heating up.

Jefferson's identification with political liberty rests primarily, of course, upon that document he composed the following June. That declaration, though it did not altogether escape the fate of being rewritten by a committee, bears the unmistakable style and verve of a now thirty-three-year-old Jefferson. The Declaration of Independence is familiar to all, but at the same time familiar to none. As Garry Wills has noted, it is a document that we see but do not read. It has not been wrestled with, argued over, phrase by phrase, inference by inference, as has the Constitution. While we may climb a mountain simply because "it is there," we feel no particular obligation to read the Declaration because it, too, is there. As we confront it in the National Archives, we bow slightly, then hurry on. Nor is this the propitious time to parse and divide, set forth and explicate, each phrase or sentence therein. In brief compass it manages to do much, revealing Jefferson's view of the nature of man, the nature of government and of society, the nature of the grievous dispute between Britain and her colonies, and the nature of the colonists' determination to end "that subordination in which they have hitherto remained." Above all else it is political liberty that is asserted, political liberty that is single-mindedly pursued, and political liberty that is thereafter won. I shall return to some of its language

---

[2]Ibid., 121-35.

[3]Ibid., 186 (to George Gilmer, 5 July 1775).

[4]Ibid., 240 (to John Randolph, 25 August 1775).

later, but will observe here that Jefferson went on record for rights and liberties with such force that he could not back away when others, in other lands or even in his own, also sought their own free and independent station.[5]

When some farmers in western Massachusetts took up arms in 1787 to achieve—as they saw it—their own political liberties and equal justice, many in the new nation were horrified by this invitation to anarchy or, perhaps, even to the reassertion of British control. John Adams, then abroad, feared for his native state, while Abigail Adams wrote to Jefferson (also abroad) in dismay and disgust of "ignorant, wrestless [sic] desperadoes without conscience or principals [sic]."[6] With what could only have been an infuriating calm, Jefferson replied that he hoped these rebels would be pardoned. "The spirit of resistance to government is so valuable on certain occasions, that I wish it to be always kept alive. It will often be exercised when wrong, but better so than not to be exercised at all." Then in utter disregard to the Adamses' sensibilities, he added: "I like a little rebellion now and then. It is like a storm in the Atmosphere."[7] To the son-in-law of John and Abigail Adams, Jefferson observed that no country should be without rebellion for more than twenty years. "The tree of liberty must be refreshed from time to time, with the blood of patriots and tyrants. It is its natural manure."[8]

Nor was Jefferson through offending his once-revolutionary fellow patriot, John Adams. When the French Revolution erupted in 1789, Jefferson was elated: this was, he wrote, "but the first chapter of the history of European liberty."[9] England would, or at least should, follow in its train. But England's Edmund Burke thought otherwise and bitterly attacked so unrestrained, so unrefined a revolution. Thomas Paine then proceeded to attack Burke, while Thomas Jefferson managed simultaneously to endorse

---

[5]For a detailed examination of Jefferson's earlier drafts of the Declaration, see Julian P. Boyd, *The Declaration of Independence* (Princeton, 1945).

[6]Lester J. Cappon, ed., *The Adams-Jefferson Letters* (Chapel Hill, 1959) 1:168 (Abigail Adams to TJ, 29 January 1787).

[7]Ibid., 172-73 (to Abigail Adams, 22 February 1787).

[8]Boyd, *Papers,* 12:355-57 (to William S. Smith, 13 November 1787).

[9]Merrill D. Peterson, ed., *The Portable Thomas Jefferson* (New York: Viking Press, 1975) 444.

Paine and insult Adams. Jefferson thought it time to assert republicanism for all the world, to rally again around "the standard of Common Sense." In trying to patch things up with his president, Jefferson acknowledged that he had made no secret of his being "anti-monarchical and anti-aristocratical," and that this would ever be his stance whether in Boston or New York, Paris or London.[10] Political liberty was a prized possession but not a private one. *The Rights of Man,* to use the title of Paine's pamphlet, were universal no less than they were inalienable. Those rights were never won without a price. "The liberty of the whole earth," Jefferson wrote in 1793, "was depending on the issue of the contest" in France. Many martyrs fell, to be sure, "but rather than it should have failed I would have seen half the earth desolated; were there but an Adam and Eve left in every country, and left free, it would be better than as is now."[11]

Religious liberty. However strongly Jefferson felt about political liberty, some would argue that he felt even more strongly about religious liberty. Certainly his vigilance in this area never relaxed, not even in the final years of his life. His homeland, Virginia, had not known much in the way of religious liberty from its earliest days down to Jefferson's own time. For one hundred fifty years, the Church of England (or Anglicanism) was the official, tax-supported, state-protected religion. All public officials, all college professors (William and Mary), all recognized clergy pledged their loyalty to this one church. Jefferson himself was baptized in this church, received its communion, participated in its liturgy, attended its college, and even served on its vestry. None of this, however, weakened his dedication to religious liberty, once he had made up his mind that this too was part of that intellectual and political revolution through which the Western world was passing. If anything, the Anglican dominance, oppression, and privilege only steeled his resolve.

Quite properly, the first battle was on his own home ground. In 1776 he, in fact, had great difficulty tearing himself away to go to Philadelphia because Virginia was in the process of adopting a new constitution, and Jefferson's first interest was there. He had even written a constitution for his "country," convinced that throwing off a bad government in Britain

---

[10]Dumas Malone, *Jefferson and the Rights of Man* (Boston, 1951) 357-58.

[11]Saul K. Padover, ed., *A Jefferson Profile as Revealed in His Letters* (New York, 1956) 92-93 (to William Short, 3 January 1793).

made no sense if a worse government arose in Virginia. Serious student of government that he was, he would forestall that possibility by providing a fundamental frame to insure the liberties of future generations. He would, for example, guarantee religious liberty by this constitutional affirmation: "All persons shall have full & free liberty of religious opinion, nor shall any be compelled to frequent or maintain any religious service or institution."[12] Jefferson wrote this, we should remember, fifteen years before the First Amendment was finally voted up, nine years before that bicentennial bill noted above was adopted, and a month or more before the Declaration of Independence was adopted. One cannot argue the power of precedent, however, for Virginia adopted not Jefferson's constitution but George Mason's—though much amended and revised.

Jefferson was disappointed in the final Virginia document on many grounds, but high among his disappointments was the failure to make religious liberty fully secure and the corollary failure to remove from his own Anglican church every vestige of privilege and power. Because of the continuing force of English Common Law, heresy was still a crime; denial of the doctrine of the Trinity, for example, was punishable by fine or prison. In the midst of a Revolution, it was unlikely that Americans would persecute Americans for novel or dissenting religious opinions, but what about when the Revolution was over? One cannot, in a matter of this magnitude, trust the temper of the times to assure the liberty of conscience.

Soon after he became governor of Virginia in 1779, Jefferson therefore introduced a bill both bold and explicit regarding religious liberty. Anglicanism was not prepared to surrender all its former perquisites, nor were most legislators prepared to abandon all tradition. Jefferson's bill thus languished for nearly seven years, as debates raged, petitions flowed, and sentiments shifted. Through the skillful floor management of James Madison, however, the Virginia legislature finally turned its back on all remaining ties to an officially approved religion. This paved the way at last for the passage, in January 1786, of the Bill for Establishing Religious Freedom. A central section, one long sentence, deserves quotation: "No man shall be compelled to frequent or support any religious worship, place, or ministry whatsoever, nor shall be enforced, restrained, molested, or burthened in his body or goods, nor shall otherwise suffer, on account of

---

[12]Boyd, *Papers,* 1:344.

his religious opinions or belief; but . . . men shall be free to profess, and by argument to maintain, their opinions in matters of religion, and . . . the same shall in no wise diminish, enlarge, or affect their civil capacities.''[13]

When Jefferson the next year (1787) published the first English edition of his one book, *Notes on the State of Virginia,* he included the text of the bill in his appendix, for he wanted all the Western world to know that Virginia had taken a stand, if somewhat tardily, for full religious liberty. Jefferson took his stand in the *Notes* as well, using language that would haunt him later in a presidential campaign. Jefferson wrote: ''The legitimate powers of government extend to such acts only as are injurious to others. But it does me no injury for my neighbor to say that there are twenty gods, or no God. It neither picks my pocket nor breaks my leg.''[14] Although that particular opinion may not have been injurious to others, it was decidedly injurious to Jefferson. He, however, contemplated no retreat, for the only effect of an established church had been to ''make one half the world fools, and the other half hypocrites.''[15]

In the same year that this edition of the *Notes* appeared, delegates to a constitutional convention were at work in Philadelphia. Their work was finished by fall, but the resultant document said little about religion. Aside from declaring that there would be no religious test for public office (and allowing one to ''affirm'' as well as ''swear''), it was silent on the subject. Madison, the moving force behind the writing of the Constitution, did not worry that this new charter carried no guarantee of religious liberty. This was a matter for the states to take care of, he believed, even as Virginia had done. He quickly sent a copy of the Constitution to Jefferson, who was then in Paris as minister to France. In December 1787 Jefferson wrote back to compliment Madison and his colaborers on their herculean effort in Philadelphia. But then to his good friend he observed: ''I will now add what I do not like. First the omission of a bill of rights providing clearly and without the aid of sophisms for the freedom of religion.''[16] He goes on to name other freedoms, but let us stop here in order to emphasize the top

---

[13]Peterson, *Portable,* 253.

[14]Thomas Jefferson, *Notes on the State of Virginia* (New York: Harper & Row, Torchbooks edition, 1964) 152.

[15]Ibid., 153.

[16]Peterson, *Portable,* 429.

priority, in Jefferson's mind, for absolute clarity with respect to religious liberty. For Thomas Jefferson it was not enough that such a right might be implied, might be reserved to the states, might be understood somehow and some way to be safe and secure. It had to be explicitly and unequivocally guaranteed.

Many other Americans joined Jefferson's camp in 1787, 1788, and 1789. Madison agreed that, if the Constitution were ratified, he would pledge to introduce a Bill of Rights in the very first legislative session of the new government. He fulfilled his pledge in 1789 and, by 1791, a sufficient number of states had ratified those ten amendments to the Constitution. The very first phrase of the very first amendment provided the federal guarantee that Jefferson had sought: "Congress shall make no law respecting the establishment of religion or prohibiting the free exercise thereof."

So, then, Jefferson could relax? Not really. In this often bloodied arena of human history, he never relaxed. In the hard-fought presidential campaign of 1800, Jefferson was not allowed to relax where religion was concerned. He was the infidel, the atheist, the enemy of biblical revelation, the potential overthrower of all ordered society and sound morality. His political enemies pointed out that he did not accept the Genesis account of creation, the universality of Noah's flood, the theory of inspiration, or the necessity of religion for the public weal. In the guise of arguing for religious liberty, he only masked his own religious hostility. Here is a man who declared that it makes no difference whether one believes in twenty gods, one god, or no god! A New York minister observed in 1800: "Let my neighbor once persuade himself that there is no God, and he will soon pick my pocket, and break not only my *leg* but my *neck*. If there be no God," he continued, "there is no law, no future account; government then is the ordinance of man only."[17] Our property will not be safe, nor will the chastity of our wives and daughters be secure, and the Christian religion itself will be "trampled upon and exploded."[18] All this will occur if the infidel be elected. The infidel was elected.

---

[17]Dickinson W. Adams, ed., *Jefferson's Extracts from the Gospels* (Princeton, 1983) 11 (quoting from William Linn, *Serious Considerations*, 1800).

[18]Ibid., quoting "A Christian Federalist," 21 September 1800. That strong feelings about Jefferson continued well into the nineteenth century is evident in Robert Baird's evaluation of him and his proposition on religious liberty. What Jefferson really wanted to do, Baird wrote, was "degrade Christianity" by putting all religions on an equal plane. Baird added: "It was this that made the arch-infidel chuckle with satisfaction." (*Religion in America* [New York, 1856] 225.)

When he became president in 1801, Jefferson waited for some opportunity to indicate that he was not hostile to religion but rather took the First
Amendment seriously—and strictly. (That he was not hostile to religion
he had tried to make clear in the *Notes* when he wrote that "it is error alone
which needs the support of government. Truth can stand by itself." There
is no evidence that his opponents quoted this in the course of the long campaign.) The opportunity he awaited presented itself near the end of his first
year in office when a group of Baptists in Danbury, Connecticut, wrote to
congratulate him on his election (not many in Connecticut were prepared
to do that!) and to ask him to appoint a day of fasting to help heal the wounds
of a bitter campaign. Jefferson appreciated the good wishes, especially since
they came from a pious religious body, but he would declare no day of
fasting or feasting or prayer or thanksgiving.

His reply to the Danbury group contained language that became more
famous than the First Amendment phrases themselves. I believe as you do,
he wrote in January 1801, that "religion is a matter which lies solely between man and his God, [and] that he owes account to none other for his
faith or his worship." I also "contemplate with solemn reverence that act
of the whole American people": that is, the First Amendment, which was
an act "of the whole American people" since they had in fact ratified it.
But then the clincher was Jefferson's gloss on the First Amendment language, namely "thus building a wall of separation between Church and
State." For Jefferson, the religious phrases of the First Amendment were
neither ambiguous nor fuzzy: they were as clear and obvious as a brick wall
that divided the civil estate on the one hand from the ecclesiastical estate
on the other. When later a Presbyterian minister rebuked him for stub-
bornly refusing throughout his two terms as president to set aside special
devotional days, Jefferson replied that this was simply not the business of
civil government or of any civil officer in that government. All religious
exercises, he wrote, are exclusively in the hands of the denominations and
the churches, "and this right can never be safer than in their own hands,
where the Constitution has deposited it."[19]

Even when he left the White House in 1809, Jefferson could not let this
liberty rest unwatched, unaffirmed. If anything, his language grew even
stronger. In 1810 he spoke of the long centuries of Christian establish-

---

[19]A. A. Lipscomb and A. E. Bergh, eds., *The Writings of Thomas Jefferson* (Washington, 1907) 11:428.

ment, from Constantine on, as a time when religion became "an engine for enslaving mankind." He viewed the role of religion for clergy as "a mere contrivance to filch wealth and power to themselves"; and if any dogma was too gross to be swallowed, then it was shoved down every throat.[20] In 1813 he told John Adams that the time had come to follow no oracle but conscience, to sweep away the "gossamer fabrics of factitious religion," for I assume that belief should be "the assent of the mind to an intelligible proposition."[21] In 1814 he stated: "Our particular principles of religion are a subject of accountability to our god alone. I enquire after no man's, and trouble none with mine."[22] The following year he went so far as to speak of "this loathsome combination of church and state."[23]

In 1816 he acknowledged that the law provided for religious liberty, but he feared that "we are yet under the inquisition of public opinion." The clergy get much credit for that, for they are in the business of "shedding darkness"; it is their only protection.[24] And in his eightieth year, Jefferson rejoiced that he lived in a country "of free enquiry and belief, which has surrendered its creed and conscience to neither king nor priest."[25] Reason is man's only oracle; once that is surrendered, we become like a ship without a rudder, "the sport of every wind. With such persons gullability [sic] which they call faith takes the helm from the hand of reason and the mind becomes a wreck."[26] One final quotation from Jefferson, cited by practically everybody, is seldom given in its clear context, which is religious liberty. In writing to Benjamin Rush in 1800, before his election to the presidency, Jefferson observed that every religious group still hoped to win some government favor and patronage, "especially the Episcopalians and the Congregationalists. The returning good sense of our country threatens abortion to their hopes, and they believe that any portion of power confided to me will be exerted in opposition to their schemes. And they

---

[20]Adams, *Extracts*, 345 (to William Baldwin, 19 January 1810).

[21]Ibid., 347 (22 August 1813).

[22]Ibid., 360 (to Miles King, 26 September 1814).

[23]Ibid., 364 (to Charles Clay, 29 January 1815).

[24]Ibid., 375 (to Margaret Bayard Smith, 6 August 1816).

[25]Ibid., 405 (to Benjamin Waterhouse, 26 June 1822).

[26]Ibid., 409 (to James Smith, 8 December 1822).

believe truly. For I have sworn upon the alter of god eternal hostility against every form of tyranny over the mind of man.''[27]

Liberty versus equality. Jefferson the libertarian is also the great egalitarian, or so at least he appears in our frequent citations from the Declaration of Independence. But is there not a fundamental antagonism between liberty on the one hand and equality on the other? Alexis de Tocqueville so argued, as have many others before and since. And if that antagonism is real, may we not expect to see in Jefferson some struggle, some pain, some inconsistency as he labors to remain loyal to both ideals? I think the answer to that last question has to be an affirmative one. Moreover, if in this contest it becomes necessary to lean more toward one than the other, I further believe that we must see Jefferson as having chosen liberty over equality. Here we enter the murky waters of racial and gender equality versus liberty. The waters are murky partly because consciousness had not been raised as high in the eighteenth century as in our own, but also partly because the limitations of observation and experience operated more severely then than now. (Even with all our advance in natural science, in anthropology, in social and pyschological measurement, we still know that no totally compelling beatific vision concerning human liberty and equality has settled upon a willing and waiting world.)

The three greatest men who ever lived were, in Jefferson's well-considered opinion, Bacon, Newton, and Locke. They emancipated him from ''idols of the tribe,'' from preconceived notions and innate ideas, from inherited and unexamined dogmas or presuppositions. Or at least they tried. They taught him to observe, measure, count, experiment, trust in the senses, and discard all that the senses did not confirm. And Jefferson tried throughout his life to be their loyal, unwavering disciple. It would be asking more of him than we ask of ourselves, however, if we were to require a constancy that never failed, a commitment that never faltered. Jefferson had much to say about Indians and blacks, little to say about women, but in all three categories of humanity we find ''Jeffersonian liberty'' ambiguous at best, severely compromised at worst. A large part of the problem was that in each instance theory pulled in one direction, experience (or political reality) in another.

With respect to the Indians, Jefferson comes off better than in the other two categories. This can be accounted for in terms of at least three Jefferson-

---

[27]Ibid., 320 (23 September 1800).

ian presuppositions. First, much armchair anthropology of the eighteenth century proclaimed a highly favorable view of the natural and the noble savage. It was civilization that corrupted, nature that redeemed; most fortunate of all were those never caught in the web of man-made artificiality and tyranny. Second, the Indian was the quintessential American. Jefferson spent much of his time in France defending America and the New World generally from bad anthropology, bad biology, and bad manners. The New World environment, it was argued from afar, was inferior in every way; the species were few in number, degenerate in development, and short in years. Jefferson countered much of this nonsense in excellent Newtonian or Baconian fashion: he counted, weighed, tabulated, recorded, and responded. If in particular the Indian were demoted or degraded, then all America was demoted and degraded, with Europe's pseudoscientists rushing in to complete the kill. Third, in the intense argument of the day concerning a single creation of the human species or multiple creations, Jefferson came down firmly on behalf of the former. (Species in the eighteenth century, one must remember, were fixed.) All humankind is of one creation and therefore of one species. The famous phrase, "All men are created equal," stood in Jefferson's first draft of the Declaration of Independence in this form: "All men are of an equal creation." That general and universal proposition worked—at least so far as the Indian was concerned.

So in 1785 Jefferson wrote to a French correspondent that the attacks on the nature and primitive genius of the American Indian had no basis in scientific fact. It is absurd to draw conclusions only from those Indians in South America who have been held in slavery for centuries. "It is in N. America we are to seek their original character; and I am safe in affirming that the proofs of genius given by the Indians [there] . . . place them on a level with Whites in the same uncultivated state." From the closest observation, Jefferson concluded, it is necessary, indeed scientific, to affirm the Indian "to be in body and mind equal to the whiteman."[28] Concerned about the extinction of many tribes and the decline in Indian population, Jefferson planned ways to introduce the aboriginal peoples to farming, to government, and to a wholly integrated society. "Let our settlements meet and blend together . . . intermix, and become one people."[29] If that sounds like intermarriage, Jefferson re-

[28]Boyd, *Papers*, 8:184-86 (to the Marquis de Chastellux, 7 June 1785).

[29]Lipscomb and Bergh, *Writings*, 10:363.

moved all doubt concerning his approval of that arrangement when, in an 1808 address to several Indian tribes, he declared that "we shall all be Americans; you will mix with us by marriage, your blood will run in our veins, and will spread with us over this great island."[30]

Jefferson acknowledged the responsibility of the stronger, better-armed Europeans in taking away hunting lands and violating tribal patterns of life. The Indians have, he said, "been overwhelmed by the current, or driven before it."[31] Yet earlier, as secretary of state in Washington's administration, Jefferson had given his support to that current. "I hope we shall drub the Indians well this summer," he wrote to Madison in April 1791, "and then change our plan from war to bribery."[32] As an obstacle to the nation's march westward, the Indians must be driven or conquered, then pacified or contained. Jefferson's political instincts operated here. In the realm of anthropology, his scientific instincts and observations persuaded him that Indians and whites could and should live together as equals, "improving our reason, and obeying its mandates." Liberty was the Indians' lot as soon as they allowed knowledge to displace ignorance and reformation to supplant tradition. "The Indians are like whites in this respect as well: they have their own anti-philosophers (we call ours Federalists!) who wish to see that nothing ever changes."[33]

With respect to women, Jefferson seldom thought of them as an anthropologist or a Baconian might. He thought as a man, a husband, a lover, or a father. And from these perspectives, a woman was a creature to enjoy, to protect, to be distracted by, to educate—at least to a degree sufficient to enable her to educate her own daughters and, if need be, sons as well. They should learn the domestic arts, of course, along with music, dance, and art. Spelling is important, Jefferson told his eleven-year-old daughter, even encouraging her to go to the extreme of consulting a dictionary when in doubt. Both sexes should learn French since it is not only the language of diplomacy, but "the depository of all science" as well.[34] Women, how-

---

[30]Ibid., 16:452.

[31]Peterson, *Portable*, 318 (from his Second Inaugural Address).

[32]Boyd, *Papers*, 20:214-15.

[33]Peterson, *Portable*, 319.

[34]Ibid., 366-67 (to Martha Jefferson, 28 November 1783). Also see Lipscomb and Bergh, *Writings*, 15:165-68 (to William Burwell, 14 March 1818).

ever, are the weaker sex, "formed by nature for attention and not for hard labour."[35] Mentally, they might be better equipped for hard labor, if they did not read so many novels and demand that books "be dressed in the figments of fancy."[36] Politics should not trouble them, nor should they be concerned with it other than "to soothe and calm the minds of their husbands, returning ruffled from political debate."[37] Women should not mix in public assemblies, for it leads to a moral decline, to say nothing of the "ambiguity of issue."[38] And to his secretary of the treasury, President Jefferson wrote in 1807 that appointing a woman to public office "is an innovation for which the public is not prepared, nor am I."[39] It *is* hard to make Thomas Jefferson a supporter of feminism. In his proposed Virginia Constitution, he does provide that laws of inheritance will apply to males and females equally.[40] But in general neither female equality nor female liberty occupied a great deal of his attention, nor on this topic is there any significant development in his thinking from early manhood to old age. Male chauvinism was one of those "idols of the tribe" not yet toppled from its pedestal.

The place of blacks in American society, however, demanded constant attention and often agonized reflection. The question here was partly anthropological once again, of course, but even more inescapably was it political, economic, and moral. Jefferson's discomfort in this area was intensified by the existence of the slave trade (that "cruel war against human nature itself") and of the institution of slavery itself on so wide a scale in his own Virginia. His discomfort was further intensified by that conflict between theory and experience here manifest in its most acute form. Nothing seemed obvious or simple; no explanation or resolution was perfect; compromises, both intellectual and political, overruled consistency. And

---

[35]Boyd, *Papers,* 13:27.

[36]John P. Foley, ed., *The Jeffersonian Cyclopedia* (New York: Russell and Russell, 1967 [1900]) 1:274 (to Nathaniel Burwell, 14 March 1818).

[37]Ibid., 2:949 (to John H. Pleasants, 19 April 1824).

[38]Ibid., 2:748 (to Samuel Kercheval, 5 September 1816). In the long letter to Burwell (n. 34 above), Jefferson affirmed that young ladies should be taught dancing, even though the skill has only a short life, for "the French rule is wise, that no lady dances after marriage."

[39]Ibid., 2:652.

[40]Boyd, *Papers,* 1:344.

even if compromise is the essence of politics, it is scarcely the genius of reason or of science, scarcely the distinguishing trait of a Bacon, Newton, or Locke.

In 1776, while preparing his draft of the July Declaration, Jefferson used remarkably strong language in condemning the trading in slaves, an evil commerce for which he held King George III responsible. It was a violation of the "most sacred rights of life & liberty," a "piratical warfare," an "assemblage of horrors,"—so horrible, in fact, that even "infidel powers" condemn what good Christian nations have done and continue to do.[41] The language was impressive, and there is no reason to believe it insincere. So strong was it, however, that the Continental Congress deleted the entire section from the final version of the Declaration of Independence. What the Declaration does not say with respect to the slave trade is most regrettable, to be sure, but this fault cannot be charged against Jefferson. It is what Jefferson does say a decade later about blacks and slavery that can be charged against him.

Before the *Notes on Virginia* appeared, however, Jefferson had persuaded Virginia in its 1783 constitutional revision to provide freedom for all children born of slaves after 1800. The next year he took a leading role in shaping the language of the Northwest Ordinance, which asserted that "neither slavery nor involuntary servitude" would be allowed after 1800 anywhere in that large territory. As David Brion Davis has remarked, if Jefferson "had died in 1784, at the age of forty-one, it could be said without further qualification that he was one of the first statesmen in any part of the world to advocate concrete measures for restricting and eradicating Negro slavery."[42] But in 1785 he began quietly to circulate the *Notes on Virginia* in France. His reluctance to make that book more widely available was based partly on his remarks regarding slavery and blacks. The mixing and mingling that Jefferson looked forward to with respect to Indians was not, in his judgment, an option with respect to blacks. "Deeprooted prejudices entertained by the whites; ten thousand recollections, by the blacks of the injuries they have sustained; new provocations; the real distinctions which nature has made; and many other circumstances, will

---

[41]Ibid., 1:426.

[42]David Brion Davis, *The Problem of Slavery in the Age of Revolution, 1770-1823* (Ithaca NY: Cornell University Press, 1975) 174.

divide us into parties, and produce convulsions, which will probably never end but in the extermination of one or the other race."[43] This dreadful consequence could only be avoided, Jefferson thought, through some intelligent plan of colonization—perhaps to South America or the West Indies, maybe Santo Domingo where the blacks were already well organized under their own government. Later, he thought more in terms of Africa, but without much confidence that this or any plan of repatriation would be accomplished soon or without great resistance.

Why was Jefferson so pessimistic with regard to blacks when he had been so optimistic with regard to Indians? Apart from the painful historic memories (and Indians, we can assume, had a few painful memories too), Jefferson claimed that nature has made too many differences between blacks and whites to permit a peaceful, happy assimilation. After describing these differences in great detail—recounting his observations of character traits, mental faculties, and physical differences—Jefferson moved gingerly, tentatively, but inexorably toward a conclusion that flew in the face of his theory regarding an equal creation. "To justify a general conclusion," Jefferson wrote, "requires many observations." Recognizing that his observations had indeed been limited, that (for example) he had never been to Africa, that blacks in America had never "been viewed by us as subjects of natural history" (and indeed in the *Notes* Jefferson himself discusses them under the subject heading Administration of Justice), any conclusion must be qualified and conditional. "I advance it, therefore, as a suspicion only, that the blacks, whether originally a distinct race, or made distinct by time and circumstances, are inferior to the whites in the endowments both of body and mind."[44] More than twenty years later, Jefferson again acknowledged that his observation had been limited to Virginia, "where the opportunities for the development of their genius were not favorable, and those of exercising it still less so." On this occasion he did add that "whatever be their degree of talent, it is no measure of their rights." Newton "was superior to others in understanding, but he was not therefore lord of the person or property of others."[45] Liberty, yes; equality, no.

[43]Jefferson, *Notes*, 132-33.

[44]Ibid., 138.

[45]Lipscomb and Bergh, *Writings*, 12:254-55 (to H. Gregoire, 25 February 1809).

This might lead one to suspect that Jefferson at some point became an active abolitionist. He did not, having reached a high point in this regard in his early forties. In the *Notes* he does bewail the effect of slavery upon both master and slave by invoking "the most unremitting despotism on the one part, and degrading submissions on the other." And he does tremble upon reflecting that God is just, and that, in the struggle between exploited and exploiter, God "has no attribute which can take side with us in such a contest." Yet it must be under the auspices of heaven that total emancipation will come.[46] Jefferson spoke more in terms of hope than of plans, more in terms of heaven than of earth. "We must await with patience," he wrote, "the workings of an overruling Providence, and hope that that is preparing the deliverance of these, our suffering brethren. When the measure of their tears shall be full, when their groans shall have involved heaven itself in darkness, doubtless a God of justice will awaken to their distress."[47] Never has Jeffersonian rhetoric sounded so hollow or struck so false a note. Slavery is an abomination, but leave it to heaven; blacks are of an equal creation but inferior; my observation is limited, partial, and distorted by abnormal circumstances, but my mind is made up. A moment earlier I suggested that we could summarize Jefferson's position as being a case of "liberty, yes; equality, no." It is now necessary to qualify it as "equality, no; liberty, later—and farther away." The most generous point that can be made regarding Jeffersonian liberty with respect to blacks is that glorious opportunities were ingloriously missed.

Academic liberty. We speak of it as "academic freedom," but that phrase in our time has such a familiar if not hackneyed sound. Everybody knows all about that, believes in it, or at least feels obliged to bow before it. This was not the case in Jefferson's day. Every colonial college had its religious orientation, if not denomination: Harvard, Yale, and Dartmouth were Congregational; Princeton, Presbyterian; Brown, Baptist; Rutgers, Dutch Reformed; Columbia, along with William and Mary, Anglican or Episcopalian. Only the College of Philadelphia lacked the sponsorship of a single denomination, but even there Anglican and Presbyterian influences were determinative, with the statue of George Whitefield on today's campus a continuing testimony to the influence of colonial revivalism as well.

---

[46]Jefferson, *Notes,* 155-56.

[47]Boyd, *Papers,* 10:63.

Two of the three items for which Thomas Jefferson most wished to be remembered were accomplished before he was forty-three years old. The third, however, was the achievement of his old age. Jefferson wanted to create a university, but one of a different sort on the American scene: one free not only of religious control but even of all sectarian influence. Dogmas drove men mad.[48] When it came to establishing a real university, a free university, Jefferson regarded academic liberty as the non-negotiable essential. He offered to the College of William and Mary the opportunity to relocate farther west, more in the center of population by 1800 and away from the "malarial swamp" of Jamestown fame. He further offered his alma mater the option of becoming the state's open, free, liberal, and public institution, with the single proviso that it sever all sectarian ties with the Anglican, now Episcopal, church. The college declined to set out on so unfamiliar, so nontraditional a course. Jefferson, who had no trouble rejecting the familiar and traditional, therefore turned with determination, if not with delight, to the concept of a wholly new institution of higher learning to be built on wholly new assumptions.

The time had come on the American scene, Jefferson believed, to "civil-ize" education: that is, to place it under civil control and in the hands of the general public. He hoped that the leading institution of higher education in every state would now be a public, not a private institution. In this respect Jefferson was to be bitterly disappointed, for in every state where a private college was found, that school remained in the hands of the relatively few. Even where state officials sat on governing boards, as at Yale, state officials did not control the institution. Moreover, such colleges resisted every effort to establish a rival public institution, maintaining that resistance successfully until well after the Civil War. When the state of New Hampshire attempted to take over Dartmouth, Jefferson applauded. But Jefferson had not taken into account the oratory of Dartmouth alumnus Daniel Webster, nor the Federalist determination of Chief Justice John Marshall. How ridiculous, Jefferson wrote the governor of New Hampshire in 1816, that "our lawyers and priests . . . suppose that preceding generations held the earth more freely than we do [and that they have] a right to impose laws on us, unalterable by ourselves." Obviously,

[48]See Robert M. Healey, *Jefferson on Religion in Public Education* (New Haven, 1962) 161.

they believe that "the earth belongs to the dead, and not to the living."[49]
Jefferson's long-distance indignation could not match Daniel Webster's
peroration delivered in that area. Dartmouth remained private, and a half-
century would pass before the state had its public university. Jefferson lost
in New Hampshire; he would not lose in Virginia.

Designing, promoting, and building the University of Virginia was the
happy occupation of Thomas Jefferson in his retirement and on into his final years. He fixed the site, laid out the grounds, became the architect, designed the curriculum, selected the library's books, chose the faculty, raised
the money, and presided over the opening ceremonies the year before he
died. In Virginia they still speak of it as "Mr. Jefferson's University." It
is, I think, hard to argue with that designation. Some months after his eightieth birthday, Jefferson wrote to John Adams: "I am fortunately mounted
on a Hobby, which indeed I should have better managed some 30. or 40.
years ago, but whose easy amble is still sufficient to give exercise and
amusement to an Octogenary rider. This is the establishment of an University, on a scale more comprehensive, and in a country more healthy and
central than our old William and Mary, which these obstacles have kept in
a state of languor and inefficiency."[50] Jefferson regarded Europe as far
ahead of America in the sciences; therefore, his professors had to come
from Europe, "thus to improve our science, as we have done our manufactures, by borrowed skill." He was much criticized for seeking faculty
abroad, chiefly "perhaps by disappointed applicants for professorships to
which they were deemed incompetent."[51] The faculty ultimately arrived
(the ship was thought for a time to be lost at sea), and in 1825 in Char-
lottesville "Mr. Jefferson's University" opened its doors to sixty-eight
students.

A quarter-century earlier Jefferson had written of his dream to Joseph
Priestley: "We wish to establish in the upper & healthier country . . . an
University on a plan so broad & liberal & *modern,* as to be worth patron-
izing with the public support, and be a temptation to the youth of other states

---

[49]Quoted in Donald G. Tewksbury, *The Founding of American Colleges and Universities before the Civil War* (New York: Teachers College, Columbia University, 1932) 152.

[50]Cappon, *Letters,* 2:599.

[51]Ibid., 2:605.

to come, and drink of the cup of knowledge & fraternize with us.''[52] Such young men did come, permitting Jefferson atop Monticello to look down with pride on his enduring monument to academic liberty. Of states already possessing private colleges in 1800, only Virginia succeeded in creating a new and lively public institution. Where other public universities were established early, such as in Georgia (1785) and South Carolina (1801), no private college existed. These states were therefore free to follow the Jeffersonian model; and in choosing such names for their sites as Athens and Columbia, they revealed their intent to pursue the pattern first envisioned by the sage of Monticello.

Jefferson the libertarian was in most respects ahead of his time, though he, like us, could not wholly cast off his own cultural captivity. As the beneficiaries of his pursuit of liberty, our obvious challenge is to carry that pursuit farther than he was able to do. Our obvious concern is that we, despite the lifelong labors of Sidney Mead, may be slipping backward.

---

[52]Richard Hofstadter and Wilson Smith, eds., *American Higher Education* (Chicago: University of Chicago Press, 1961) 1:175.

Alliances for Progress: Some Imperialist Aspects of American Indian Policy, 1789-1839

William G. McLoughlin

"Trade is the great lever by which to direct the policy and conduct of the Indian tribes." —*Governor William Clarke*
of Missouri, 1814

"I am directed by your great father, the President of the United States, to endeavor by Reasoning with the chiefs of the Cherokies, to reconcile them to a survey for the purpose of ascertaining the practicality of a canal through their country. . . . suppose this took five or even ten years and the expense [was] two millions of dollars (and this is believed to be a moderate estimate), would not the circulation of that some [sum] of money in the Cherokee Nation be an advantage . . . and besides, a stimulant to Industry?
—*Hugh Montgomery*,
federal agent to the Cherokee chiefs
26 September 1827

Sidney Mead has been a historian in the grand mode—a man who sees history whole and who strives to give his readers "the big picture." His astute essays and books have synthesized and surveyed American history, placing his sharp analytical inquiries in the broad context of our past. From *Nathaniel W. Taylor* and *The Lively Experiment* to *The Old Religion in the Brave New World,* Mead has concentrated on the years 1750 to 1850 when the United States was taking shape socially, religiously, politically, and intellectually. Unlike today's "microhistory" and "test case" cliometrics, Mead's work has always searched for the major patterns in our culture. When we read Mead's work, whether it is his short, seminal essay on denominationalism or a whole volume on *The Nation with the Soul of a Church,* we realize that this wide-ranging approach to historical development does more to illuminate our past than a host of discrete but unrelated "building blocks." Mead belongs to the designers of our past, not to its technicians. Those of us who have admired and learned from his work acknowledge the breadth and depth of a master craftsman. The following essay tries to build on his work and his style by indicating a pattern in early Indian-white relations in North America that has striking similarities to United States' attitudes toward the non-Anglo-Saxon peoples of Central and South America in this day. Any tribute to Sidney Mead should express his example to "think big."

"Manifest Destiny" in terms of territorial expansion has been a basic aspect of Western civilization at least since the first European settlements in North and South America. Students of the policies of Europeans toward Native Americans have considered it axiomatic that "land greed," "land hunger," or "population expansion" was the controlling factor in divesting the Indians of their territory.[1] This is especially prevalent in discussions of the westward expansion of the United States after 1789. "Westward the course of empire takes its way" the Euro-Americans believed, and they found numerous justifications for dispossessing the weaker peoples who stood in their way. George Harmon, Francis P. Prucha, Bernard Sheehan, Albert K. Weinberg, and other historians of westward expansion have explained it in demographic terms—the urge of Western settlers to find virgin land to farm. As Sheehan puts it, "The uncontrollable force of frontier settlements" made the national government more than willing to employ "force and manipulation" to accede to the demands of its migrating citizens.[2]

---

[1]See Albert K. Weinberg, *Manifest Destiny* (Chicago: Quadrangle Books, 1963) 72-100; Francis P. Prucha, *American Indian Policy in the Formative Years* (Cambridge: Harvard University Press, 1962) 3, 139.

[2]Bernard W. Sheehan, *Seeds of Extinction* (Chapel Hill: University of North Carolina Press, 1973) 4, 9, 147.

But this is only one side of the story of white territorial aggrandize-
ment. The pressure for expansion did not come only from the Westerners;
it was instigated just as insistently from the central government in Washington. The federal government began by sponsoring the building of interstate turnpikes with federal money in the 1790s in order to "open up the
West" to settlement; it continued its quasimercantilist sponsorship of private business ventures throughout the next half-century. The national bank
and protective tariffs were only the first steps in the government's continued efforts to spur trade and commerce in the infant nation. Improvement
of rivers and harbors, expansion of inland waterways, and special grants
of land or tax abatements to groups of private developers were common in
this period. By 1815 most frontier farmers had abandoned Jefferson's ideal
of the self-sufficient yeoman farm for a cash-crop system that made the
farmer a businessman, and the first factories had opened the way for rising
cities and growing international trade. Inevitably the Indian nations became engrossed in this process of national economic development—not
only by offering possibilities for expanding wheat, corn, cattle, and cotton
production but through the development of the mineral resources and trade
routes through their territory. Private entrepreneurs and missionary associations received encouragement and assistance from the federal government in any venture that promised to make Indian land more productive
and to integrate "progressive" Indians into the economic development of
the United States.

In its efforts to accommodate and encourage both the cash-crop farmers to get their crops to market and the risk-taking entrepreneurs to develop
Indian resources, the federal government stood ready to assert all of its
considerable power upon the Native Americans. In many cases this led to
military intervention and internal manipulation of Indian leaders. Indian
nations that tried to resist the economic development of their resources were
deliberately destabilized. Frederick Merk has argued that the aggressive,
imperialistic thrust of American expansionism was always tempered by the
humanitarian ideal of "mission." The federal government, he argues, truly
wanted to "uplift" the Native Americans and to spread the blessings of
republican government and Christian morality among them and other
"backward" peoples.[3] But when the Indian nations declined to act in a

---

[3]Frederick Merk, *Manifest Destiny and Mission in American History* (New York: Vintage, 1966) 3-14.

manner that allegedly served both their needs and those of white businessmen and farmers, the federal government did not hesitate to employ any form of subversive activity (bribery, monetary imposture, intimidation, subsidized factionalism, paid secret agents, and military force) to support "progress." The Indian was officially designated a child or ward of the Great Father in Washington. He was to be cajoled into submission if possible and tricked or forced into it if recalcitrant.

The ideology of "uplifting the savage" in order to integrate him into equal citizenship required that he adopt the white man's concept of progress through commercial and industrial growth. This was to begin with a shift from fur trading to farming, then to move toward a market economy as surpluses of cash crops developed, and then to include domestic manufactures such as spinning and weaving, cheese making, and hide tanning supplemented by the inauguration of small-scale craft skills (blacksmiths, wheelwrights, tinsmiths, carpenters, coopers, and so forth). Turnpikes would be introduced for trade, followed by canals and railways. Commercial services would be required—taverns, inns, mail posts, ferries, stores, and banks. Ultimately this would lead to corporate activities by private investors who would develop the timber and mineral resources within the Indian nations. To transform the Indians into cash-crop farmers was only the first step toward integrating them into the infrastructure of Western development.

Cultural traditions and values led most Indians to resist the more advanced stages of economic development. One-horse farming for subsistence was grudgingly accepted as necessary for survival, but increasing pressures brought by the federal government and private enterprise to push them into total acculturation frequently produced stubborn reactions against the policy of "civilization." Acculturation seemed a malignant rather than benignant force, and those who came to resist it developed their own ideology of separatist nationalism to oppose it. White Americans expressed surprise and anger at this and indignantly described the resisters as "backward" and "barbarous." American taxpayers had spent millions to assist the Indian nations to become civilized and to help integrate their communities into the economy of the United States. They were not to be thwarted by savages. In the clash of cultures, a typical colonial situation resulted. The mother country, believing that its national growth, its national security, and its benevolent intentions were being wrongly resisted, turned increasingly to coercive measures. Government officials looked for "hostile" or "subversive" or "rebellious" elements within the Indian nations and tried to suppress them. The government built up its relations with "friendly" leaders. Ultimately it redefined its relationship with the Indian nations, concluding that they had no right to the permanent possession of their land but were only "tenants at will," liable to forcible removal at any such time as they ceased to subordinate their own development to the good of the dominant culture. Ironically, no sooner had the United States broken its own colonial ties to the British empire than it began to create an empire of its own over the Indian nations. What rights, after all, did a savage people conquered in a just war have?

There were many other strands to the emerging colonialist pattern in Indian relations that historians have noted: the racist overtones of white versus red peoples; the ethnocentrism of Christians trying to eradicate "pagan" cultural patterns; and the religious "fundamentalism" or "traditionalism" among the subject people that generated hostile uprising against foreign domination. More attention should be given to the role of federally sponsored economic development and the increasingly harsh interventionism of the War Department and Executive branch ("the home office," as it were) over the restless natives. Convincing evidence of this can be taken from the government's relations with the Cherokee Nation. Located in the South, the Cherokees became more highly "civilized" or "acculturated" than any other native people in the first half-century after 1789. They also developed the most effective resistance to total assimilation. Part of their pattern of acculturation included the employment of black slaves on their farms and plantations in imitation of their white neighbors. Furthermore, the Cherokees had a high proportion (eventually amounting to one-quarter) of their people who were of mixed ancestry or whites married to Cherokees. This produced an English-speaking elite and made it easier for whites to enter the nation and do business with it. The Cherokee Nation was rich in resources: some good cotton-growing land, much timber, navigable rivers, silver, gold and lead, salt peter caves (a source of gunpowder), salines, iron ore. It was strategically located in one of the first and most rapidly growing frontier regions at the juncture of North Carolina, Georgia, Alabama, and Tennessee. They rapidly developed one of the most stable, efficient, and honest governing systems of any Indian nation, and through land sales accumulated a large and regular income of goods and cash that provided the means for their internal economic development. An ambitious white entrepreneur was able to find more government assistance in the Cherokee Nation than in most other Indian nations, for the Cherokees became the prize example of successful Indian adaptation to progress.

In the years before the dominance of cotton production, the South was as eager as the Old Northwest to develop a diversified economy, experiment with manufacturing, and utilize its natural resources. Henry Clay's "American System" of government-subsidized internal improvements appealed as much to Southern farmers and entrepreneurs as to those in the North. It is within this framework of a semimercantilist economic philosophy that I want to reexamine the first half-century of American Indian policy. Furthermore, one must remember that cash crops like tobacco, hemp, rice, sugar, and cotton were themselves an early form of agribusiness. They demanded the creation of an efficient system for transportation of goods, of reliable marketing mechanisms, and of a stable, flexible banking system. These commercial interests (abetted by avid land speculation) fostered a ruthless approach to relations with the Indian nations who possessed so much of the South's land in these years. More than eighty percent of the land area south of Kentucky was in Indian hands in 1789. It was not the small pioneer farmers who needed canals, turnpikes, railways, and steamboats so much as the large-scale plantation owners and the rising businessmen, merchants, and bankers. Private enterprise and corporate investors, not land-hungry farmers, wanted to develop the mineral resources within the Indian nations. Through private initiative in Washington, through political patronage of state and local politicians and, above all, through intensive lobbying in Congress, these entrepreneurial interests pushed the federal government to impose an imperial policy upon Indian affairs. The fact that economic resources were located on Indian land was considered only a minor problem at first because Indian economic development and that of the United States were assumed to go together. The difficulty lay in the decision of the federal government to treat the Indian peoples as foreign nations.

In 1789 when Henry Knox, George Washington's secretary of war, began formulating the first Indian policy, he specifically stated that "the Indians, being the prior occupants [of the Western lands] possess the right to the soil. It cannot be taken from them unless by their free consent." He went on to say that "the independent nations and tribes of Indians ought to be considered as foreign nations, not as the subjects of any particular

state" or of the United States.[4] The United States may, by treaty arrangements, have expected the Indian nations to trade exclusively with it; but
according to the Constitution, the nature of this arrangement was to be the
same as the federal government's control of the trade among the various
states of the Union, and it was generally agreed that the states in 1789 retained a good deal of their sovereign power. The Indian nations interpreted
Article I, Section 8 of the American Constitution to place them on the same
footing as the states of the Union, if not on the same footing as foreign
nations. Section 8 states that "Congress shall have power to regulate commerce with foreign nations and among the several states and with the Indian tribes." Acting upon these assumptions, the United States allied itself
to the Indian nations by treaties, guaranteed their boundaries, offered them
economic aid, acknowledged their right to self-government, and loaned or
gave them money to promote their internal development, education, and
prosperity.

On the one hand, Knox's policy was designed to ally the Western Indian nations to the new republic so that they would not form alliances with
Britain, France, or Spain; on the other hand, it was designed to persuade
white voters that the United States had only benevolent intentions toward
the aborigines. The benevolent purpose was to transform the Indian's
economy from reliance upon the fur trade to reliance upon husbandry,
spinning, weaving, and a market economy. Knox assumed that within half
a century the Indians would become so acculturated that they would will-
ingly give up their independent status and accept denationalization in exchange for citizenship in the United States. Implicit in the policy was the
belief that what was good for the development of the United States was
good for the Indian nations. But Knox did not leave this to chance.

"In the administration of the Indians," he told Washington in 1789,
"every proper expedient that can be devised to gain their affections and
attach them to the interest of the Union, should be adopted." Because their
hunting was almost depleted, Knox said, the government should impart
"our knowledge of cultivation and the arts to the aboriginals," persuade
them to adopt "a love for exclusive property," and encourage them to sell
off those tracts of land that they are not cultivating. The Indian nations were

---

[4]Henry Knox to George Washington, *American State Papers: Indian Affairs*, ed. Walter Lowrie and Walter S. Franklin (Washington DC, 1834) 1:53. Hereafter cited as ASP.

to use the money derived from the sale of these lands for the capital investment needed to transform their economy.[5]

Although Knox began by saying that "the independent nations and tribes of Indians ought to be considered as foreign nations," and no land should be taken from them except by treaties voluntarily entered into with the federal government, he went on to assert that "as the settlements of the whites shall approach near to the Indian boundaries established by treaties, the game will be diminished and the lands, being valuable to the Indians only as hunting grounds, they will be willing to sell them . . . for small considerations." The key to this program was for the federal government to provide the Indian nations with extensive economic aid in the form of plows, hoes, axes, seed, sheep, cattle, spinning wheels, looms, and eventually gristmills, sawmills, and cotton gins. This would lead to cash-crop surpluses and livestock surpluses, as elsewhere in the West, which would permit the Indians to develop a market economy. "The establishment of commerce with the Indian nations . . . is most likely to conciliate their attachment" to the United States.

A resident federal agent, serving as a kind of ambassador, would distribute these implements of husbandry and domestic manufacture within each Indian nation. In addition, he would have funds to hire farmers, spinners, and weavers to instruct Indian women how to grow cotton, spin it, and weave it into clothing for their families. Gifts of cattle, sheep, and hogs would stimulate the production of livestock for sale. He would also hire blacksmiths, coopers, wheelwrights, tinsmiths, tanners, sawyers, and millers to help the Indian men to sustain horse-and-plow farming. The agent would also license all white citizens who wished to trade with the Indians in order to assure that they were honest and reliable. Moreover, trading posts, subsidized by the government of the United States and managed by a government factor (or storekeeper), would provide manufactured goods and farm supplies so that the Indians would have a yardstick by which to measure the prices of private traders. The storekeepers would be allowed to extend credit to Indian farmers to enable them to make the investments needed to establish themselves.

In addition to the storekeeper and the resident agent, Knox proposed to encourage and support missionaries. Their purpose would be threefold:

---

[5]Ibid., 1:54, 13.

they would provide schools to teach reading and writing; they would provide moral training in the principles and practices of Christianity, and they would serve as vocational training personnel. "Missionaries of excellent moral character," Knox said, "should be appointed to reside in their nation[s], who would be well supplied with all the implements of husbandry and the necessary stock for a farm." These mission stations should be federally supported in order to educate Indian boys to be farmers and Indian girls to become farmers' wives. The missionaries should be regarded as paid agents of the federal government; they would serve as "the instruments to work on the Indians" in order to secure their allegiance to and gratitude toward the United States. "They should be their friends and fathers," as well as the eyes and ears of the government in every Indian town where they resided.[6] No one has ever calculated exactly how much money the federal government poured into these various forms of economic aid to Indian nations, but one federal agent to the Cherokees calculated that, directly and indirectly, at least half a million dollars came to that nation between 1801 and 1822.[7]

The resident agent of the War Department was the key figure in this elaborate bureaucracy governing Indian affairs. "Once established among them," Knox wrote, "they would possess the opportunity and most probably the power of regulating events as they should arise. They would acquire a knowledge of the characters of the influential chiefs and of the proper mode of managing them. Occasions would frequently occur of administering to their wants and fixing their gratitude. In short, agents so stationed and acting purely for the mutual interests of the United States and the Indians would soon attain a respectable and preeminent influence [over them]."[8] The key terms here were "managing them" and "mutual interests." As ambassadors to the Indian nations, the resident agents were to manage affairs so that the interests of the United States would become the preeminent interests of the Indians. Until 1815 these American ambassadors to the Indian nations were primarily concerned to prevent Indian al-

---

[6]Ibid., 1:54.

[7]Return J. Meigs to John C. Calhoun, 17 August 1822, Microfilm Records of the Cherokee Indian Agency in Tennessee, 1801-1835 (M-208), reel 9, Records of the Bureau of Indian Affairs (RG 75), National Archives, Washington DC. Hereafter cited as M-208 with date and reel number.

[8]ASP 1:259-60.

liances with European nations; after the War of 1812 their primary concern was to advance American economic interests.

I am not concerned here with the specifics of land acquisition except to note that Indian nations were always reluctant to sell their land. Though it was useless as a basis for fur trading, the Indians were smart enough to see that future generations of Indians might want to farm on it and that its timber and mineral resources were valuable. Some chiefs frankly saw land sales as a form of tribal income for their own capital development and encouraged it. Nonetheless, many times treaty commissioners returned empty-handed from negotiations. By 1818 the Cherokees were determined to hold on to every acre they had left. Having sold more than 25,000 square miles of their territory in the preceding thirty years, their chiefs told the secretary of war, "We consider ourselves a free and distinct nation," and they were determined not to dispose of one more foot of their homeland.[9] Ten years later, they set an example for rising Indian nationalism by adopting their own constitution and asserting "the sovereignty and jurisdiction" of their own elected legislature.[10] Sale of Cherokee land was made punishable by death. More germane to the argument here, the Cherokees passed a law in 1825 stating "that all gold, silver, lead, copper or brass mines which may be found within the limits of the Cherokee Nation shall be the public property of the Cherokee Nation" and should be developed only under the direction of the legislature for the benefit of the nation.[11] Native Americans came to see the virtues of separatist nationalism and to understand well the nature of capital investment and exploitation by the 1820s because they had seen it in action.

In 1789 the Cherokees occupied 49,000 square miles of territory. They numbered about 10,000 persons or 3,000 families. During the next twenty years they successfully moved from a fur-trading to a farming economy. They cleared plots of land, built log cabins, obtained horses and plows, grew corn, wheat, and cotton; their women learned to spin, sew, and weave to make the clothes for their families. Some Cherokees became artisans;

---

[9]Cherokee memorial to Joseph McMinn, 30 June 1818, Letters Received by the Secretary of War: Main Series, 1801-1870 (M-221), reel 71, #0284, Records of the Office of the Secretary of War (RG 107), National Archives, Washington DC.

[10]The Cherokee Constitution is printed in *Laws of the Cherokee Nation* (Tahlequah, Cherokee Nation: 1852) 118-30.

[11]Ibid., 50.

some engaged in trade; and by 1809 the wealthier members of the nation owned 583 black slaves who labored for them in many capacities.[12] Still, their economic transition was slow and uneven. Until the 1820s they were subject to perennial periods of near starvation whenever droughts, floods, frosts, pests, and windstorms ruined their crops. During such periods the Cherokees needed food for famine relief, and the federal government often provided it. However, federal officials did not hesitate to use the leverage they obtained from such humanitarian gestures to force the Cherokees to grant them economic favors in exchange.

For example, in the years 1799 to 1803, the Cherokees had firmly resisted all efforts to permit a federal turnpike to be built through the heart of their country that would connect Athens, Georgia, to Nashville, Tennessee. The treaty commissioners sent to negotiate for this right-of-way said that the United States did not intend "to extinguish your right but to give value to your land and make it immediately productive to you."[13] The Cherokees were reluctant to increase their commerce with the rough whites in the neighboring frontier towns who plied them with liquor, cheated, abused, and stole from them. Jefferson's secretary of war, Henry Dearborn, kept pointing out to their chiefs that they could hardly expect to ask the government for food relief as well as gratuitous economic assistance in the form of plows, hoes, and spinning wheels, and then refuse to grant the United States the small favor of building a mutually advantageous road through their country. The chiefs replied, "I expect you will think [agree] we have a right to say yes or no as answer."[14] Jefferson admitted this when he explained his failure to Congress in 1802: "All these nations are known to be very jealous on the subject of their lands . . . though our overtures to them were moderate and respectful of their rights, their determination was to yield no accommodation."[15]

Nonetheless, Jefferson persisted. His secretary of war told the resident agent among the Cherokees, Colonel Return J. Meigs, to get tough: "It

---

[12]For Cherokee economic growth in slaves and other property, see W. G. McLoughlin and Walter H. Conser, Jr., "The Cherokees in Transition," *Journal of American History* 64:3 (December 1977): 678-703.

[13]ASP 1:656-57.

[14]Ibid., 657.

[15]Ibid., 656-57.

may not be improper to inform the Chiefs that from their conduct . . . they must not expect any particular favors from the United States.''[16] Faced with the curtailment of their economic assistance and famine relief, the Cherokees finally yielded in 1803 and allowed the road to be built. During the next decade the Cherokees had many experiences with white entrepreneurs who offered, they said, similar mutual advantages in economic development. Their first experiences were with itinerant traders who asked permission to establish permanent stores in the nation. They seldom found these traders as accommodating as their own native traders. They met many traveling blacksmiths, school teachers, and carpenters who thought they could make more money from gullible or ignorant Indians than in white settlements. They met whites who offered to be sharecroppers on Indian land, where they could live without paying taxes until they saved enough to move out and buy their own farms. They met whites who wanted to establish taverns, inns, or ferries along their roads. As early as 1802 the Cherokees were leasing salt-peter caves to enterprising whites who agreed to pay rent in gunpowder procured from the mines. They rented salines to whites and in 1810 a man named James Ore received permission to mine for lead in the nation.[17] All of the aspects of a market economy were evident in the Cherokee Nation by 1810. By then the Cherokees developed their own entrepreneurs who owned trading posts, had large plantations, owned boats that traded to New Orleans, and took large droves of horses and cattle to sell in neighboring white communities. In 1809 the resident agent published a statistical chart of Cherokee progress in which he listed the existence of thirteen gristmills, three sawmills, three salt-peter works, two powder mills, and five schools.[18] Five years later a white man named John Fergus started a fulling mill in the nation.[19]

One of the major aspects of government-sponsored private enterprise among the Cherokees was the effort to start an iron foundry to manufacture cannon and other military materiel for the United States Army. The entrepreneur behind this venture was Colonel Elias W. Earle of South Carolina. Earle had traded for years among the Cherokees and discovered that there

---

[16]Henry Dearborn to Return J. Meigs, 7 and 30 April 1802, M-208, reel 1.

[17]Samuel Riley to Return J. Meigs, 26 February 1810, M-208, reel 5.

[18]A copy of this statistical table is located in the Moravian Archives, Winston-Salem NC.

[19]John Fergus to Return J. Meigs, 6 March 1814, M-208, Reel 6.

were large deposits of iron ore along the Tennessee River near the mouth of Chickamauga Creek. However, instead of going to the Cherokee Council, as most entrepreneurs did who wanted to operate such a concession, Earle went directly to President Jefferson and the secretary of war. They were eager to assist him and the corporate investors he had gathered in South Carolina to back the venture. The secretary of war, Henry Dearborn, instructed the federal agent to negotiate a treaty with the Cherokee chiefs that would grant Earle outright possession of six square miles in the heart of their nation. Meigs gathered a group of twenty-three chiefs together in December 1807, and after some bribery, threats, and cajolery, they signed a treaty disposing of the thirty-six square miles for $2500 (although Meigs admitted that it was land worth five dollars an acre). Meigs told Dearborn that "when the land for Iron works was ceded, it was foreseen that they must famish without corn, and it was one strong inducement" to them to sign when a gift of 1,000 bushels of corn was added to the purchase price.[20]

The great majority of the 100 or more chiefs in the Cherokee Nation were angry when they learned of this "sham treaty" and wrote to the president about it. When he nonetheless recommended it to the Senate for ratification, the chiefs wrote to the Senate.[21] Meanwhile Earle and his backers raised the money to gather the first men and equipment to start the iron foundry. However, when he tried to march his first caravan of workers, slaves, and supplies to Chickamauga Creek, he was stopped at the Cherokee border by a group of chiefs who opposed the project. The federal agent was about to call out the army to provide safe passage for Earle's company when some Tennessee entrepreneurs discovered that the tract that had been negotiated for Earle lay within the state of Tennessee; the people of Tennessee opposed granting this economic concession to a citizen of South Carolina. Tennessee's senators prevented ratification of the treaty and Earle's project collapsed. Nonetheless, the War Department deducted several thousand dollars from the Cherokee annuity to compensate Colonel

---

[20]Return J. Meigs to Henry Dearborn, 24 March 1808, M-208, reel 4.

[21]Cherokee Chiefs to George Clinton, 16 February 1808, Letters Received by the Secretary of War (unregistered), 1789-1861 (M-222), reel 3, #1154, Records of the Office of the Secretary of War, National Archives, Washington DC. Hereafter cited as M-222 with date and reel and frame numbers.

Earle for the trouble and expense he had been caused when his wagon train was stopped by the irate chiefs.[22]

After 1810 the Cherokees generally welcomed the building of additional roads through their nation so that they could get their produce and livestock to market more easily, but they tried to build roads by incorporating their own turnpike companies and loaning them money out of their treasury to undertake these public works for the good of their nation. Whenever the federal government built a turnpike, it expected to hire white contractors and to grant white men the franchises for inns, taverns, and ferries along it. In 1808 the Cherokee legislature told the War Department, "It is not our wish that any part of our lands should be leased or rented by any company of individuals" to maintain inns or "stands" along the turnpikes within Cherokee boundaries.[23] The Cherokees wanted their own citizens to benefit from these enterprises, not foreigners. But it was no easy task, for in most cases the governors of the states surrounding the Cherokee Nation expected the War Department to allow them to allocate franchises as part of the political patronage that accompanied state support for the project.

Whenever Cherokee resistance hardened against pressure for economic concessions, the federal agent was quick to find what he called "progressive," "friendly," or "well-disposed" chiefs whom he could manipulate into a faction that would urge the Cherokee legislature to cooperate with their benefactors in Washington. The agent found ways to influence the chiefs in these factions. A good example of this occurred in 1806-1807 when the War Department wanted to purchase the last of the Cherokee hunting grounds in middle Tennessee and northern Alabama. Colonel Meigs had cultivated the friendship of a group of chiefs in the Lower Town region of the nation led by a chief named Doublehead. Doublehead had received a great deal of personal economic aid from Meigs; he ran several large plantations, owned many slaves, and engaged in trade down the Mississippi to New Orleans. He had asked Meigs to supply him with a boat for his trading and expected him to acquiesce.[24] In 1806 the

[22]Return J. Meigs to William Eustis, 15 December 1810, M-208, reel 5; and Charles Royce, *The Cherokee Nation of Indians* (Chicago: Aldine Publishing Co., 1975) 71-73.

[23]Cherokee Chiefs to Thomas Jefferson, 4 June 1808, M-222, reel 3, #1343.

[24]Doublehead to Return J. Meigs, 20 November 1802, M-208, reel 1.

War Department authorized Meigs to have the federal storekeeper in the Cherokee Nation extend $500 worth of credit to Doublehead with the understanding that the debt would be wiped off once a treaty for the hunting grounds was concluded. In addition, Meigs worked out certain codicils to be inserted in the treaty that would benefit Doublehead and his friends (but which the Cherokee council would never be shown). President Jefferson, upon the conclusion of the treaty for the sale of the hunting ground, gave Doublehead a special gift of $1,000 "in consideration of his active influence in forwarding the views of Government in the introduction of the arts of civilization among the Cherokee Nation, and for his friendly disposition towards the United States and for the purpose of enabling him to extend his useful example among the Red People."[25]

When all of these machinations became known in 1807, a group of chiefs in the Upper Town region of the nation called a council and deposed the leaders of the Lower Town faction. They then voted to assassinate Doublehead for treason to the nation. Three chiefs carried out that decision. Colonel Meigs was furious at the death of his compliant ally. He termed the opposing faction a "rebellious party" acting against the progress of their nation and its friendly relationship with the United States. Calling together the frightened chiefs of Doublehead's faction, Meigs made an agreement with them to arrest the leader of the "rebels," a chief named James Vann, on trumped-up charges of assault against a white citizen. The United States Army was called out to arrest Vann and jail him for trial in Tennessee. "If Vann is properly brought to Justice," Meigs wrote the secretary of war, "it will have a very good effect; [it] will silence his partizans—negotiations with the Cherokees will [then] be conducted with ease."[26] Unfortunately for Meigs, the charges against Vann did not stick. Ultimately the rebellious party gained control of the nation and Meigs had to learn to work through it.

The use of the government trading post as a source of bribery and economic pressure upon the Cherokees and other tribes has been well docu-

---

[25]Henry Dearborn to Return J. Meigs, 8 January 1806, Letters Sent by the Secretary of War Relating to Indian Affairs, 1800-1824 (M-15), reel 2, p. 153, Records of the Bureau of Indian Affairs, National Archives, Washington DC. Hereafter cited as M-15 with reel and page numbers.

[26]Return J. Meigs to John Sevier, 23 October 1808, M-208, reel 4.

mented.[27] Apart from buying the cooperation of individual chiefs, it could be used to intimidate the whole nation. Although the Cherokees, by sale of land, accumulated an annuity or annual stipend from the government of between $6,000 to $10,000 upon which to fund their own economic growth, many individual Cherokees ran up large debts at the government trading post or with private traders. When Meigs, in 1807, wanted to alter secretly the boundary line of the treaty that ceded the hunting grounds, he informed the War Department: "The Cherokees, being in debt to the United States $1803, I offered to cancel that debt as compensation for the alteration of the line."[28] The five chiefs who agreed to this alteration did not inform the Cherokee legislature because it was their own debts that were thus wiped out. Thomas Jefferson encouraged storekeepers at Indian trading posts to allow huge debts to build up amounting to many thousands of dollars—so large that the tribal annuities could not possibly cover them. Then he demanded immediate payment and insisted that land be sold to do this. John Hooker, the Cherokee storekeeper, explained this maneuver to a Cherokee chief. He said "that when he was at the Norward [Washington D.C.] that in a conversation with Mr. Jefferson, he [Jefferson] asked him if he [Hooker] could get the Cherokees to run into debt to the amount of ten or twelve thousand dollars in the public store." Hooker answered that he could, if necessary, run up a debt of "fifty thousand." "Well, says he [Jefferson], that is the way I entend to get there cuntry, for to get them to run in debt to the public store and [then] they will have to give there land for payment."[29]

In some cases wealthy chiefs concluded a treaty and then deducted from the money owed to the tribe enough to pay their own debts first. This happened to the Cherokees in 1806 when a delegation of fourteen chiefs was sent to Washington to make a treaty. The government paid them $10,000 in cash for a tract of land, but none of this was ever placed in the tribal treasury. The delegation voted to use $2,000 of this money to pay their hotel bills and other travel expenses and the other $8,000 to pay off their individual debts to private traders and to the public storekeeper. When the Cherokee council learned of this, they complained to the secretary of war:

---

[27]Prucha, *American Indian Policy*, 88.

[28]Return J. Meigs to Henry Dearborn, 28 September 1807, M-208, reel 4.

[29]Samuel Riley to Return J. Meigs, 29 November 1806, M-208, reel 3.

"The last deputation that was at the city of Washington agreed that the debts due to their old traders should be paid out of our annuity. . . . a few individuals run in debt to a few favorite Merchants in the neighborhood of the Garrison [where the public store was] who gets the whole of the money, and the nation never receives one cent of benefit from [its land sale]."[30] Until the Cherokees managed to gain control over their own treasury after 1813, they were subject to another form of economic manipulation by the resident agent. The War Department turned over to the agent each year the $6,000 to $10,000 annuity for transmission to the Cherokees. But before he delivered this money, he deducted from it all claims against the tribe by white citizens. These claims might be made for stolen horses or cattle, for property theft, for damaged property, or for infringement of some contractual arrangement. Meigs also deducted money from the annuity to pay slaveowners for any slaves who were killed by Cherokees. Such fiscal control was a strong incentive for cooperation.

During the Panic of 1819, when it was difficult to obtain specie, the agent paid the annuity in paper money printed by state banks. The Cherokee treasurer complained that because paper money circulated at five to six percent below par, the nation was being cheated out of a large part of its income. "I will again complain to yourself [about] the kind of money you have paid to the Nation these last two years annuity," wrote treasurer Charles Hicks to the agent in June 1821. "I find the southern bank bills are already begun to depreciate their nominal standard from 4, 5, 6, and 7 per unit below par."[31] When the agent ignored the complaint, the Cherokee legislature passed a law directing its treasurer "not to receive into the Treasury from the Agents of the United States . . . any other description of money than Specie, Treasury [notes] or Notes of the United States Bank."[32] However, the agent continued to do what was most convenient for him.

The ultimate use of the tribal annuity as a means of economic pressure to force compliance with the government wishes came during the presidency of Andrew Jackson in 1831. Jackson was trying to compel the Cher-

---

[30]Cherokee Chiefs to Thomas Jefferson, 4 June 1808, M-222, reel 3, #1343.

[31]Charles Hicks to Return J. Meigs, 28 June 1821, M-208, reel 9, and Charles Hicks to Joseph McMinn, 4 May 1823, M-208, reel 9.

[32]*Laws,* 83.

okees to sign a treaty to sell all their land and remove to Arkansas Territory. He instructed the secretary of war not to pay any further annuities into the Cherokee treasury. Instead, he divided the $6,000 stipend by the total number of Cherokee individuals and ordered the agent to pay forty-two cents to each Cherokee who came to the agency to collect it. This tactic was designed specifically to prevent the Cherokees from paying attorneys whom they hired to bring test cases before the United States Supreme Court regarding Cherokee sovereignty and treaty rights.

Over the years, as the Cherokee Nation increased in stability and prosperity, it developed a centralized governmental system with an elaborate bureaucracy. By 1823 it had established an elected, bicameral legislature, a supreme court and district courts, a jury system, a police force, and a national treasury all operating under written laws. Although this system provided effective control over Cherokee affairs, it proved very costly to run. In 1819 the Cherokee legislature decided to lay taxes on its citizens and others doing business in the nation in order to help provide additional revenue. Poll taxes were laid on all male citizens and licensing taxes were laid on all traders, white and Cherokee. Some of the white traders refused to pay the taxes levied upon them and appealed to the War Department. When the Cherokee courts ordered the Cherokee police to confiscate goods from these traders and sell them to pay their taxes, the traders brought suit for illegal distraint of their private property by an Indian nation.[33] The War Department asked the attorney general for an opinion, and he asserted that under the treaties Indian nations did not have the power to lay taxes on white citizens because the federal agent was the only proper licensing and control authority over whites within Indian nations. The Cherokees sent a memorial to Congress stating that by international law and under the Constitution of the United States, they had the right to lay taxes for internal revenue as did any state in the Union: "The Cherokee Nation possess the same right of making municipal regulations for their internal government for the purpose of creating a revenue as any other nation. . . . The Cherokee are not foreigners but original inhabitants of America and . . . they now inhabit and stand on the soil of their own territory. . . . they cannot recognize the sovereignty of any State within the limits of their terri-

---

[33]This question of internal taxation is discussed in detail in W. G. McLoughlin, *The Cherokee Ghost Dance: Essays on the Southeastern Indians, 1789-1861* (Macon GA: Mercer University Press, 1984) 193-215.

tory."[34] In defense of this position they cited Article I, Section 8 of the Constitution. But the War Department instructed the resident agent to deduct from the Cherokee annuity in 1824 sufficient funds to pay back the merchants whose goods had been confiscated, and to tell the Cherokees that they must repeal the law that laid taxes on white citizens within their boundaries.

In order to strengthen their position against the oppressive power of the United States, many Indian nations in the West tried to confederate. The Cherokees were particularly eager to work with other Indian nations in the Old Southwest to prevent the sale of Indian land. The lack of clarity about boundaries between the Indian nations made it easy for the federal government to persuade one nation to sell off land that was claimed by another. In 1785, 1796, and 1805 the Cherokees formed tentative alliances with other tribes in order to foil efforts to pit them against each other. The War Department and the resident agents asserted every possible form of pressure to break up these confederacies. In 1805, for example, the secretary of war heard that the Southeastern Indians were forming "a general confederacy for preventing any particular nation from disposing of their lands without the consent of the whole of the nations combined."[35] He sent word to all the resident agents in these nations, ordering them to "use every prudent measure in your power for preventing such combination."[36]

On the whole the War Department was successful in this. However, in 1825 the Cherokees formed an alliance with the Creek Nation and provided it with substantial aid in resisting the sale of its land in Georgia. This was done when three well-educated Cherokee leaders—Major Ridge, John Ridge, and David Vann—agreed to serve as secretaries and counselors to the Creeks in their negotiations (because the Creeks had few good bilingual chiefs whom they could trust). The secretary of war threatened the Cherokee Council with punitive action if it did not order these three Cherokees to desist. "There is great reason to apprehend," wrote the secretary, "that John Ridge and David Vann, natives of the Cherokee Nation, are

---

[34]Charles Hicks and John Ross to Hugh Montgomery, 11 December 1825, Letters Received by the Office of Indian Affairs, 1824-1880 (M-234), reel 72, #0762, Records of the Bureau of Indian Affairs (RG 75), National Archives, Washington DC. Hereafter cited as M-234 with reel and frame numbers.

[35]Henry Dearborn to Return J. Meigs, 20 June 1805, M-208, reel 3.

[36]Idem.

very improperly interfering in the affairs of the Creek Nation and by their
Counsel creating and keeping up a feeling in that Nation dangerous to its
peace and hostile to the best views of the government with respect to it.
[This is] highly disapproved of by the President and cannot be permitted.
[The President expects you] to apply the corrective in this matter [or it will]
lead to consequences that would seriously affect the tranquility and happiness of the Cherokee Nation.''[37] The War Department sent its chief
troubleshooter, Thomas L. McKenney, to warn the Creeks that they must
not permit the Cherokees to influence their actions. McKenney managed
to persuade the principal chief of the Creeks that these Cherokee allies were
secretly plotting to depose him. The principal chief believed McKenney,
ordered the Cherokees out of the nation, and proceeded to sign a treaty giving the government what it wanted.[38]

Although the United States did not like the Cherokees to meddle in
Creek affairs, it had no qualms about employing Creeks to meddle in Cherokee affairs. In 1823 Chief William McIntosh of the Creeks was sent to a
treaty conference in the Cherokee Nation to offer large bribes to the leading Cherokee chiefs. McIntosh was at first welcomed to the conference because he was married to a Cherokee, but when he offered bribes he was
exposed and fled back to his own nation. The treaty commissioners from
the United States pretended that they were totally unaware of McIntosh's
actions, though where he would have obtained authorization to offer
$29,000 in bribes was never explained.[39]

Several years later, when the United States was trying to encourage individual Cherokees to move to Arkansas (an action that had a very destabilizing effect upon internal affairs), the War Department secretly hired two
of the Cherokees then living in Arkansas to travel around the Cherokee Nation in the East telling their friends how advantageous it would be for them
to emigrate. The War Department promised to give every Cherokee who
agreed to emigrate a new gun, a new blanket, a brass pot, and five pounds

[37]George Barbour to Little Prince, 23 June 1827, Letters Sent by the Office of Indian
Affairs, 1824-1882 (M-21), reel 4, pp. 78-82, Records of the Bureau of Indian Affairs (RG
75), National Archives, Washington DC (hereafter cited as M-21 with reel and page numbers); George Barbour to Cherokee Council, 25 June 1827, M-21, reel 4, p. 83.

[38]This incident is fully discussed in Thurman Wilkins, *Cherokee Tragedy* (New York:
Macmillan Co., 1970) 144-52.

[39]Ibid., 142-44.

of tobacco. The two agents, James Rogers and Thomas Maw, were soon detected and exposed. They nearly lost their lives for their efforts.[40]

The ultimate form of imperial intimidation of client nations is of course military intervention, and in the end it was at the point of bayonets that the Cherokees were forced on the Trail of Tears in 1838-1839. However, force had been used or threatened against them before that time. In 1807, for example, when the rebellious young chiefs deposed Doublehead and tried to take control of the council, the federal agent ordered the nearby army garrison to prepare to enter the country to restore the legitimate government (that is, the well-disposed chiefs in Doublehead's faction). At the same time he also wrote to the governor of Tennessee, John Sevier, asking him to prepare to call out the Tennessee militia for action in case the rebellious faction proved too strong for the small army garrison. This action was avoided, but the government was always prepared to use it if necessary.

In 1819, when Governor James McMinn of Tennessee was acting as a government agent to promote the sale of Cherokee land and instigate removal to the West, he became frightened by the vigorous opposition of the Cherokee rank and file. One of his assistants was assaulted, and he told the War Department that his own life was in danger. Consequently, he ordered the army garrison to surround the negotiating council with troops to prove that the government would meet force with force. Intimidated, the Cherokees agreed to send a delegation to Washington to negotiate a sale of land as a means of staving off removal, even though they had said they would never sell another foot.[41]

The presence of United States troops at the garrison near the federal agency in any Indian nation was originally designed to protect the Indians from hostile actions by white frontiersmen as well as to prevent Indian uprisings. Protection of the borders of Indian nations was written into all treaties, but it was a difficult and dangerous task. Whites commonly entered and settled on Indian land, assuming that they had a perfect right to use whatever land the Indians were not using. At any given time between 1789 and 1839 there were literally hundreds of white intruders in the Cherokee Nation; they felled timber, built log cabins, planted corn, and grazed their cattle until the federal Indian agent (usually prior to a treaty negotiation)

---

[40]See Hugh Montgomery to Peter B. Porter, 31 October 1828, M-234, reel 72, #0639.

[41]ASP 2:481-88.

would order out the troops for the purpose of removing them. Yet even army troops were not always safe from frontiersmen who believed they were defending their homes.[42]

Moreover, it became a common means of intimidation by the War Department and its agents to threaten to refuse to call out the army to protect Indian borders from intruders. Once it became known that they would not be evicted, white frontiersmen would have flocked by the thousands into Indian land and wreaked havoc with good order there. Because Indians could not testify in any trial against a white man, these intruders could assault, rob, dispossess, and even murder Indians with impunity once the army garrison was withdrawn. Although this threat was not carried out until Jackson's day, it was frequently expressed by angry treaty negotiators and federal agents who accused the Cherokees of failing to realize how grateful they should be to the United States for protecting their borders.

Finally, something should be said about the destabilizing role of missionaries in the Indian nations. Robert Berkhofer and others have documented the problems that arose once a "Christian faction" was formed and a "Pagan faction" was criticized by missionaries.[43] At least three times between 1789 and 1839, the Cherokee Nation was disrupted by confrontations between those favorable to missionaries and those opposed to them.[44] Although technically, under the treaties, an Indian nation had the right to eject missionaries, it was not to their advantage to do so, and the War Department strenuously objected when any nation tried it. It was all too easy to argue that only the backward, pagan, full bloods opposed mission schools, while the enlightened, Christian converts were supportive of them. In most of the Indian nations, however, the majority of the people adhered to traditional beliefs. Cultural subversion by missionaries in the pay of the federal government, as Berkhofer points out, was promoted by the ethnocentric assumption that the only way an Indian could be civilized was for him to give up everything that made him an Indian—his religion,

---

[42]See Prucha, *American Indian Policy*, 139-88.

[43]See Robert K. Berkhofer, *Salvation and the Savage* (New York: Atheneum, 1976) 125-51.

[44]For discussions of the traditionalist uprising among the Cherokees, see W. G. McLoughlin, *Cherokees and Missionaries* (New Haven: Yale University Press, 1984) chs. 4, 8, and 9.

his dress, his language, his sports, his social customs, his behavior, and his values.[45]

Although most missionaries claimed to be apolitical, the whole purpose of the mission enterprise was to teach the Indians that adaptation to the economic assumptions of the capitalist system was imperative. One missionary, the Reverend Gideon Blackburn, specifically undertook projects for the secretary of war. Blackburn was a Presbyterian from Tennessee who established two schools in the Cherokee Nation after receiving funds from President Jefferson. In 1809 he explored the navigable rivers of the Cherokee Nation at the request of the secretary of war. He well knew that once a river was found to be navigable between two or more states, the United States would declare it open to traffic by white citizens no matter how much the Indians might object to such intrusions through their nations. Blackburn and his brother were in the whiskey-trade business, however, and were looking for means to expand their business.[46]

It is true, of course, that some missionaries sided with the Indian nations against their denationalization and against their removal to the West. Missionaries were shocked in 1830 to find that Andrew Jackson was willing to break all treaty guarantees, intimidate the Indians, and compel them to leave their homes. As soon as missionary opposition showed itself, President Jackson declared that he no longer considered them government agents. As a result, seven missionaries in the Cherokee Nation were arrested in 1831 by the state of Georgia and two were sent to the penitentiary for refusing to sign an oath of allegiance to obey Georgia laws directed at denationalization.[47] Jackson thought they deserved their sentences for refusing to support the government's policy.

At the other extreme, some missionaries functioned as secret agents of the government during the removal crisis. The Reverend Alexander Talley, a Methodist missionary among the Choctaws, not only urged them to sign a removal treaty in 1831, but wrote the treaty himself.[48] After 1830

---

[45]Robert K. Berkhofer, *The White Man's Indian* (New York: Knopf, 1978).

[46]See W. G. McLoughlin, "Parson Blackburn's Whiskey," *Journal of Presbyterian History* 62:4 (Winter 1979): 427-45.

[47]See McLoughlin, "Civil Disobedience and Social Action among the Missionaries to the Cherokees," in *Cherokee Ghost Dance,* 423-49.

[48]See Angi Debo, *The Rise and Fall of the Choctaw Republic* (Norman: University of Oklahoma Press, 1934) 52-57.

no white citizen in an Indian nation could be a free agent. Like the Indians, they had to toe the line of national policy or become subject to reprisals.

Had the Southeastern Indian nations who occupied most of the cotton belt been truly free and sovereign, they could have become rich from the sale of their land. However, they were not allowed to sell it at market price. The government set the price for Indian land, and as the secretary of war said, "We never pay more than two cents an acre for Indian land."[49] The justification for this was that the land being sold by the Indians was "waste land," meaning land no longer fit for hunting and not yet under cultivation. But this was a strange way of evaluating land. It is not the value of land to the owner but its value to the prospective buyer that establishes its market price. Consequently all Indian land sales, most of them effected under duress, defrauded the Indians. Occasionally some Indian leaders would suggest that they survey their land and sell it in small parcels as white land speculators did. The War Department told them that they were not entitled to do this and absolutely refused to purchase any land under such circumstances. Most Indian nations were not interested in dividing their land in severalty. Had they done so, any Indian landholder could have sold it to whites as his own private property. Therefore, none of the tribes gave up the traditional practice of holding all tribal land in common.

Historians have generally given three interlocking reasons for the decision to remove the Indians to the West in 1830. The first was the increasing pressure from frontier settlers wanting land; the second was the increasing value of land in the West; and the third was the growing reluctance of the Indian nations to sell any more land—a position the whites chose to attribute to their unwillingness or inability to become civilized. However, there was a fourth and equally cogent reason for Indian removal. It was not that the Indians did not want to become farmers and adopt the agrarian life-style of the white man, but rather the fact that the pace of commercial farming and the market economy had grown much more intense, more regional, and large-scaled. Business ventures and interstate trade were linking the rural areas to new urban areas, the West to the East, Appalachia to New Orleans and the Gulf ports. The Erie Canal, completed in 1825, was the major symbol of this new step toward urban industrialism in a region that had formerly been isolated and self-contained. In the next decade

---

[49]Henry Dearborn to Return J. Meigs, 8 October 1805, M-15, reel 2, p. 117.

the first railroads and the Mississippi steamboats were to complete the process in the Old Northwest and the Old Southwest. Economic nationalism was at hand and the Indians were not ready to be submerged into it.

The best illustration of this was the continued refusal of the Cherokee Nation in the 1820s to allow railways or canals to be built through their land by big companies investing millions of dollars and backed by state and federal subsidies. This matter was first broached to the Cherokees at negotiations in July 1826 when John Quincy Adams, at the insistence of businessmen from Georgia and Tennessee, asked the Cherokees to allow surveyors to look for a route for canals or horsedrawn railways that would link their two states and provide eastern Tennessee with quicker access to the Gulf of Mexico.[50] The Cherokee Council refused. The request was renewed in the fall of that year and again in 1827. The state of North Carolina also joined in these efforts on behalf of its Western citizens. Typical of many letters that the federal agent, Hugh Montgomery, sent to the Cherokee legislature urging it to reconsider its position was the one written on 26 September 1827. Montgomery wrote concerning "a canal Connecting the waters of the Tennessee with the Chatahoochee" and argued that it would not only enrich the region and enhance the commerce of the United States, it would also mean tremendous economic advantages for the Cherokee Nation.

> The New York canal, 250 miles long, was completed in about three years, . . . but suppose this took five or even ten years and the expense [was] two millions of dollars (and this is believed to be a moderate estimate), would not the circulation of that some [sum] of money in the Cherokie Nation be an advantage to every person in it by affording a ready cash market for every lb. of Beef, Pork, Butter and cheese . . . etc. and a ready employ and good wages . . . and besides a stimulant to Industry?[51]

Montgomery also noted that "this is not all," for the canal would provide a cheap and "convenient Road to market" for Cherokee goods and it would aid the nation "in Receiving supplies . . . at Reduced prices." In short, canals and railways would link the Cherokee economy to the regional and national economy and bring new riches to all.

---

[50]James Barbour to Hugh Montgomery, 19 July 1826, M-21, reel 3, p. 149.

[51]Hugh Montgomery to the Cherokee Chiefs, 26 September 1828, M-208, reel 10.

The Cherokees, realizing that the profits from building and operating such a canal would go principally to enrich the white men who built it and maintained it, refused to allow even a survey to take place.[52] Such stubborn resistance to the most enticing aspects of American national progress could not be tolerated. By 1827 the people of Georgia and Tennessee were ready to deny that Indian nations had any right to control their land. Three months after the Cherokees refused to heed Montgomery's advice, the Georgia legislature voted that all Cherokee land within its boundaries belonged to the sovereign state of Georgia and that the state intended to assert its jurisdiction over it. A year later General Jackson of Tennessee was elected president with the full support of the states of the Old Southwest. He had long been committed to the denationalization and removal of the Indians. The charge that the Indian nations had become *imperia in imperio* was simply a statement that they could not be allowed to hinder the nation's economic growth. As Jackson put it bluntly in 1833, the Indians "have neither the intelligence, the industry, the moral habits, nor the desire of improvement which are essential to any favorable change in their condition. Established in the midst of another and superior race, and without appreciating the causes of their inferiority or seeking to control them, they must necessarily yield to the force of circumstances and ere long disappear."[53]

When John Marshall and the Supreme Court ruled in 1831 that the Cherokees were a "domestic dependent nation," the Cherokees emphasized the term *nation* and Jackson the term *dependent*. It was almost the same attitude with which President James Monroe had treated the newly independent nations of Latin America in his famous "doctrine" of 1823. Starting from the position that their territorial integrity was dependent upon the power of the United States, and implying that as protectorates the United States would guarantee their boundaries, the State Department developed policies in Latin America that gradually evolved along the same path that had marked the nation's treatment of the Native American nations. What was necessary for American economic progress was necessary for Latin American progress.

---

[52]Part of the resistance to the surveys resulted from a traditionalist uprising in the Cherokee Nation in the years 1824-1827 that culminated in a movement called White Path's Rebellion. See McLoughlin, *Cherokees and Missionaries*, 213-39.

[53]Andrew Jackson, "Message to Congress," 3 December 1833, *Congressional House Documents* (Washington: Gales and Seaton, 1833) 254:14.

In 1789 the federal government had promised to provide economic assistance to the undeveloped Indian nations and ultimately to treat their people as equals. But whenever an Indian nation refused to comply with some
economic request of the government, it found the ties of economic assistance tightened to enforce compliance. If economic pressure was insuffi-
cient, bribery, internal factionalism, political destabilization (sometimes
promoted by secret agents), and eventually military intervention were utilized. The Indian nations were told that they did not know what was best
for them, that they did not know how to develop their own internal resources, and that white entrepreneurs must be allowed to do it for them.
When they resisted, the United States did not hesitate to establish control
by force. ''You see,'' the secretary of war said to the Cherokees in 1819,
''that the Great Spirit has made our form of society stronger than yours,
and you must submit to adopt ours if you wish to be happy by pleasing
him.''[54] What he meant was that the Indian nations were subservient to the
more powerful military, political, and economic might of the United States
and that the development of Indian communities must always be subservient to its growth. By 1830 it was clear: Indian ''nations'' had no sovereignty, no self-determination, no independence. Long before the removal
of the Indians, it was clear that their land and people were considered fit
only to serve the needs of the dominant Anglo-Saxon imperialists.

---

[54]ASP 2:190.

·● Part III ●·

Exploring
the Boundaries

Soaring with the Gods: Early Mormons and the Eclipse of Religious Pluralism

Richard T. Hughes

Sidney E. Mead observed in *The Lively Experiment* that one of the defining themes of American Christianity during the nation's early years was a profound sense of "historylessness," a perspective shaped by three assumptions: "the idea of pure and normative beginnings to which return was possible; the idea that the intervening history was largely that of aberrations and corruptions which was better ignored; and the idea of building anew in the American wilderness on the true and ancient foundations." Reinforcing this restoration perspective was the radical newness of the American experiment, which worked to erase not only continuity with Europe but also with the historic churches. Thus, many Christians imagined they were beginning again "at the point where mankind had first gone astray—at Eden, the paradise of man before the fall."[1]

Alongside this theme lay another that Mead developed in much greater detail, namely the persistent refusal of many religionists in America to ac-

---

[1]Sidney E. Mead, *The Lively Experiment* (New York: Harper & Row, 1963) 108-10. Regarding this theme, see also Mead, "The Theology of the Republic and the Orthodox Mind," *Journal of the American Academy of Religion* 44 (March 1976): 105-13.

cept either the legitimacy or the premises of religious pluralism. Indeed, Mead argued that antipathy toward pluralism was especially strong in the early nineteenth century when the religious premises for pluralism were "drowned in the great tidal wave of revivalism that swept through the country" at that time.[2]

Mead recognized the relation between these themes when he noted that the fact of religious pluralism, with its vast free market of souls, determined that each sect would compete with all the others by claiming that it "most closely conformed to the Biblical patterns."[3] The relation between these themes was more intimate even than that, though. In the first place, while practically every sect and denomination may have used the appeal to biblical patterns as an effective weapon in denominational rivalry, some groups took upon themselves the restoration ideal as a defining characteristic, a raison d'être. This was the case, for example, with Mormons, Separate Baptists, Shakers, Disciples, and "New Light" Christians of both the South and the East. And in the second place, restoration in their hands often became the basis not just for rivalry and competition, but also for opposing both the fact and premise of religious pluralism itself. Accordingly, many restorationists argued that a return to the ancient order of things would bring not only a unity of the church but also a unity of civilization under the lordship of Jesus Christ. Alexander Campbell, for example, argued that "there is now a scheme of things presented, in what is called the *Ancient Gospel,* which is long enough, broad enough, strong enough, for the whole superstructure called the Millennial Church—and . . . it will alone be the *instrument* of *converting* the whole human race." Campbell also suggested that this conversion would finally "subvert all political government," including that of the pluralistic American nation.[4] Or again, the Mormon missionary Parley P. Pratt foresaw in 1851 that through the progress of the Mormon restoration all governments, kingdoms, and tribes

[2]Cf., e.g., Mead, *The Nation with the Soul of a Church* (New York: Harper & Row, 1975) 49 and 74; idem, *The Lively Experiment,* 53.

[3]Mead, *The Lively Experiment,* 110.

[4]Alexander Campbell, "Millennium—No.1," *Millennial Harbinger* 1 (February 1830): 55-56; idem, "An Oration in Honor of the Fourth of July," 1830, in *Popular Lectures and Addresses* (St. Louis: John Burns, 1861) 374-75.

would be "dissolved—destroyed—or mingled into *one* —one body politic—*one* peaceful empire—*one* Lord—*one* King—*one* interest all."[5]

How does one account for this radically ecumenical thrust with its antipluralist dimension? From a theological perspective, restorationists commonly appealed to Jesus' prayer for the unity of believers. But what prompted them to heed that prayer so devoutly, it seems to me, was the radical newness of the religious situation in America during that period. After all, Americans in the early nineteenth century were people not far removed in time from the established churches of the nations from which they had come. Whatever else one might choose to say about those old-world environs, they at least provided *cosmos*. One knew where one stood, and one stood invariably in the bosom of *the* church. In contrast, the "brave new world"[6] launched on these shores was religiously chaotic in the extreme. Clearly, one compelling way to bring order and cosmos to a messy, disorderly, and chaotic pluralism was to present the "ancient order of things" as a firm ecumenical foundation. Therefore, in Mead's words,

> it is notable that the most successful of the definitely Christian indigenous denominations in America, the Disciples of Christ, grew out of the idea of a "new reformation" to be based, not on new insights, but on a "restoration" of the practices of the New Testament church—on which platform, it was thought, all the diverse groups of modern Christianity could unite as they shed the accumulated corruptions of the church through the centuries.[7]

While the disciples may have been the most successful of the indigenous American traditions for their time, none presents to the historian a more richly textured restorationist/ecumenical perspective than does the Church of Jesus Christ of Latter-day Saints in its early years. And no single Mormon spokesperson more clearly explained the restorationist premises for Mormon antipluralism than did Parley P. Pratt, one of the original Twelve Apostles of the Latter-day Saints. It is therefore to the early Mor-

---

[5]Parley P. Pratt, "The Millennium," in *Millennial Star;* reprinted in Parker Pratt Robison, ed., *Writings of Parley Parker Pratt* (Salt Lake City: Parker Pratt Robison, 1952) 259-60.

[6]Cf. Mead, *The Old Religion in the Brave New World* (Berkeley: University of California Press, 1977).

[7]Mead, *The Lively Experiment*, 111.

mon understanding of restoration and its relation to the problem of pluralism, and especially to Parley Pratt's understanding of these themes and of
their relation to one another, that we now turn.

I

The intimate connection between the early Mormon understanding of
restoration and the problem of religious pluralism is apparent in the event
that prompted the beginnings of this faith: the first vision of Joseph Smith.
Profoundly distressed by the competing claims of America's frontier sects,
fifteen-year-old Joseph retired to the woods in the spring of 1820 to ask
the Lord which of the churches he should join. Significantly, the Lord replied that he "must join none of them, for they were all wrong" and "all
their creeds were an abomination in his sight."[8] Following that vision, Jo-

---

[8]Joseph Smith, *History of the Church of Jesus Christ of Latter-day Saints,* vol. 1 (Salt
Lake City: The Deseret Book Co., 1927) 6.

Marvin Hill has also observed the close and intimate connection between primitivism
and antipluralism in the Mormon experience. In his 1968 Ph.D. dissertation Hill wrote that
most interpreters have "failed to see that within the primitive gospel beliefs was an antipluralistic tendency, largely resulting from a reaction to the fiercely divisive and strife-pro-
moting effects of sectarian revivalism." ("The Role of Christian Primitivism in the Origin
and Development of the Mormon Kingdom, 1830-1844," Ph.D. dissertation, University
of Chicago, 1968, 4.) Hill also recognized the antipluralistic dimensions of the "first vision." Thus, he wrote that through this vision Joseph "in effect turned his back upon the
prevailing religious pluralism in the United States, rejecting it as the source of confusion
and religious doubt in his own mind" (55). Significantly, Hill's dissertation was written
under the direction of Professor Sidney E. Mead.

Arguing along similar lines, Gordon Pollock saw early Mormonism as a response to
the social, economic, and religious chaos that characterized early-nineteenth-century
America. ("In Search of Security: The Mormons and the Kingdom of God on Earth, 1830-
1844," Ph.D. dissertation, Queen's University, 1977, 6ff.) Regarding the Mormon response to religious pluralism, Pollock wrote, "The intense competition between sects was
the application to religion of the free-market system which characterized the American
economy. . . . In the face of quarreling and competing sects those who became Mormons
did so because they accepted its claim to be the one, true and authoritative religion in the
world" (22-23).

For other assessments of the restoration theme in early Mormonism, cf. Richard Bushman, *Joseph Smith and the Beginnings of Mormonism* (Urbana: University of Illinois Press,
1984) esp. 179-88; Peter Crawley, "The Passage of Mormon Primitivism," *Dialogue* 13
(Winter 1980): 26-37; Marvin Hill, "The Shaping of the Mormon Mind in New England
and New York," *BYU Studies* 9 (Spring 1969): 351-72; Jan Shipps, *Mormonism: The Story
of a New Religious Movement* (Urbana: University of Illinois Press, 1985) esp. 67-85; and
F. Mark McKiernan, Alma R. Blair, and Paul M. Edwards, eds., *The Restoration Movement: Essays in Mormon History* (Lawrence KS: Coronado Press, 1973).

seph became a seeker, earnestly searching for the restoration of the one true church that once had flourished but now had disappeared from the face of the earth.

As a seeker, Joseph was hardly unique. The fact is that Seekerism as a religious phenomenon abounded in America in the 1820s, especially in New York where the Smith family lived. Typical was Solomon Chamberlain of Lyons, who had long been convinced that "faith was gone from the earth" and that "all Churches were corrupt,"[9] or Wilford G. Woodruff, who became convinced in 1830 that Christ's church was not to be found on the face of the earth.[10] Joseph's own parents reflected this same perspective. His father, Joseph Smith, Sr., dreamed of a barren earth that signified "the world which now lieth inanimate and dumb, in regard to the true religion or plan of salvation."[11] And Lucy Mack Smith, his mother, concluded that all the churches were "unlike the Church of Christ, as it existed in former days," and there was not, therefore, "then upon the earth the religion I sought." Thus, Joseph and Lucy refused to "subscribe to any particular system of faith, but contended for the ancient order as established by our Lord and Savior Jesus Christ, and his Apostles."[12]

It is clear that for many, if not most, of these seekers, religious pluralism was the source of their despair. George Burnham of Greenville, New York, bewailed the "multitude of sectarian divisions," which for him provided proof that American Christianity "is not the *house of God,* while thus divided against itself—and is not the *body of Christ* which cannot be divided."[13] Joseph Smith, in his later years, recalled the days of his youth when "the different religious parties . . . created no small stir and division amongst the people, some crying, 'Lo here!' and others, 'Lo, there!' " Indeed, he wrote of those early years in his *History of the Church.*

---

[9]Bushman, *Joseph Smith,* 149-50. For a more expansive delineation of Seekerism in the Smith milieu, cf. Hill, "Role of Christian Primitivism," 49-61.

[10]Cf. Thomas G. Alexander, "Wilford Woodruff and the Changing Nature of Mormon Religious Experience," *Church History* 45 (March 1976): 2.

[11]Lucy Smith, *History of the Prophet Joseph* (Salt Lake City: Improvement Era, 1902) 55.

[12]Ibid., 33 and 45.

[13]George L. Burnham, *Voice of Truth,* 27 July 1844; cited in David L. Rowe, "A New Perspective on the Burned-Over District: The Millerites in Upstate New York," *Church History* 47 (December 1978): 415.

So great were the confusion and strife among the different denominations, that it was impossible for a person young as I was, and so unacquainted with men and things, to come to any certain conclusion who was right and who was wrong. . . . In the midst of this war of words and tumult of opinion, I often said to myself, what is to be done? Who of all these parties are right; or, are they all wrong together?[14]

As Roger Williams did 200 years before, Smith concluded that they were "all wrong together." Indeed, the similarities between Smith and Williams are profound. Both concluded that the true apostolic and primitive church had vanished from the face of the earth. Further, both concluded that the church had grown so completely corrupt during the centuries that no man or group of men could possibly restore it to its original purity. Both Smith and Williams eagerly longed for a latter-day prophet or apostle, bearing authority from the throne of God, who would restore the church to its original state.

But there the similarities break down, for Smith and Williams differed profoundly in two major respects. Most obvious is the fact that Williams died a seeker, still longing and searching for the prophet and the restoration. On the other hand, Smith himself became that prophet and by 1830 claimed that God, through him, had restored the Church of Christ once again to the earth. The other difference pertains to motivation. Williams found the church of his day a corrupt abomination and a gross departure from the primitive model precisely because it compelled and coerced the consciences of men and women. For Williams, therefore, the premise of religious freedom was essential to recovery of the apostolic church. Put another way, true religion, for Williams, was religion born of persuasion, not of coercion.[15] Ironically, however, it was the prevalence of persuasion in the competitive free market of souls that convinced Joseph Smith, and a host of other seekers in the new American nation, that the true church

---

[14]Smith, *History*, 1, 3-4. Further testifying to the pervasiveness of Seekerism among early Mormons are the statistics of Laurence Yorgason, who has found that sixty-two percent of those who eventually became Mormons had earlier changed their church affiliation at least twice. Yorgason, "Some Demographic Aspects of One Hundred Early Mormon Converts, 1830-1837" (M.A. thesis, Brigham Young University, 1974, 49-50); cited in Alexander, "Wilford Woodruff," 3.

[15]Regarding the restoration vision of Roger Williams, see C. Leonard Allen, " 'The Restoration of Zion': Roger Williams and the Quest for the Primitive Church" (Ph.D. dissertation, University of Iowa, 1984).

had disappeared. As Mother Smith said, the claims and counterclaims of the various sects made "them witnesses against each other." In this context of vacuous relativity, what was needed was authority: a clear word from God that would subdue the confused and errant words of men.[16]

Nowhere was the quest for authority more evident than in the conversion of Parley P. Pratt. Living in Ohio in 1829, Pratt heard Sidney Rigdon, a follower of Alexander Campbell, proclaim faith in Jesus Christ, repentance toward God, baptism for remission of sins, and the gift of the Holy Ghost. "Here was the ancient gospel in due form," Pratt later wrote in his *Autobiography.* Yet he was not content. By what authority could Rigdon establish this ancient gospel? He was neither prophet nor apostle. "Who is Mr. Rigdon?" Pratt asked. And "who is Mr. Campbell? Who commissioned them?" On what basis could one determine that their ancient gospel was any more authentic than the ancient gospel of, say, the Baptists or of some other group with a primitivist orientation? What Rigdon and Campbell lacked, in Pratt's view, was "the *authority* to minister in holy things— the apostleship, the power which should accompany the form."[17] After reading the *Book of Mormon,* however, and after learning that God had annointed Joseph Smith as his prophet in the latter days, Pratt exulted that "I had now found men on earth commissioned to preach, baptize, ordain to the ministry, etc., and I determined to obey the fulness of the gospel without delay."[18]

Indeed, for Pratt and for other early Mormons, the fact that God had restored to earth the ancient gospel through the agency of a latter-day prophet rendered perfectly irrelevant the tumult of words and the strifes and contentions of preachers and sects. Campbell, the Baptists, Rigdon, and others might preach their *opinions* concerning the ancient gospel. But God had bestowed on Joseph Smith, Jr. the authority of the priesthood both to baptize and to confer the gift of the Holy Ghost in the latter days. Further, God had communicated with Joseph in visions and revelations, had called him to translate the *Book of Mormon* from the Golden Plates buried

---

[16]Mario S. De Pillis has argued that the quest for authority was from the beginning the fundamental issue in Mormonism. "The Quest for Religious Authority and the Rise of Mormonism,"*Dialogue* 1 (March 1966): 68-88.

[17]Parley P. Pratt, *The Autobiography of Parley Parker Pratt* (Chicago: Law, King & Law, 1888) 32.

[18]Ibid., 42.

by ancient American Christians, and had annointed him both prophet and apostle. In this way, to the Mormon mind, God had established once again the true Church of Jesus Christ upon the earth, sanctioned not by human opinion, nor by the inventions of men, but by the authority of heaven itself.

This notion of restoration made it abundantly clear that God had sanctioned His one, true church, and that others were false. This dichotomy, which allowed no room for abstractions, ambiguities, or shades of gray, found clear expression in the *Book of Mormon:* it asserted that "there are save two churches only; the one is the church of the Lamb of God, and the other is the church of the devil; wherefore, whoso belongeth not to the church of the Lamb of God belongeth to that great church, which is the mother of abominations; and she is the whore of all the earth."[19] It was a short step from this premise to the notion that the wrath of God would be "poured out upon . . . the great and abominable church of all the earth."[20]

Fundamental to this antipluralist posture was the peculiarly Mormon understanding of restoration. While Puritans, Baptists, and "Christians," for example, sought simply to emulate the faith and practices of the ancients, Mormons embraced a scheme of restoration that was cosmic in its scope, that penetrated space to the ends of the earth and the outer boundaries of the universe itself, and that encompassed time from its very beginning to its final end. Indeed, Mormons referred to their vision as the "restoration of all things."[21]

II

In the annals of the Latter-day Saints, no one has articulated this vision more cogently and descriptively than Parley P. Pratt. Born in Burlington, Otsego County, New York, on 12 April 1807, Pratt moved in 1827 to Ohio where he made common cause with Sidney Rigdon and the Campbellite "restoration movement" that Rigdon espoused. Returning to New York in 1830 on a preaching mission, Pratt discovered the *Book of Mormon,* converted, and

---

[19]1 Nephi 14:10.

[20]Ibid., 14:17.

[21]Jan Shipps has argued that Mormonism was not like the Christians or Disciples, a mere imitation of primitive Christianity, but rather was a radical tear "across history's seamless web to provide humanity with a new world wherein God is actively involved" (cf. 72). It is largely for this reason that she describes Mormonism as a "new religious movement."

was baptized by Oliver Cowdery on 1 September 1830 in Seneca Lake. From that initiation into the fellowship of Latter-day Saints, Pratt would become one of its most significant proponents. Ordained one of the Twelve Apostles on 1 February 1835, Pratt essentially was a missionary throughout his life. He preached throughout the United States, and in England, Canada, the Pacific Islands, and South America. On 13 May 1857, he was murdered while on a preaching tour near Van Buren, Arkansas.[22]

Pratt made his most lasting contribution through his numerous pamphlets written in defense of the Mormon faith. In fact, he is often considered the ''father of Mormon pamphleteering.''[23] Beyond this, scholars generally acknowledge that two of his pamphlets in particular furnished the most cogent, noncanonical expressions of the Mormon faith to appear in the nineteenth century. His 1837 work, *A Voice of Warning*,[24] has been judged ''the most important of all noncanonical Mormon books''[25] and ''the most important missionary pamphlet in the early history of the church.''[26] In fact, Peter Crawley argues that while this was not the first Mormon tract, ''it was the first systematic statement and defense of the fundamentals of Mormonism. More than this it erected a standard for all future Mormon pamphleteers, setting down a formula for describing the tenets of Mormonism as well as biblical proof-texts, arguments, examples and expressions that would be used by others for another century.''[27] This work went through at least eight editions by 1860. By 1842 the *Times and Seasons* reported that a first edition of 3,000 copies had been exhausted as well as

[22]Cf. Pratt, *Autobiography;* and Andrew Jenson, *Latter-day Saint Biographical Encyclopedia*, vol. 1 (Salt Lake City: Andrew Jenson History Company, 1901) 83-85.

[23]David J. Whittaker, ''Early Mormon Pamphleteering'' (Ph.D. dissertation, Brigham Young University, 1982, 58). For the source of this designation of Pratt, Whittaker cites an unpublished essay by Peter Crawley, ''Parley P. Pratt: The Father of Mormon Pamphleteering.''

[24]Parley P. Pratt, *A Voice of Warning and Instruction to All People, Containing a Declaration of the Faith and Doctrine of the Church of the Latter-day Saints, Commonly Called Mormons* (New York: W. Sandford, 1837).

[25]Crawley, ''The Passage of Mormon Primitivism,'' 33.

[26]Introduction to *Key to the Science of Theology / A Voice of Warning* (Salt Lake City: Deseret Book Co., 1978) i-ii.

[27]Crawley, ''The Passage of Mormon Primitivism,'' 33.

a second edition of 2,500 copies.[28] The editor of its most recent edition suggests that this book "undoubtedly contributed to the conversion of thousands of seekers to Mormonism."[29]

Pratt's other major work was *The Key to the Science of Theology*.[30] Published in Liverpool, England, in 1855, this work was one of the earliest attempts to bring together systematically the various disparate elements of Mormon theology. Clearly, it was among the most successful attempts, for the book was in great demand and remained through the early twentieth century "one of the leading statements of Church doctrine."[31]

Significantly, Pratt consistently defined Mormon theology in terms of restoration. But what did he mean by this term? Pratt addressed this question frequently and forthrightly. "Now we can never understand what is meant by restoration; unless we understand what is lost or taken away."[32] What had been lost was dialogue with God and communion with heavenly beings. Pratt contrasted the ancients and the moderns in this regard: "Witness the ancients, conversing with the Great Jehovah, learning lessons from the angels, and receiving instruction by the Holy Ghost, in dreams by night, and visions by day, until at length the veil is taken off. . . . Compare this intelligence, with the low smatterings of education and worldly wisdom, which seem to satisfy the narrow mind of man in our generation."[33] The key to the science of theology, then, was for Pratt precisely "the key of divine revelation,"[34] and it was this key that Mormons claimed to have restored.

From this perspective, Pratt and his Mormon colleagues could only view as extraordinarily deficient the restoration efforts of Disciple leaders

[28]Whittaker, "Early Mormon Pamphleteering," 59 n. 30.

[29]Introduction to *Key*, i.

[30]Parley P. Pratt, *Key to the Science of Theology: Designed as an Introduction to the First Principles of Spiritual Philosophy; Religion; Law and Government; as Delivered by the Ancients, and as Restored in This Age, for the Final Development of Universal Peace, Truth and Knowledge* (Liverpool: F. D. Richards, 1855). Unless otherwise indicated, all of the following references are to the 1855 edition.

[31]Introduction to *Key*, 1978 ed., ii; and Whittaker, "Early Mormon Pamphleteering," 62-63.

[32]Pratt, *Voice*, 147.

[33]Ibid., 154-55.

[34]Pratt, *Key*, 26-27.

Thomas and Alexander Campbell. For Pratt, these "restorers" were part of the problem, not part of the solution. After all, a fundamental premise of these men was their conviction that the gifts of the spirit had expired with the original apostles. In their view, therefore, the object of restoration was not recovery of the gifts of the spirit, or of divine revelation, but rather of the forms and structures that the spirit had inspired.

Thus, both Thomas and Alexander Campbell directly attacked Mormon claims to have restored the gifts of the spirit. When Sidney Rigdon converted to the Latter-day Saints, Thomas Campbell challenged him to debate, claiming that he would demonstrate that "imposition of hands for communicating the Holy Spirit, is an unscriptural intrusion upon the exclusive prerogative of the primary apostles."[35] Alexander Campbell simply ascribed Rigdon's claims to spiritual gifts to insanity. "Fits of melancholy succeeded by fits of enthusiasm accompanied by some kind of nervous spasms and swoonings which he has, since his defection, interpreted into the agency of the Holy Spirit, or the recovery of spiritual gifts, produced a versatility in his genius and deportment which has been increasing for some time."[36]

Whether Pratt ever read these specific attacks is unknown, but he clearly responded to the common claim that spiritual gifts had ceased with the deaths of the apostles. To him, miraculous gifts partook of the essence of the Christian faith, and to claim these gifts had ceased was tantamount to admitting that the church had ceased to exist. In fact, this is exactly the point Pratt wanted to make: "When the miracles and gifts of the divine Spirit ceased from among men, Christianity ceased, the Christian ministry ceased, the Church of Christ ceased." Then Pratt launched an attack of his own. "That ministry which sets aside modern inspiration, revelations, prophecy, angels, visions, healings, &c., is not ordained of God; but is anti-Christian in spirit. In short, it is that spirit of priestcraft and kingcraft, by which the world, for many ages, has been ruled as with a rod of iron."[37]

---

[35]Thomas Campbell, open letter to Sidney Rigdon, Painesville, Ohio *Telegraph,* 15 February 1831, in Francis W. Kirkham, *A New Witness for Christ in America: The Book of Mormon,* vol. 2 (Independence MO: Press of Zion's Printing and Publishing Co., 1951) 93.

[36]Alexander Campbell, "Sidney Rigdon," *Millennial Harbinger* 2 (7 February 1831): 100.

[37]Pratt, *Key,* 108-109.

From Pratt's perspective, the central defect of Protestants and traditional restorers like Campbell was their fixation on the Bible. For Pratt and his Mormon colleagues, the Bible was not the ultimate authority in religion, nor was it the final source of power or of knowledge. Rather, the Bible simply pointed beyond itself to the God who was the final arbiter of ultimate things. While the Scriptures were true and good and useful, Pratt argued, "they are not the fountain of knowledge, nor do they contain all knowledge, yet they point to the fountain, and are every way calculated to encourage men to come to the fountain and seek to obtain the knowledge and gifts of God."[38] The chief function of the Bible, Pratt argued, was not to provide guidelines or blueprints for forms, structures, or static institutions, but rather to show the divine power behind them. By this power, Pratt contended, Enoch was translated, Moses freed a nation, Joshua conquered, David excelled the wisdom of the East, and Jesus Christ himself conquered death and hell. And by this same divine power, "A Joseph in modern times has restored the fullness of the gospel; raised the church out of the wilderness; restored to them the faith once delivered to the saints."[39]

It was precisely because early Mormons pointed not to a book, but to the divine power behind all books (including both the Bible and the *Book of Mormon*), that Mormon theology could grow and evolve as Joseph announced his many revelations that continued from the First Vision until his 1844 death in Carthage, Illinois. Those early Mormons who resisted theological change and growth and defected to a more static tradition simply never understood the premises of the Mormon restoration ideal.

Indeed, Pratt specifically excluded from the Mormon faith the authority of antiquity, even Christian antiquity. Mormons had no interest in patterning their faith and practice after a particular time, but looked instead to the God who had worked wonders in all times. Thus, "they [Mormons] claim no authority whatever from antiquity," Pratt proclaimed.[40] Instead, "the Lord uttered his voice from the heavens, an holy angel came forth and restored the priesthood and apostleship, and hence has arisen the church

[38]Pratt, "The Fountain of Knowledge" in *Writings,* 20-21.

[39]Ibid., 19-20.

[40]Pratt, *Late Persecution of the Church of Jesus Christ, of Latter Day Saints. Ten Thousand American Citizens Robbed, Plundered, and Banished; Others Imprisoned, and Others Martyred for Their Religion. . . . Written in Prison* (New York: J. W. Harrison, 1840) iii.

of the saints.''[41] In contrast, traditional restorers had fixed their gaze on a particular age or institution—for example, the church of the first century—and had missed the divine reality that had inspired not only the primitive church but also the patriarchs, the prophets, and Christ himself. Pratt therefore criticized those traditional restorers as having ''fallen into this one inconsistency, viz., of patching new cloth on to old garments; and thus the rent has been made worse.'' Alexander Campbell, for example, had ''attempted to restore the ordinances without the priesthood, or gifts of the spirit.''[42] In contrast, Pratt described the Church of Jesus Christ of Latter-day Saints as ''a NEW 'TREE'—NEW 'FRUITS,'—'NEW CLOTH,' and 'NEW GARMENTS,'—'NEW WINE' and 'NEW BOTTLES'—'NEW LEAVEN' and a 'NEW LUMP,' 'A NEW COVENANT' and spirit; and it may roll on till we have a new heaven and a new earth, that we may dwell forever in the new Jerusalem, while old things pass away, and all things are made new, even so. Amen.''[43]

This is not to suggest that Pratt thought that Campbell could have restored the divine power and initiatives if he had tried. Indeed, he could not unless God had chosen him for the task. Like Roger Williams before him, Pratt was convinced that once the priesthood and spiritual gifts had been lost from the earth, they could be restored only at God's own initiative. In short, ''the man or men last holding the keys of such power . . . [must] return to the earth as ministering angels, and select . . . certain individuals of the royal lineage of Israel, to hold the keys of such Priesthood, and to ordain others, and thus restore and reorganize the government of God, or His kingdom upon the earth.''[44] But this would only take place in the fullness of time or, as Mormons liked to say, ''the times of restitution of all things.'' Indeed, this latter phrase was part of the text by which Mormons typically justified their restoration agenda, Acts 3:20-21 (KJV): ''And he shall send Jesus Christ, which before was preached unto you: whom the heaven must receive until the times of restitution [restoration] of all things, which God hath spoken by the mouth of all his holy prophets since the world began.''

---

[41]Pratt, ''Grapes from Thorns, and Figs from Thistles,'' reprinted from the *Millennial Star* in *Writings*, 303.

[42]Ibid.

[43]Ibid., 303-304.

[44]Pratt, *Key*, 70.

It was only because God alone had determined this extraordinary time that reformations, protests, and religious revolutions had failed time and again. In a particularly cogent passage Pratt wrote,

> Protests upon protests! reforms and re-reforms; revolutions, and struggles, exertions of every kind, of mere human invention, have been tried and tried in vain. The science of Theology, with all its keys and powers, once lost, could never, consistent with the ancient Prophetic testimony, be restored to either Jew or Gentile, until the full time should arrive—"*The times of restitution of all things.*" Then, and not till then, could the science, the keys, the powers of Theology, be restored to man. No individual or combined human action could obtain or restore again these keys—this science. A mighty angel held the keys of this science for the last days.[45]

Pratt was convinced that he lived in the last days—"the times of restitution of all things"—and that God had annointed Joseph Smith as apostle and prophet in order to begin a restoration that soon would be completed when the millennium dawned. Further, Pratt was convinced that the Mormon restoration was radically dissimilar to all other restoration attempts. If other would-be restorers focused on particular books, persons, or ancient times, Mormons treated all particular, sacred manifestations as transparencies that pointed beyond themselves to ultimate reality. Even as other restorers, upon their own initiative, sought to recover mere finite forms, God had called and enabled Mormons to recover communion with the infinite itself.

From this perspective, early Mormonism may well be understood as a romantic rejection of the spirit of Common Sense rationalism so prevalent in America in the early nineteenth century.[46] Alexander Campbell's restoration movement was rational to the core, calling for the application of human reason to the biblical text and limiting authentic religion to that sphere. In so doing, the Campbell movement was as clear an expression of the spirit of Common Sense rationalism as one could hope to find in American religion in the early nineteenth century. On the other hand, Mormonism sought to transcend the cognitive and the rational and to soar with the gods in the realm of the infinite and the eternal. In this sense Mor-

---

[45]Ibid., 18-19.

[46]This is a very different argument from that made by Robert N. Hullinger in *Mormon Answer to Skepticism: Why Joseph Smith Wrote the Book of Mormon* (St. Louis: Clayton Publishing House, 1980). The burden of Hullinger's argument is that Mormonism was essentially a response to skepticism and Deism.

monism was an expression of Romanticism in revolt against the constrictions of Common Sense. Many commentators on Mormonism have noted the literalism of the Mormon tradition. However, literalism was secondary to their romantic visions, which were primary. Put another way, the Saints took quite literally a romantic theology that came to them in visions, dreams, and revelations, mediated through a latter-day prophet. And this was a very different sort of literalism from the rational, New Testament-oriented literalism that characterized Campbell and his Disciples of Christ.

With this singular restoration vision, Mormons addressed the problem of religious pluralism, which they found so disconcerting. In fact, religious pluralism, they thought, simply would not exist if the "science of theology"—communion with angels and gods—had not been lost. In their view, pluralism was merely a symptom of the human confusion that inevitably resulted when divine authority disappeared. According to Pratt, "The reason for all the division, confusion, jars, discords, and animosities; and the reason of so many faiths, lords, baptisms, and spirits . . . is all because they have no Apostles, and Prophets, and other gifts, inspired from on high . . . , for if they had such gifts . . . they would be built up in one body, . . . having one Lord, one faith, and one Baptism."[47] Indeed, the final objective of the Mormon restoration was recovery of the one body, the one faith, and the one baptism.

This quest for *ultimate* power and *ultimate* authority, descending from the very heavens themselves, was the genius of the Mormon restoration ideal. Yet it is undeniably true—and fundamentally important—that early Mormons sought recovery of infinite and ultimate authority precisely through recovery of the finite forms that the infinite had inspired in all ages past. This was the meaning, then, of the phrase "restitution of all things." We now turn, therefore, to this other side of Mormon primitivism, namely, the recovery of finite structures and forms, and the implications of this concrete, tangible restoration for Mormon attitudes toward religious pluralism in America.

III

If Parley Pratt condemned Alexander Campbell for attempting to restore the outward ordinances without the gifts of the spirit, he also con-

---

[47]Pratt, *Voice*, 118-19.

demned the Quakers for attempting to restore the gifts of the spirit apart
from outward ordinances.[48] Pratt's dual judgment here is highly significant, for it symbolized the extent to which the finite and the infinite were
inseparably related in the early Mormon imagination.

Indeed, to encompass sacred, finite forms *was* to encompass the infinite precisely because, as Joseph revealed in May of 1844, "there is no
such thing as immaterial matter, all spirit is matter."[49] Conversely, early
Mormons argued that all matter is eternal. Thus, Parley Pratt simply rejected creation ex nihilo. The fact is, he said, "the original elements of
matter are eternal,"[50] "uncreated and self-existing."[51] The very term *creation*, Pratt argued, is misleading. God no more created the world than he
created Himself. He simply organized preexisting elements into a coherent
whole or universe.[52]

If inanimate matter was uncreated, Pratt contended, then obviously so
was humanity. Pratt scoffed at the Genesis notion that God made man from
the dust of the ground and Eve from Adam's rib. Moses knew better, he
said. But because humankind, immature as it was, could not view the Almighty face to face, Moses "was forced again to veil the past in mystery,
and . . . assign to man an earthly origin." In so doing, Moses resembled
a watchful parent who "would fain conceal from budding manhood, the
mysteries of procreation . . . by relating some childish tale of newborn life,
engendered in the hollow trunk of some old tree." The real truth, which
Moses refused to tell, was that "man is the offspring of Deity."[53]

As the "offspring of Deity," humankind possessed the power to recover—or restore—the deific original from which it had sprung. Pratt thus
exhorted his hearers and readers to "burst the chains of mortality which
bind thee fast; unlock the prison of thy clay tenement which confines thee

---

[48]Pratt, "Grapes from Thorns," in *Writings*, 303.

[49]*Doctrine and Covenants*, 131:7. Cf. also Smith, *History*, 6:302-17, and Smith's funeral sermon for King Follett, 7 April 1844.

[50]Pratt, "Immortality and Eternal Life of the Material Body" in *Writings*, 28. Likewise, Joseph himself had declared in 1833 that "the elements are eternal" (*Doctrine and
Covenants*, 93:33).

[51]Pratt, "The World Turned Upside Down," in *Writings*, 65.

[52]Pratt, *Key*, 47-48.

[53]Ibid., 49-50.

to this groveling, earthly sphere of action; and robed in immortality, wrapped in the visions of eternity, with organs of sight and thought and speech which cannot be impaired or weakened by time or use; soar with me amid unnumbered worlds which roll in majesty on high.''[54] Pratt even suggested that God's saints would, ''like the risen Jesus, ascend and descend at will, and with a speed nearly instantaneous.''[55]

This constellation of ideas—that spirit is matter, that matter is eternal, and that men sprang from God and can become gods themselves—constitutes the basis of the early Mormon understanding of restoration. Therefore, if the Saints would ultimately ''ascend the heights'' and ''descend the depths'' and ''explore the lengths and breadths of organized existence''[56]—something the gods themselves had done in the primordium—should not the Saints embrace this cosmic perspective in their restoration? Unwilling to be confined to a single book or to a single sacred epoch, as were traditional restorationists, early Mormons sought ''the restoration of all things.'' Like bees sucking nectar first from this flower and then from the next, early Mormons moved at ease from the primitive church to Moses to the prophets to Abraham to Adam and then to the millennium to come. Many interpreters of Mormonism have commented on this amalgamation of sacred times, an amalgamation so complete that it appears as sheer confusion. To early Mormons such as Parley Pratt, however, it was far from confusion, but rested instead on an inner logic and consistency that simply baffled those whose gaze was riveted to the finite particulars of religious faith.

To early Mormons, after all, the finite ordinances of every sacred age equally partook of the infinite. Nothing, therefore, could be more consistent than to practice Christian baptism in a baptismal font resting on twelve oxen symbolizing the twelve tribes of Israel. Likewise, from this peculiarly Mormon perspective, there was no inconsistency whatever in restoring at one and the same time the ancient rite of baptism for the remission of sins and the patriarchal practice of polygamy. Nor was there anything unseemly, to them, in their intention to worship in a restored ''Jewish'' temple built on the site of the Garden of Eden. One must remember what motivated Mormons in the first place: their quest for infinite and therefore

---

[54]Pratt, ''The Fountain of Knowledge,'' in *Writings,* 18. Cf. *Key,* 32-33.

[55]Pratt, *Key,* 155-56.

[56]Pratt, ''The Fountain of Knowledge,'' in *Writings,* 18.

ultimate authority. To saturate themselves with the infinite by sucking its nectar from the various finite blossoms of every sacred age only made sense.

Granted, none of these perspectives made sense to those whose restoration premises were governed by Common Sense rationalism. Thus, Alexander Campbell was appalled that Jews in the *Book of Mormon* were "called Christians while keeping the law of Moses, the holy Sabbath, and worshipping in their temple at their altars and by their high priests,"[57] and that "the Nephites . . . were good christians, . . . preaching baptism and other christian usages hundreds of years before Jesus Christ was born!"[58] Likewise, Walter Scott, Campbell's colleague in New Testament-oriented restoration, criticized the *Book of Mormon* for confounding "history with prophesy, . . . putting in the mouths of his fictitious seers the language of the apostles."[59] From the consistency of their perspective, however, neither Smith nor Pratt would even have winced at these critiques, which failed entirely to speak to the heart of the Mormon faith. For to Smith and Pratt, patriarchal polygamy, Jewish temple rites, and Christian baptism were all finite and material ordinances that had been, during some sacred epoch, ordained of God and that now shared one common function: to bring the power and authority of the infinite into the world of the Latter-day Saints. To Common Sense restorationists such as Campbell and Scott, this perspective was spiritual gibberish and religious nonsense.

It all made wonderfully good sense to early Mormons, however, for one fundamental reason: their conviction that they lived in the last days and on the threshold of the millennial dawn. Indeed, their millennial awareness lent both purpose and meaning to the Mormon restoration ideal. Pratt argued that "God has sent us . . . to prepare his way, and to make straight his paths—by gathering in the children of God from all the jarring systems in which they are now organized, and planting them in one fold by the ministration of the ordinances in their ancient purity."[60] When that task was accomplished, Pratt proclaimed, "then shall the Lord Jesus Christ, the great Messiah and King, descend from the heavens in his glorified, im-

---

[57]Alexander Campbell, "Delusions," *Millennial Harbinger* 2 (7 February 1831): 93.

[58]Ibid., 87.

[59]Walter Scott, "Mormon Bible—No. 1," *The Evangelist*, n.s. 9 (1 January 1841): 18-19.

[60]Pratt, *Late Persecution*, 171.

mortal body, and reign with his saints, and over all the kingdoms of the earth, one thousand years."[61]

Further, this final age was not just one dispensation among others. Rather, as the last age, it should embrace all the others, tying together with cords of infinity the perfections of all previous sacred times. The twelve apostles made it clear that "this [present] dispensation comprehends all the great works of all former dispensations."[62] Standing, therefore, on the threshold of the age of infinite perfections, Mormons sought to reenact the sacred dramas of all prior ages and to saturate themselves with the nectar that all the sacred flowers of all previous times had produced. All of this made wonderfully good sense to those who stood in the shadow of the end.

With respect to religious pluralism, it is fundamentally important that early Mormons consistently tied restoration of the infinite to restoration of particular, finite forms, rites, and institutions. Indeed, Mormons found in Zion and its temple an institutional complex that, from their perspective, embraced all rites and ordinances of all sacred epochs, that encompassed time from beginning to end and earthly space from pole to pole, that obligated all men and women of all ages and nations to respond positively to the gospel of the Saints, and that provided means for their inclusion into the Mormon fold.

The city of Zion was preeminently the link between heaven and earth and between primordium and millennium. In the first place Zion was no mere human concoction, but rather a city that would literally descend from heaven itself. According to the *Book of Moses* in the *Pearl of Great Price*, Enoch built the city of Zion, which the Lord took with Enoch unto Himself and which one day would descend to the earth as New Jerusalem, the center of the millennial kingdom.[63] This heavenly city would be restored and rebuilt in Jackson County, Missouri, adjacent to the site of the primordial Garden of Eden in Davies County, Missouri.[64] Further, Parley Pratt ar-

---

[61]Pratt, "Proclamation of the Gospel," in *Writings*, 163.

[62]"An Epistle of the Twelve Apostles, to the Brethren Scattered Abroad on the Continent of America," in Smith, *History*, 4:437.

[63]*The Book of Moses* 7, esp. vv. 21, 23, and 62-65.

[64]For Jackson County, Missouri, as Zion, see Smith, *History*, 1:189, and *Doctrine and Covenants*, 57:1-3. For Davies County as the Garden of Eden, see *Doctrine and Covenants*, 107:53-57, 116.

gued that Zion was the hinge between the ancient order of things and the millennial dawn; hence restoration of this city was absolutely essential to the second coming of Christ. "When this city is built the Lord will appear in his glory, and not before," Pratt announced. "So from this we affirm, that if such a city is never built, then the Lord will never come."[65]

Further, Joseph Smith envisioned the construction of city after city, all modeled after New Jerusalem and built in adjacent plats, and in this way, he told the Saints, they would "fill up the world in these last days." Parley Pratt reflected this charge when, writing on behalf of the apostles, he declared that God "has commanded us to . . . build up holy cities and sanctuaries—And we know it."[66] Thus, a British brother reported a dream of a conference of the Saints wherein

> it was motioned by Joseph Smith and seconded by John the Revelator, "That forty-eight new cities be laid out and builded, this year, in accordance with the prophets which have said, 'who can number Israel? Who can count the dust of Jacob? Let him fill the earth with cities.' "[67]

While these visions all seem millennial, one must not forget their fundamentally restorationist underpinnings rooted in Enoch's Zion of old. Moreover, that Zion, even in ancient times, stood opposed to religious pluralism and symbolized unanimity rather than diversity is evident from the *Book of Moses* 7:18: "And the Lord called his people ZION, because they were of one heart and one mind, and dwelt in righteousness; and there was no poor among them."

Finally, during the Nauvoo period of Mormon history, Joseph Smith introduced into Mormon practice and theology two ordinances that would make Mormonism more expansive still. Significantly, both ordinances could be performed only in the Temple. The first was the doctrine of baptism for the dead, included in a revelation of 19 January 1841, in which Joseph also announced the Lord's command to build the Nauvoo Tem-

---

[65]Pratt, *Voice*, 177.

[66]Smith, *History*, 1:358. Pratt, "Proclamation of the Twelve Apostles," in *Writings*, 13.

[67]*Millennial Star* 6 (1845): 140-42; cited in Robert Flanders, "To Transform History: Early Mormon Culture and the Concept of Time and Space," *Church History* 40 (March 1971): 111-12. Flanders's article is a seminal statement of early Mormon attempts to collapse both space and time into their restored millennial kingdom.

ple.[68] Not content to extend their restored, millennial kingdom through space, by this doctrine Mormons might also extend the kingdom backward through time and thereby erase whatever religious pluralism existed in ages past. Regarding this doctrine Pratt proclaimed that "in the world of spirits . . . are . . . Catholics, and Protestants of every sect. . . . There is also the Jew, the Mohametan, the infidel. . . . All these must be taught, enlightened, and must bow the knee to the eternal king."[69] In this way, as Klaus Hansen has noted, the living and the dead would be linked together "in one gigantic chain of family and kinship that would ultimately bind together the entire human race."[70]

If baptism for the dead might potentially erase religious pluralism from ages past, the doctrine of celestial marriage promised the rule of the Saints even in other worlds, in other ages to come. In a sermon of 16 May 1843, Joseph Smith declared that if "a man and his wife enter into an everlasting covenant and be married for eternity . . . , they . . . will continue to increase and have children in celestial glory."[71] In the revelation of this doctrine, Joseph announced that those males who take a wife "by the new and everlasting covenant . . . shall inherit thrones, kingdoms, principalities, and powers, dominions, all heights and depths. . . . Then shall they be gods, because they have no end."[72]

Clearly, through this expansive, cosmic theology, early Mormons addressed the problem of religious pluralism not only for their own age but also for ages past and time to come. Their posture in this regard rested squarely on the issue of authority. Other reformers, even restorers, acted on their own, apart from divine authority, guidance, and direction. But the Latter-day Saints responded to God Himself, who spoke to them through His prophet in dreams, visions, and revelations, as He had to saints of old.

---

[68]Smith, *History*, 4:277; *Doctrine and Covenants*, 124:27-39. Cf. Robert Flanders, *Nauvoo: Kingdom on the Mississippi* (Urbana: University of Illinois Press, 1965) 190-91.

[69]Pratt, *Key*, 128-29.

[70]Klaus J. Hansen, *Mormonism and the American Experience* (Chicago: University of Chicago Press, 1981) 103.

[71]Smith, *History*, 5:391-92.

[72]*Doctrine and Covenants*, 132:19-20. The revelation regarding celestial marriage was never made public by Joseph Smith during his own lifetime; Brigham Young announced it in 1852. Cf. Flanders, *Nauvoo*, 274-75.

Restoration among Mormons, therefore, essentially involved soaring with the gods while others grovelled on earth. It involved appealing to the sacred while others could appeal only to the profane. In this context, it was only appropriate that the particular rites and ordinances that Mormons chose to restore were rites and ordinances that would bring heaven to earth, collapse both primordium and millennium into their own time and place, and tie the Saints to God's work in all time past. This, ultimately, was the theological basis for the political rule of the Saints.

IV

In 1841 Parley Pratt addressed a dire warning to the Queen of England. He told Victoria that the world was "on the eve of a REVOLUTION," that a "new nation will be established over the whole earth, to the destruction of all other kingdoms," that if the rulers of England would "hearken to this message, they shall have part in the glorious kingdom," but "if they will not . . . they will be overthrown with the wicked, and perish from the earth."[73] Earlier, in 1837, Pratt had incorporated these themes into his widely influential missionary tract, A Voice of Warning, which was intended to be just that: a voice of warning. There Pratt proclaimed that the Mormon restoration "is the gospel which God has commanded us to preach. . . . And no other system of religion . . . is of any use; every thing different from this, is a perverted gospel, bringing a curse upon them that preach it, and upon them that hear it." Indeed, all who refused the Saints' message "shall alike feel the hand of the almighty, by pestilence, famine, earthquake, and the sword: yea, ye shall be drunken with your own blood . . . until your cities are desolate . . . until all lyings, priestcrafts, and all manner of abomination, shall be done away."[74]

How can one account for the fact that the Saints could entertain such violent, coercive visions? This question is both underscored and complicated by the fact that Mormons consistently proclaimed their faith in religious freedom. For example, a general assembly of the Saints voted unanimously in Kirtland, Ohio, in 1835 that governments should "secure to each individual the free exercise of conscience" and that human law has

---

[73]Pratt, "A Letter to the Queen," in Writings, 97, 100, and 108.

[74]Pratt, Voice, 140-42. This chapter, which is the pivotal "warning" section of A Voice of Warning, is altogether deleted from the 1978 edition.

no right "to bind the consciences of men." That same "Declaration" affirmed the total illegitimacy of mingling "religious influence with civil government, whereby one religious society is fostered and another proscribed."[75] Further, as a candidate for the presidency of the United States in 1844, Joseph Smith promised to "open the prisons, open the eyes, open the ears, and open the hearts of all people, to behold and enjoy freedom—unadulterated freedom."[76]

Here, then, are two dominant threads in the intellectual garment of the early Saints: a coercive, sometimes even violent antipluralism, alongside a ringing affirmation of the right of all people to freedom of conscience in matters of religion. How can one reconcile these two themes?

Several observations are in order. First, Mormons themselves suffered intense persecution, including physical violence, at the hands of other Americans, and therefore took steps to defend their lives and property. Thus, the Kirtland "Declaration" of 1835 affirmed that "all men are justified in defending themselves . . . from the unlawful assaults and encroachments of all persons in times of exigency, where immediate appeal cannot be made to the laws, and relief afforded."[77] It would be fair to suggest that the persecutions they suffered and the steps they took for defense at the very least made violence, and the possibility of violence, a factor in their perspective. But how did they cross the line from the rhetoric and reality of defensive violence to a rhetoric of coercion?

A second observation: early Mormons such as Parley Pratt were missionaries whose task was made urgent by what they perceived as an imminent end to a profane and fallen world. In this apocalyptic context it was God, not they, who would avenge the wicked and stiff-necked of this earth. Indeed, many interpreters of Mormonism have rooted the coercive visions of the Saints precisely in their apocalypticism. Thus, for example, Klaus Hansen viewed the creation of the Council of Fifty as a consequence of Mormon millennialism.[78] And Grant Underwood, while faulting Hansen for rooting millennial perspectives in social deprivation, nonetheless con-

---

[75]*Doctrine and Covenants*, 134.

[76]Smith, *History*, 6:208-209.

[77]*Doctrine and Covenants*, 134:11.

[78]Klaus J. Hansen, *Quest for Empire: The Political Kingdom of God and the Council of Fifty in Mormon History* (Lincoln: University of Nebraska Press, 1974) 23.

curs with Hansen on the point at issue and argues that "Mormon millennialism disposed the Saints to a . . . conspiratorial view which . . . leagued the whole sectarian world with Lucifer."[79]

But even these explanations, as helpful as they are, leave much unexplained. For what reason would God smite the wicked and exalt the Saints? To what final court would Pratt appeal for the legitimacy of his apocalyptic vision? And why would a God of a freedom-affirming people smite those of different faiths at all?

In fact, the ideological basis for the coercive rhetoric of early Mormons was their restoration sentiment, not their millennialism. After all, early Mormons could hardly claim to differ from other religious groups on the basis of a millennium that was yet in the future. But they could—and did—put an infinite distance between themselves and their religious neighbors by identifying themselves with a constellation of sacred and primordial pasts while others were confined to the finite realm of history and time. Put another way, early Mormons, by rooting themselves in the primordial past, simply removed themselves from history and the historical process and claimed instead that they sprang full blown from the creative hands of God. In April of 1830, they said, their prophet had restored to earth the ancient church with all its gifts, miracles, and visions.

This perspective spoke to the Saints in a decisive way regarding the dilemmas posed by religious pluralism in American life. In the first place, the Saints at one level were fully committed to freedom of conscience for all human beings so long as this fallen and profane world should last. But in the millennial age, as with other childish things, religious pluralism would be put away. In this scenario, millennialism was not the source either of Mormon perfectionism or of coercive rhetoric. The role of the millennium, instead, was simply to provide a stage on which the great cosmic drama, pitting the "church of the Lamb" against "the church of the devil," could be brought to its final conclusion.

In the meantime the Saints could anticipate the coming age when, as Pratt predicted, "a universal Theocracy will cement the whole body politic. One king will rule. One holy city will compose the capitol. One tem-

---

[79]Underwood faults Hansen's social-deprivation perspective in "Early Mormon Millenarianism: Another Look," *Church History* 54 (June 1985): 222-23. But see also Underwood, "Millenarianism and the Early Mormon Mind," *Journal of Mormon History* 9 (1982): 45.

ple will be the centre of worship. In short, there will be one Lord, one Faith, one Baptism, and one Spirit.''[80] And in anticipation of that golden age, they could proceed to establish the political kingdom of God that would one day rule with Christ. As Orson Pratt, Parley's brother, wrote in 1851: ''The kingdom of God . . . is the only legal government that can exist in any part of the universe. All other governments are illegal and unauthorized.''[81] This activity and conviction finally rested on the notion that through their restoration, early Mormons had burst the bounds of time, history, and finitude that for centuries had imprisoned humankind. As Parley observed, they had ''burst the chains of mortality'' and now soared with the gods ''amid unnumbered worlds which roll in majesty on high.'' Here indeed was a radical form of that common nineteenth-century vision that Mead described as ''building anew in the American wilderness on the true and ancient foundations.''

---

[80]Pratt, *Key,* 135.

[81]Orson Pratt, *The Kingdom of God* (Liverpool, 1851) 1. The antipluralism implicit in the early Mormon vision of the kingdom of God should not be surprising, especially given the Old Testament, theocratic roots of this vision. Indeed, Richard Bushman has argued effectively that the ''templates for Book of Mormon politics'' were biblical, not American. Bushman notes that ''Book of Mormon government by Jacksonian standards was no democracy. . . . Looking at the Book of Mormon as a whole, it seems clear that most of the principles associated with the American Constitution are slighted or disregarded altogether.'' Bushman concludes that ''Book of Mormon political attitudes have Old World precedents, particularly in the history of the Israelite nation.'' Bushman, ''The Book of Mormon and the American Revolution,'' *Brigham Young University Studies* 17 (Autumn 1976): 16-19.

One might argue that the doctrine of degrees of salvation, announced in a revelation of 16 February 1832, was in some sense an accommodation to religious pluralism. Thus, the Saints would inherit celestial glory; the ''honorable men of the earth, who were blinded by the craftiness of men'' would inherit a lesser, terrestrial glory; and those ''who received not the gospel of Christ'' would inherit a still-lesser terrestrial glory (*Doctrine and Covenants,* 76). If this was indeed a concession to religious pluralism, one finds a similar concession in Parley Pratt, who envisioned a millennial kingdom that would encompass the ''heathen nations,'' but these would ''be exalted to the privilege of serving the Saints. . . . They will be the ploughmen, the vine-dressers, the gardeners, builders, etc. But the Saints will be the owners of the soil, the proprietors of all real estate, . . . and the kings, governors, and judges of the earth'' (*Key,* 134). It is possible to find in these sorts of visions evidence of the tension that plagued a people who, at one level, valued religious pluralism but who, at another level, anticipated its final collapse. At any rate, the sort of pluralism inherent in these visions is hardly the kind of pluralism implicit in the First Amendment and plowed into the history of the American experience.

·● 8 ●·

On Battling over the Intentions and Morality of the Nation's Founders

Ronald B. Flowers

In America a holy war is currently in progress. In the minds of those who are waging it, the very survival of the nation is at stake. One of the generals in the army of righteousness has called the war a "battle for the mind."[1] The goal is to wrest the nation from the secularists, into whose hands it has fallen, and to return it to its original, God-fearing morality.

Much of Sidney Mead's writing has relevance to such controversies. He has shown that there is a religious undergirding to the American nation, yet that it is a nonparticular religion, a religion-in-general, based upon the Enlightenment concept of "nature's God." The problem has been that those who have held more particular theological views have tended to disparage this "religion of the Republic," especially when they have realized that it made their specific theology essentially irrelevant to the welfare of the nation, no matter how important it might be to individuals and the perpetuation of ecclesiastical structures.[2] Mead's view is summarized in two

---

[1]Tim LaHaye, *The Battle for the Mind* (Old Tappan NJ: Fleming H. Revell Co., 1980).

[2]Cf. Sidney E. Mead, *The Old Religion in the Brave New World: Reflections on the Relations between Christendom and the Republic* (Berkeley: University of California Press, 1977) esp. 40-41, 69-71, 79; Sidney E. Mead, *The Nation with the Soul of a Church* (New York: Harper & Row, 1975) 1-47.

quotations: "I have become convinced that the religion of the American culture—what I have called 'the religion of the Republic'—is not the Christianity exhibited in the form of any or all of the denominations in our religiously pluralistic society."[3] "The species of religion incarnated in the denominations with their massive institutional inertia, is not the religion that actually sets and legitimates the norms of our society . . . the theology of the denominations does not legitimate the political and legal structure of the commonwealth."[4]

This controversy broke out in a virulent form beginning in the mid-1970s and has continued, often with pyrotechnic dimensions, into the present. The controversy pits the "New Christian Right" against "secular humanism."[5] So the dispute is not exactly as Mead described it. It is not a denomination criticizing the "religion of the Republic" so much as it is Christianity, understood in a Fundamentalist/strict Evangelical way, charging that the "religion of the Republic" has been captured by secular humanism. The Christian Right claims too much for the "religion of the Republic" by identifying it with some form of the Judeo-Christian tradition and too little in not seeing the range of moral values within it. The purpose of this article is to describe, with interpretive comments along the way, two dimensions of this altercation: attacks on the United States Supreme Court and pleas for morality in government.

In the view of the Christian Right, a principal culprit in the secularizing of the nation is the Supreme Court and ultimately the entire judiciary system, since it follows the precedents established by the Supreme Court. Some

---

[3]Mead, *Nation with the Soul of a Church*, 5.

[4]Mead, *The Old Religion*, 69.

[5]The history of the rise of the "New Christian Right" and how it defines its enemy and goals are treated in the following survey articles: George M. Marsden, "Preachers of Paradox: The Religious New Right in Historical Perspective," in *Religion in America: Spiritual Life in a Secular Age*, ed. Mary Douglas and Douglas Tipton (Boston: Beacon Press, 1982) 150-68; James McBride, " 'There Is No Separation of God and State': The New Christian Right's Perspective on Religion and the First Amendment," in *Cults, Culture, and the Law: Perspectives on New Religious Movements*, ed. Thomas Robbins, William C. Shepherd, and James McBride (Chico CA: Scholars Press, 1985) 205-24. Cf. also A. James Reichley, *Religion in American Public Life* (Washington: The Brookings Institution, 1985) 311-31; and Ronald B. Flowers, *Religion in Strange Times: The 1960s and 1970s* (Macon GA: Mercer University Press, 1984) 1-137, 164-75.

decisions stand out as beacons of secularism. *Roe* v. *Wade*[6] said that a woman's right to privacy and her own personhood means that her right to decide whether or not to end a pregnancy is fundamental. Consequently, during the first trimester the state may only require that the abortion be performed by a licensed physician. *Engel* v. *Vitale*[7] and *Abington Township School District* v. *Schempp*[8] declared that prayers, whether or not they were composed by government officials, could not be required by law in public schools.[9] *Lemon* v. *Kurtzman*,[10] *Committee for Public Education and Religious Liberty* v. *Nyquist*,[11] *Meek* v. *Pittenger*,[12] and *Wolman* v. *Walter*[13] forbade a variety of programs to provide federal or state aid to parochial schools. To the Christian Right the results and implications of these cases were staggering. The abortion decision elevated personal choice to a level that takes precedence over human life. The prayer decisions removed traditional theism from public schools, thus "establishing" secular humanism. The aid decisions, through the tyranny of economics, not only limit parents' free exercise to send their children to church schools, but force the children into public schools, where the state's religion—secular humanism—is established. (In this frame of reference, "traditional theism" teaches absolute moral standards derived from God: moral choices are based on God's law, not on human whim. "Secular humanism" rejects belief in God and replaces it with belief in human wisdom and interests. Consequently, moral standards are based only on self-interest and are relative rather than absolute.[14]) All of this happened because the Supreme Court

---

[6]410 U.S. 113 (1973).

[7]370 U.S. 421 (1962).

[8]374 U.S. 203 (1963).

[9]It should be noted, however, that the Court did not forbid voluntary prayer and approved the teaching of religion as part of the curriculum of the public schools.

[10]403 U.S. 602 (1971).

[11]413 U.S. 756 (1973).

[12]421 U.S. 349 (1975).

[13]433 U.S. 229 (1977).

[14]John W. Whitehead and John Conlon, "The Establishment of the Religion of Secular Humanism and Its First Amendment Implications," *Texas Tech Law Review* 10 (1978): 24-25, 29-31. Cf. also LaHaye, *Battle for the Mind*, 25-46, 125-40.

has used too broad an interpretation of the Establishment Clause of the First Amendment.

Opponents of this trend have argued that the way to reverse it is for the Court to base its decisions only on the intention of the framers of the Constitution; that is, when the Court departed from the original meaning of the First Amendment, secularism began to creep into its decisions. This argument—that judicial decisions should be based on a literal reading of the text of the Constitution—a kind of judicial fundamentalism, is not a new one, but recently has gained momentum. The most powerful recent presentation of this perspective is a book by Robert L. Cord[15] that makes two principal arguments: (1) the founders of the Constitution did not intend absolute separation of church and state and (2) recent Supreme Court justices have not done their homework. In reference to the first, Cord analyzes the language of the debates, including the recommendations of state-ratifying conventions, leading up to the final formulation of the First Amendment. He concludes that

> regarding religion, the First Amendment was intended to accomplish three purposes. First, it was intended to prevent the establishment of a national church or religion, or the giving of any religious sect or denomination a preferred status. Second, it was designed to safeguard the right of freedom of conscience in religious beliefs against invasion solely by the national Government. Third, it was so constructed in order to allow the States, unimpeded, to deal with religious establishments as they saw fit. There appears to be no historical evidence that the First Amendment was intended to preclude Federal governmental aid to religion when it was provided on a nondiscriminatory basis. Nor does there appear to be any historical evidence that the First Amendment was intended to provide an *absolute separation or independence* of religion and the national state. The actions of the early Congresses and Presidents, in fact, suggest quite the opposite.[16]

From that assertion he proceeds with an analysis of the actions of Presidents Jefferson and Madison (those usually thought to have had the most influence in the formation of the First Amendment) after the ratification of the Bill of Rights. He argues that their political behavior shows that they

---

[15]Robert L. Cord, *Separation of Church and State: Historical Fact and Current Fiction* (New York: Lambeth Press, 1982). Cord does not write as a devotee of the "New Christian Right," but rather as a political scientist and historian. But his book well serves the Christian Right's agenda.

[16]Ibid., 15 (emphasis in original).

believed such a separation was not absolute. For example, they encouraged legislation for the government to aid churches in their work with the Indians and supported government-paid chaplains in the national Congress. Madison even proclaimed national days of prayer and thanksgiving—a practice that Jefferson would not support.[17]

However, there is another point of view—labeled the strict separationist—about the meaning of the First Amendment. This position argues that the words of Jefferson and Madison show that they believed in absolute separation between church and state; therefore, even nondiscriminatory aid to religion was prohibited. According to the Constitution, government may try to achieve only secular goals and employ secular means to reach those goals, never religious means.[18] Cord (along with other "intentionalists") does not believe the historical evidence will bear that construction.

When he turns to the Supreme Court, Cord argues that the justices in the last forty years have been either fools or knaves because they have adopted the strict separationist view. They were fools because they did not do their homework and did not know the intention of the founders or knaves because they knew the founders' intention and ignored it. The problems stem from the Court's opinion in *Everson* v. *Board of Education*.[19] In that case Justice Hugo Black, writing for the Court, described the scope and application of the Establishment Clause in a famous passage.

> The "establishment of religion" clause of the First Amendment means *at least* this: Neither a state nor the Federal Government can set up a church. Neither can pass laws which aid one religion, *aid all religions,* or prefer one religion over another. Neither can force nor influence a person to go to or remain away from church against his will or force him to profess a belief or disbelief in any religion. No person can be punished for entertaining or professing religious belief or disbelief, for church attendance or non-attendance. *No tax in any amount, large or small, can be levied to support any religious activities or institutions, whatever they may be called, or whatever they may adopt to teach or practice religion. Neither a state nor the Federal Government can, openly or secretly, participate in the affairs of any religious organizations or groups and vice versa.* In the words

---

[17]Ibid., 19-82.

[18]Cf. Leo Pfeffer, *Church, State, and Freedom,* rev. ed. (Boston: Beacon Press, 1967) esp. 91-180.

[19]330 U.S. 1 (1947).

of Jefferson, the clause against establishment of religion *was intended to erect a "wall of separation between church and State."*[20]

The passages emphasized in this quotation are those with which Cord disagrees. Black's construction prohibited what Cord thinks the founders would allow: aid to all religions on a nondiscriminatory basis and tax monies to support such aid. In writing the opinion of which the quoted passage is the cornerstone, Justice Black relied on the history of the First Amendment's creation. Cord argues that if the entire history of the period is examined, the evidence will not support the broad interpretation of the Establishment Clause set forth in *Everson*. The principal problem, from the intentionalist point of view, is that virtually all subsequent Establishment Clause cases have rested on the *Everson* reasoning. These decisions, in giving no aid to religion, have tended to sanitize various programs and institutions from religion (the public schools being the principal example).[21] This has led to a secularized society. It is necessary that the Supreme Court return to the intention of the founders, with their much narrower view of the Establishment Clause, in adjudicating cases.

The intentionalist view reached the Supreme Court itself in 1985. Justice William Rehnquist, writing a lengthy dissent in a school-prayer case, *Wallace* v. *Jaffree,* reproduced Cord's argument.

> The Framers intended the Establishment Clause to prohibit the designation of any church as a "national" one. The Clause was also designed to stop the Federal Government from asserting a preference for one religious denomination or sect over others. . . . As its history abundantly shows, however, nothing in the Establishment Clause requires government to be strictly neutral between religion and irreligion, nor does that Clause prohibit Congress or the States from pursuing legitimate secular ends through nondiscriminatory sectarian means.[22]

The fact that this argument appeared in a Supreme Court decision, albeit a dissent, sent shock waves through strict separationist students of church-state relationships.

This effort to recover the original meaning of the Establishment Clause is not the only summons to return to the intention of the founders. In order

---

[20]330 U.S. sec.1, 15; Cord, *Separation of Church and State,* 109.

[21]Cord, *Separation of Church and State,* 103-239.

[22]105 S.Ct. sec. 2479, 2520 (1985).

to understand the argument that follows, it is necessary to review the judicial concept of "incorporation."

Intentionalists and nonintentionalists agree that the founders intended the Bill of Rights to apply only to the federal government. All involved believed that they were creating a limited government, one in which the individual states retained considerable sovereignty.[23] This is particularly true in reference to religion. The states were left free to deal with religion as they chose. Four states maintained government support of religion after the First Amendment was ratified in 1791.[24]

That the founders' understanding persisted is shown by many opinions of the Supreme Court. One of the more famous is *Barron* v. *Baltimore*.[25] Barron sued the city of Baltimore for taking some of his private property for public use without just compensation, contrary to the Fifth Amendment of the Constitution, which he claimed applied to Baltimore as much as to the United States Government. Chief Justice John Marshall wrote that the amendment was applicable only to the federal government and Barron could not sue Baltimore under its provisions.

More pertinent to the religion clauses is *Permoli* v. *New Orleans*.[26] A Catholic priest, who had been fined for violating the city's ban on exhibiting a corpse in a public place when he conducted a funeral, sued, claiming the city had denied him his constitutional right to the free exercise of religion. The Court denied the action because the federal constitution did not apply to the states; for relief Permoli would have to rely on state laws.

In the aftermath of the Civil War, the Fourteenth Amendment became part of the Constitution in 1868. Congress wanted to improve the condition of black people, to forbid discrimination in civil rights on account of race, and to extend citizenship to former slaves. Embedded in the language meant to accomplish those goals is this important line: "Nor shall any State deprive any person of life, liberty, or property, without due process of law."

In the twentieth century, many argued that the liberties contained in the Bill of Rights were specifications of the liberties guaranteed to the citizens

---

[23]Pfeffer, *Church, State, and Freedom*, 139-41.

[24]Leonard W. Levy, "The Original Meaning of the Establishment Clause of the First Amendment," in *Religion and the State: Essays in Honor of Leo Pfeffer*, ed. James E. Wood, Jr. (Waco TX: Baylor University Press, 1985) 71-77.

[25]32 U.S. (7 Peters) 243 (1833).

[26]3 Howard 589 (1845).

of states by the Due Process Clause of the Fourteenth Amendment; that is, that amendment "incorporated" the liberties enumerated in the Bill of Rights. The first Supreme Court decision implementing incorporation was *Gitlow* v. *New York,*[27] which applied the Free Speech Clause of the First Amendment in favor of one who claimed that New York had denied him freedom of speech and the press.

In the area of religion, *Cantwell* v. *Connecticut*[28] was the first explicit incorporation case. It applied the Free Exercise Clause to the states in the case of a Jehovah's Witness who had been arrested for street preaching without the required permission from civil authorities. The Court held that the federal Constitution will not allow a state to impose a prior restraint on a religious activity. The first case incorporating the Establishment Clause was *Everson* v. *Board of Education.* [29] This issue was whether a city may provide tax funds to parents to assist them in sending their children to parochial schools on public buses. In saying yes (public transportation is a public service the same as police and fire protection, which cities supply to churches) the Court applied the Establishment Clause to local and state government. So *Everson* is important not only because it articulated a broad, absolutist interpretation of the Establishment Clause (too broad, from the intentionalists' point of view), but it also applied that interpretation to the states. This, as we have seen, has led to the secularizing of society, at least in the view of the Christian Right.[30]

It is obvious that one way to get around such a broad application of the Establishment Clause to the states would be to abolish the concept of incorporation. Many have proposed for some time that incorporation is not inherent in the Fourteenth Amendment, that it is logically inconsistent with reference to the Establishment Clause (how can a state's right be imposed as a prohibition on the state?), and that it interposes federal judges between the people and their local and state legislatures.[31]

[27]268 U.S. 652 (1925).

[28]310 U.S. 296 (1940).

[29]330 U.S. 1 (1947).

[30]For an extensive history of the concept and process of incorporation, see Henry J. Abraham, *Freedom and the Court: Civil Rights and Liberties in the United States,* 4th ed. (New York: Oxford University Press, 1982) 28-91.

[31]Representative of this literature is Joseph M. Snee, SJ, "Religious Disestablishment and the Fourteenth Amendment," *Washington University Law Quarterly* (December 1954):

The administration of Ronald Reagan has held the expectation that judges should be "strict constructionists" who practice judicial restraint in applying the Constitution.[32] This attitude solidified with the appointment of Edwin Meese as attorney general. In a speech before the American Bar Association, he asserted that the administration would like to reverse the doctrine of incorporation. Mr. Meese set the tone of his speech with these words:

> It is important to take a moment and reflect upon the proper role of the Supreme Court in our constitutional system. The intended role of the judiciary generally and the Supreme Court in particular was to serve as the "bulwarks of a limited constitution." . . . As the "faithful guardians of the Constitution," the judges were expected to resist any political effort to depart from the literal provisions of the Constitution. The text of the document and the original intention of those who framed it would be the judicial standard in giving effect to the Constitution.[33]

Turning specifically to the topic of religion and incorporation, he referred to *Barron* v. *Baltimore* with approval, noted that the idea of incorporation rests on an "intellectually shaky foundation,"[34] and then said:

371-407. For a review of objections to incorporating the Establishment Clause and attempts to answer them, see Justice Brennan's concurring opinion in *Abington School District* v. *Schempp* 374 U.S. sec. 203, 253.

[32]Speaking to a group of U.S. attorneys, Mr. Reagan summarized his views: "I want judges of the highest intellectual standing who harbor the deepest regard for the Constitution and its traditions, one of which is judicial restraint." *Weekly Compilation of Presidential Documents* 21 (21 October 1985): 1278. Attorney General Meese has explained that the value of "strict construction" is that it adheres to the text of the Constitution, which is much better than basing decisions on the whims and social theories of judges. "To allow constitutional text and the intentions of the framers to be nudged aside by the moral speculations of judges and advocates is to acquiesce in the misguided notion that a written Constitution can somehow be made viable only by ignoring or supplanting it." Furthermore, "The danger inherent in transforming the meaning of the Constitution and loosening its strictures in the name of some supposedly more benevolent and modern vision is that such tampering inevitably increases the power of government." Edwin Meese III, Address before the American Bar Association, London, 17 July 1985, transcript Superintendent of Documents Classification no. J1.34:M47/Lond., 4, 5.

[33]Edwin Meese III, Address before the American Bar Association, Washington, 9 July 1985, transcript Superintendent of Documents Classification no. J1.34:M47, 2.

[34]Ibid., 13.

And nowhere else has the principal of federalism been dealt so politically
violent and constitutionally suspect a blow as by the theory of incorporation. . . . The point, of course, is that the Establishment Clause of the First
Amendment was designed to prohibit Congress from establishing a national church. The belief was that the Constitution should not allow Congress to designate a particular faith or sect as politically above the rest. But
to have argued, as is popular today, that the amendment demands a strict
neutrality between religion and irreligion would have struck the founding
generation as bizarre. The purpose was to prohibit religious tyranny, not
to undermine religion generally.[35]

In offering a remedy to the Supreme Court's overly broad interpretation of
the Establishment Clause, Mr. Meese said:

What, then, should a constitutional jurisprudence actually be? It should be
a Jurisprudence of Original Intention. . . . This belief in a Jurisprudence
of Original Intention also reflects a deeply rooted commitment to the idea
of democracy. The Constitution represents the consent of the governed to
the structures and powers of the government. . . . A Constitution that is
viewed as only what the judges say it is, is no longer a Constitution in the
true sense. . . . It has been and will continue to be the policy of this administration to press for a Jurisprudence of Original Intention.[36]

With this argument we are again drawn back to a consideration of the
founders, this time applying their work only to the federal government,
leaving the states to their own devices in matters of religion.[37]
There are, however, some difficulties with the attempt to recover the
founders' intentions. One argument is that to raise the question of the intent of the founders is to raise the wrong question. H. Jefferson Powell[38]
has shown that the principle of the interpretation of law in the eighteenth

---

[35]Ibid., 14.

[36]Ibid., 15, 17. Cf. also the testimony of Grover Rees, Senate Committee on the Judiciary, *Hearings on a Proposed Constitutional Amendment to Permit Voluntary Prayer
S.J.Res. 199*, 97th Cong., 2d sess., 1982, 347, 370. For an overview of the Reagan administration's policies toward the judiciary, see Ted Guest et al., "Justice under Reagan," *U.S.
News and World Report*, 14 October 1985, 58-65, 67.

[37]Interestingly, Professor Cord does not argue against incorporation, but would apply
his more limited approach to the Establishment Clause to state and local laws as well as
federal (*Separation of Church and State*, 101).

[38]H. Jefferson Powell, "The Original Understanding of Original Intent," *Harvard Law
Review* 98 (March 1985): 885-948.

and early nineteenth centuries was based on common law. In that tradition the intent of the law was found within the words of the law itself, not in the motivations and subjective purposes behind the law. The modern practice of looking to the "legislative history" of a law was virtually nonexistent. The words of the document meant what they said: *they* contained the intent of the authors. The other way of knowing the meaning of a law, beyond the meaning of the words themselves, was judicial precedent—how the law was commonly applied.

The framers of the Constitution were familiar with these views stemming from English common law and agreed with them.

> The Philadelphia framers' primary expectation regarding constitutional interpretation was that the Constitution, like any other legal document, would be interpreted in accord with its express language. . . . The framers shared the traditional common law view . . . that the import of the document they were framing would be determined by reference to the intrinsic meaning of its words or through the usual judicial process of case-by-case interpretation.
>
> In accepting the common law's objective approach to discerning the meaning of a document, the framers did not endorse strict literalism as the proper stance of future interpreters. The framers were aware that unforeseen situations would arise, and they accepted inevitability and propriety of construction.[39]

Consequently, in this view, relying on the debates of the founders—analyzing every permutation of language as the religion clauses evolved, which is normally done by scholars on both sides in this debate—is an illegitimate exercise, from the viewpoint of the crafters of the Constitution. Indeed, James Madison stated, "As a guide in expounding and applying the provisions of the Constitution, the debates and incidental decisions of the Convention can have no authoritative character."[40] Thus, from this perspective, Justice Hugo Black, author of *Everson,* is no more a knave than Robert Cord, since both relied on historical arguments in a way the framers would not approve.

If one does examine legislative history, commonly done today, one can argue that it does generally support the Supreme Court's view of the Es-

---

[39]Ibid., 903-904, footnotes omitted.

[40]Letter from James Madison to Thomas Ritchie, 15 September 1821, quoted ibid., 936.

tablishment Clause.[41] Leonard Levy shows that the debates on the ratification of the First Amendment do not give a clear definition of
establishment. It is clear that some state-ratifying conventions asked for a
provision in a Bill of Rights that would prevent the preference of one religion over others, often called a ''national religion.'' Most intentionalists
interpret this to be the meaning of *establishment*.[42] It may be, however,
that the states' language reflects only what was their *primary* historical understanding of establishments. A widely read book in the late eighteenth
century was Joseph Priestley's *History of the Corruptions of Christianity*,
which called attention to the medieval church's ability, through doctrine
and power, to hold common people in subjection. Jefferson, among others,
was greatly influenced by this book.[43] A twentieth-century reader can conclude with certainty that the states were fearful of a single church's being selected for government sponsorship. One cannot conclude that such was all
they were concerned about as they contemplated establishment.[44]

As one searches for the meaning of establishment in the minds of the
founders, one notes a logical inconsistency in the intentionalist argument.
The framers wrote the Establishment Clause (indeed, the entire Bill of
Rights) as an expression of a strong desire for limited government. Before
the passage of the First Amendment, the Constitution gave absolutely no
power to government to legislate in the area of religion. If the narrow, intentionalist interpretation is adopted, that means the First Amendment gave
Congress power to legislate on religion, so long as it did not promote or
support a particular group. That would have been inconsistent with their
overarching concern to create a limited government, so one can argue that
they must have intended a broader scope for the Establishment Clause than
the narrow interpretation allows.[45]

Some intentionalists argue that the Supreme Court has done a bad job
of history not only when chronicling the intent of the founders, but also
when the justices recite the list of horrors that were inflicted on people who

---

[41]Levy, ''Original Meaning of the Establishment Clause,'' 43-83.

[42]Cord makes much of these state requests (*Separation of Church and State*, 6-8, 11).

[43]William Warren Sweet, ''Natural Religion and Religious Liberty in America,'' *Journal of Religion* 25 (January 1945): 50-51.

[44]Levy, ''Original Meaning of the Establishment Clause,'' 52.

[45]Ibid., 46, 61.

lived 350 years ago in areas that had an established church. The Court should know that persecution does not necessarily result from establishment. They could surely learn this from looking at modern benevolent establishments such as those in England, Denmark, and Scotland.[46] But this is to ask the justices to do what the intentionalists have argued against. Intentionalists have wanted to adhere to the original constitutional language and interpret it literally. This argument asks justices to consider modern circumstances in reaching their decisions, to interpret the founders' text assuming what they may not have known. (One notes again that Priestly's book on the abuse of church power was widely known.) However, Levy has shown that the framers did not know the circumstance of "benevolent establishment." Nowhere in America after 1776 did a state have an establishment of the traditional European type. There were establishments in six states; in three Protestantism was established and in three Christianity, with government benefits flowing to all equally. This means that even though the founders knew of the nondiscriminatory kind of establishment that intentionalists say the clause permits, the founders prohibited *any* "law respecting an establishment of religion," which suggests that they preferred the broad understanding the Court has maintained since *Everson*.[47]

Not only does the lack of a definition concerning what the founders meant by *establishment* make the intentionalists' argument interesting but less than compelling, so does the fact that their argument, particularly in its anti-incorporation form, makes the Constitution static, rather than dynamic, law. Time progresses, changes occur; American culture is much different from what it was in the late eighteenth century. It is virtually impossible that the founders could have foreseen the pervasive state or the public schools of the type we have in the twentieth century, for example. But the Constitution must be made to speak to these times; one cannot simply judicially turn back the clock and impose strictly held eighteenth-century ideas on the twentieth.[48] The concept of the right of privacy is an example. This right is not specifically mentioned in the Constitution, but

---

[46]Cf. the review of Cord's book by F. W. O'Brian in *Union Seminary Quarterly Review* 38 (1984): 451-59 at 457. Cord does not make this point.

[47]Levy, "Original Meaning of the Establishment Clause," 65-77.

[48]Cf. Terrance Sandlow, "Constitutional Interpretation," *Michigan Law Review* 79 (April 1981): 1033-72 for a very liberal statement of the necessity to make the Constitution responsive to modern times.

it has been recognized as an extension of other constitutional principles. It is an extension of the First Amendment guarantee of freedom of speech and of the press, the Third Amendment prohibition against peacetime quartering of soldiers without the householder's consent, the Fourth Amendment prohibition of unreasonable searches and seizures, and the Fifth Amendment privilege against self-incrimination.[49] In *Griswold* v. *Connecticut*[50] the Court decided that the privacy of married couples forbade a state from prohibiting the use of birth-control devices or counseling another in the use of them, while *Olmstead* v. *United States*[51] and *Katz* v. *United States*[52] show the necessity of privacy considerations when electronic eavesdropping devices are available.[53] The framers could never have conceived of such issues as the modern judiciary must consider.

One could argue that these examples show the need to adjust in the face of some modern technology; there were specific causes for adaptation. Is there any comparable specific cause in the area of religion? Yes, there is: pluralism. Of course, religious pluralism has existed since virtually the beginning of the colonial period. But subsequent American creativity and massive immigration have produced a society much more religiously diverse than that of the late eighteenth century.[54] Religious diversity has even caused modification of the understanding of religion in some Supreme Court decisions.[55] This diversity makes an "aid all religions" understanding of the Establishment Clause much more difficult, since there are such divergent beliefs and social goals among the many religions of the nation.[56]

---

[49]43 *Lawyer's Edition* 2d 875; 14 *American Law Reports* 2d 755.

[50]381 U.S. 479 (1965).

[51]277 U.S. 438 (1928).

[52]389 U.S. 347 (1967).

[53]Abraham, *Freedom and the Court,* 140-44.

[54]In 1978 there were at least 1,200 religious groups in America. Cf. J. Gordon Melton, *The Encyclopedia of American Religions,* 2 vols. (Wilmington NC: McGrath Publishing Co., 1978).

[55]E.g., *United States* v. *Seeger* 380 U.S. 163 (1965) and *Welsh* v. *United States* 398 U.S. 333 (1970), cases in which conscientious-objector status was based on nontraditional religious belief. Cf. Laurence Tribe, *American Constitutional Law* (Mineola NY: The Foundation Press, 1978) 826-28.

[56]Cord acknowledges that increasing religious diversity may change the interpretation of the Establishment Clause: "The religious pluralism that now exists in the United States

The willingness to incorporate the First Amendment into the Fourteenth shows the flexibility needed to keep up with changing times. Attorney General Meese, in advocating a "jurisprudence of original intention," has argued against incorporation[57] and against interpreting the Constitution in the light of present times. "I know that it is sometimes said that the problems of our time, of 1985, are complex—far more complex than the problems of 1787. . . . And it is in the light of these ostensibly very different circumstances that some would urge us to relax our commitment to the principles of our two hundred year old Constitution."[58] The answer he gives is that the problems of this time are no more complex, no more vexing, than the problems the founders faced.[59] But that misses the point. It is not that our problems are more complex than those the founders faced, but that they are new. New questions require fresh thinking. The other response he makes to the flexibility argument is that the principles included in the Constitution were already tried and true, "the product of

---

has as a consequence made the historic prohibitions of the Establishment Clause more delimiting of governmental actions. Today, because of the present *religious diversity* in the nation, public-sponsored activities that were nondiscriminatory in the past can no longer be reconciled with the First and Fourteenth Amendments' ban against placing any purely sectarian activity identified with one religious tradition into a preferred position." (*Separation of Church and State*, 165; emphasis in original.) He applies this to the abolition of the Lord's Prayer and Bible reading in public schools (*Abington School District* v. *Schempp*), which shows again that he is not a clone of the Christian Right.

[57]Being an intentionalist, he would certainly be willing to go back to the intention of the authors of the Fourteenth Amendment. There is strong evidence that some of the Congress at that time had the idea that this amendment would apply the Bill of Rights to the states. Cf. Abraham, *Freedom and the Court*, 30-46. The trouble with "intention" arguments is that they lose much of their force if one cannot show a unanimous viewpoint among the authors.

It is interesting to note that one of the strongest advocates of incorporation was Justice Black, the author of *Everson* (ibid., 35-38). But Black regarded himself a strict constructionist of the Constitution. In referring to that document, he said: "I believe the Court has no power to add to or subtract from the procedures set forth by the Founders. . . . I shall not at any time surrender my belief that the document itself should be our guide, not our own concept of what is fair, decent, and right." Quoted in Sidney H. Asch, *The Supreme Court and Its Great Justices* (New York: Arco Publishing Co., 1971) 191.

[58]Meese, American Bar Association speech in London, 9.

[59]Ibid., 10.

several centuries of experience" (since the Magna Charta).[60] The implication is that they have the stature of timeless truths. A remark I heard Hans
Küng make in a lecture on paradigm shifts in theology is applicable here:
those who want to rely on ancient, timeless truths should remember that
the sun and stars are just as they always have been, but since Copernicus,
we can never understand them as the ancients did.

Again, the controversy reached the Supreme Court. Justice Stevens reminded Mr. Meese that no justice in the last sixty years has questioned the
validity of incorporation.[61] Justice Brennan took issue with the "jurisprudence of original intention" and made the point being argued here: changing cultural/historical circumstances demand a dynamic, not static,
interpretation of the Constitution.

> We current Justices read the Constitution in the only way that we can: as
> Twentieth Century Americans. We look to the history of the time of fram-
> ing and to the intervening history of interpretation. But the ultimate ques-
> tion must be, what do the words of the text mean in our time. For the genius
> of the Constitution rests not in any static meaning it might have had in a
> world that is dead and gone, but in the adaptability of its great principles
> to cope with current problems and current needs. What the constitutional
> fundamentals meant to the wisdom of other times cannot be their measure
> to the vision of our time.[62]

Finally, the existence of Article V, which contains the procedure for
amending the Constitution, shows that the framers realized that changing
times might give rise to a need to modify the Constitution, to change or go
beyond what they themselves had wrought. It seems strange that it should
be denied to the courts, which the framers created to adjudicate cases and
controversies under the Constitution, what they clearly gave to the Congress and to the people. If one wants to go back to the intention of the framers, what one finds there is the recognition that times change and that the

---

[60]Ibid., 10, 1-2.

[61]John Paul Stevens, Address to the Federal Bar Association, Chicago, 23 October 1985,
9.

[62]William J. Brennan, Jr., "The Constitution of the United States: Contemporary Ratification," Address at Georgetown University, 12 October 1985, 7.

law of the land needs to be relevant to those changes.[63] Of course, it is a constitution that is being adjudicated and its text must be taken absolutely seriously. But it must not be frozen in any era, since the experience of the American people is dynamic. The controversy is best summarized by constitutional law professor Laurence Tribe.

> Just as the constitutional choices we make are channeled and constrained by who we are and by what we have lived through, so too they are constrained and channeled by a constitutional text and structure and history, by constitutional language and constitutional tradition, opening some practices and foreclosing others. To ignore or defy those constraints is to pretend to a power that is not ours to wield. But to pretend that those constraints leave us no freedom, or must lead us all to the same conclusions, is to disclaim a responsibility that is inescapably our own.[64]

The other dimension of the holy war against secularism—broader and less technical than questions of the intention and interpretation of law, but related to them—is the question of the moral content of American government. The thrust of this argument is that the founders intended to base the government on religious values. Some say that it was Christianity. "The religion of the first amendment is traditional theism and, in particular, Christianity."[65] "A government resting squarely on Christian principles. . . . The Constitution was designed *to perpetuate* a Christian order."[66]

Others say that the source of the values is the Judeo-Christian tradition. The secretary of education, speaking of the relationship between religion, values, and the preservation of a free society, said:

> And that relationship is this: Our values as a free people and the central values of the Judeo-Christian tradition are flesh of the flesh, blood of the blood. . . . No one demands doctrinal adherence to any religious beliefs as a condition of citizenship, or as a proof of good citizenship, here. But

---

[63]Mr. Meese mentioned the amendment process in his speech to the American Bar Association in London (8), saying that the framers made the process difficult "lest the Constitution be rendered 'too mutable.' " In that he is correct, but the existence of the process is still a recognition of the dynamic character of law.

[64]Laurence Tribe, *Constitutional Choices* (Cambridge MA: Harvard University Press, 1985) vii-viii.

[65]Whitehead and Conlon, "The Establishment of Secular Humanism," 2.

[66]Rus Walton, *One Nation under God* (Old Tappan NJ: Fleming H. Revell Co., 1975) 16, 23 (emphasis in original).

at the same time we should not deny what is true: that from the Judeo-Christian tradition come our values, our principles, the animating spirit of our institutions.[67]

Still others use *biblical* to refer to the basis of American values, although that term seems to be interchangeable with *Judeo-Christian tradition.* ''It is improper to say that America was founded on Christian principles, for that would unnecessarily exclude the Jewish community. America was founded on biblical principles, all of which are found in the Old Testament and therefore should not exclude any but the most anti-God, antimoral humanist thinkers of our day.''[68] In separating church and state, the framers never intended to divorce the government from religion.[69] Still, that is what has happened; laws and court decisions have tended to cut American government off from the inherent morality of the tradition. The result is a secular society.

That this point can be argued in a muted way—without being as shrill as the Christian Right, yet showing great force and sensibility—was shown by Richard John Neuhaus.[70] He argued against the ''myth of the secular society.'' The founders recognized the existence of religion and believed that the government they were creating rested on the values of that religion, which Neuhaus calls ''biblical'' or ''Judeo-Christian.'' There has been a desacralization of society. In law that has had the effect of robbing the law of that which legitimizes it. The law has become empty, merely a codification of competing interests, and that has contributed mightily to the ''naked public square.'' Neuhaus says that the public square cannot remain naked because the public will not stand for it. The Christian Right, whom he calls ''triumphalists'' and who are a minority in America, and the majority of the population, who are growing increasingly aware that something is wrong, will not allow a morals/values vacuum to exist. So he calls for a reawareness of the traditional values of America.

---

[67]William J. Bennett, Address to the Knights of Columbus, Washington DC, 7 August 1985, 9, 12.

[68]Tim LaHaye, *Battle for the Mind*, 37-38. Cf. also Jerry Falwell, *Listen, America!* (Garden City NY: Doubleday and Co., 1980) 16, 27.

[69]Falwell, *Listen, America!*, 53-54; Reichley, *Religion in American Public Life*, 112-13. The existence of the Free Exercise Clause shows that there is much truth to that.

[70]Richard John Neuhaus, *The Naked Public Square: Religion and Democracy in America* (Grand Rapids MI: Wm. B. Eerdmans Publishing Co., 1984).

Sidney E. Mead has shown that there is a "religion of the Republic," complete with moral values. Its source was the religion of the Enlightenment, the faith of many of the founders. In content it differed from both Judaism and Christianity: it rejected both that Jesus was a deity and that the Bible was divinely inspired—the only revelation of God to humanity. This view took the natural-theology position that the world, creation, is God's revelation. It is clear that the framers believed in God, that they were not atheists. As an extension of that, they believed in a life of virtue.[71] Although this religion was not Judaism, Christianity, or the Judeo-Christian tradition, it was not incompatible with any of them. For the founders, the existence of God was an unquestioned proposition, as was the responsibility of humans to obey God's will, which was learned from nature and interpreted by reason.[72] Religious belief produced good works. "They could not conceive of 'salvation' apart from exemplification in overt responsibility for the being and continued well-being of their society and commonwealth."[73] This Enlightenment religion had a moral dimension. For example, in describing his religious views, Benjamin Franklin said: "I never doubted, for instance, the existence of the Deity; that he made the world, and govern'd it by his Providence; that the most acceptable service of God was the doing good to man; that our souls are immortal; and that all crime will be punished, and virtue rewarded, either here or hereafter. These I esteem'd the essentials of every religion."[74] Even one of the most radical of the rationalists of the time, in summarizing one of his works, said: "The moral duty of man consists in imitating the moral goodness and beneficence of God, manifested in the creation toward all his creatures. That seeing, as we daily do, the goodness of God to all men, it is an ex-

---

[71]Mead, *The Old Religion*, 83-84; Mead, *Nation with the Soul of a Church*, 117-20. A summary of the faith of the founders is also found in Peter L. Benson and Dorothy L. Williams, *Religion on Capital Hill: Myths and Realities* (San Francisco: Harper & Row, 1982) 89-94. Incidentally, these authors, who tried to determine the influence of religion on Congress, take great exception to Tim LaHaye when he says that Congress is filled with secular humanists (*Battle for the Mind*, 172). They indicate "that the majority of Congress is a believing Congress" and do not deserve the label "secular humanist," although their sample was only 80 out of 535. (*Religion on Capital Hill*, 58-59, 20.)

[72]Mead, *The Old Religion*, 83-84.

[73]Ibid., 87.

[74]Benjamin Franklin, "Autobiography," in *The American Enlightenment*, ed. Adrienne Koch (New York: George Braziller Co., 1965) 62.

ample calling upon all men to practise the same toward each other; and consequently, that everything of persecution and revenge between man and man, and everything of cruelty to animals, is a violation of moral duty."[75]

Enlightenment religion held that God is absolute, but humans are limited in every respect. Our knowledge, even of God and religious morals, is finite and incomplete, and could be classified only as opinion. Opinion on religion could never legitimately be coerced, since one could not claim absolute authority; consequently, it could only be shared with others by persuasion. This reliance on persuasion made the freedoms of religion, speech, and the press necessary. These freedoms are not only rights of human beings, but are "unalienable"—inherent in the human situation created by God and thus they cannot be legitimately either given or taken away.[76]

This morality is usually summarized by that classic statement in the Declaration of Independence: "We hold these truths to be self-evident, that all men are created equal and are endowed by their Creator with certain unalienable Rights, that among these are Life, Liberty, and the pursuit of Happiness." This is a theological statement. It recognizes the existence of God. It further says that God has given rights to all humans and that it is the duty of the state to actualize them in the lives of its citizens. Of course, the concrete expression of that by the founders was the authorship of the Constitution and the Bill of Rights.

The point is that there is moral content to the system of government in the United States, what one might call civil ethics. If the government does not allow its citizens to enjoy these rights, then it is acting contrary to the will of God, that is, that the unrighteous nation or government leader thus violates the moral laws built into nature. The nation stands under the judgment of God. "Under judgment does not signify that God is angry with America, although I should suppose he is indeed angry with much that is done by Americans and in the name of America. Rather, under judgment means most importantly that there is a transcendent point of reference to which we as a people are accountable."[77] Exactly. Sidney Mead summa-

---

[75]Thomas Paine, *Age of Reason, Being an Investigation of True and Fabulous Theology*, pt. 1 (New York: Thomas Paine Foundation, n.d.) 67.

[76]Mead, *The Old Religion*, 84-85.

[77]Neuhaus, *Naked Public Square*, 76.

rizes this "transcendent point of reference" as this: human beings are finite, as are their laws and governments. "This is the premise of all democratic institutions. It is the essential dogma of the religion of the Republic. . . . In the Republic 'the people' is the emperor. Churches exist in the Republic to remind this sovereign ruler, 'You, too, are mortal; you are not God.' "[78] Mead likens this religion, with its moral precepts, to the mainspring of the society. "When the mainspring is broken the society runs down. . . . *the* theology of the Republic is that of 'Enlightenment.' . . . And it is not clear that this mainspring is broken."[79]

Even though the mainspring of moral precepts is not broken, it is possible for the nation to forget this heritage. The holy warriors and moral majoritarians may have oversimplified the issues and/or overstated their case, but in their call for a recovery of morality in the United States they have raised important issues. They have stimulated debate at both the popular and academic levels. This is certainly consistent with a democratic form of government. One reason the founders established the freedoms of speech and press was to allow for the free debate of ideas in the social and political arenas, with the confidence that truth would triumph in the exchange. So, in that sense, the Christian right has done the nation a service. But this raises the further question of what is the proper role of churches, Christianity, or even the Judeo-Christian tradition in relation to the "religion of the Republic" and its supposed corruption?

The role of religious institutions should be to challenge the government to be true to its own religious/moral heritage, to admonish the government to actualize the unalienable rights in the lives of all citizens. "If religion is supposed to do anything in the social order, surely it is to explicate those rules and general principles that should guide the shaping of our life together. That is not all that religion does, nor is it the most important thing it does, but it is the warrant for its participation in the public square."[80] By educating constituencies and by speaking out on public issues, religious institutions and leaders can contribute to the creation of a moral and humane society by both referring back to the moral code of the

---

[78]Mead, *Nation with the Soul of a Church*, 9-10.

[79]Mead, *The Old Religion*, 70-71.

[80]Neuhaus, *Naked Public Square*, 235.

"religion of the Republic" (this is the proper form of intentionalism) and saying to the government and any political figure, "You, too, are finite."

But while pointing up the necessity for humble and humane government, religious institutions and leaders must also remember that any church, denomination, or religious pressure group is also finite and does not have the complete truth. The particularities of its theology and/or religious practices cannot be incorporated into or imposed on government policy.[81] The public influence of religious groups must be by persuasion, not by coercion. Neither the government nor any part of it can be transformed into an extension of any sect or specific theology.[82]

In the 1980 presidential campaign, when the Moral Majority and other conservative Christian political-action groups were appearing, many said that they should not be doing what they were doing because it was a violation of the separation of church and state. Of course, that was wrong. The Free Exercise Clause grants any and all religious groups the right to be involved in the public arena. This principle was clearly expressed by Supreme Court Justice Brennan:

> That public debate of religious ideas, like any other, may arouse emotion, may incite, may foment religious divisiveness and strife does not rob it of constitutional protection. The mere fact that a purpose of the Establishment Clause is to reduce or eliminate religious divisiveness or strife, does not place religious discussion, association, or political participation in a status less preferred than rights of discussion, association and political participation generally. "Adherents of particular faiths and individual churches frequently take strong positions on public issues including . . . vigorous advocacy of legal or constitutional positions. Of course, churches

---

[81]Cf. nn. 2-4 and accompanying text.

[82]It must be conceded that some of the holy warriors, for all their talk of a Christian (Fundamentalist) America, seem to see this point. Although Tim LaHaye, *Battle for the Mind*, says "a humanist is just not qualified to be elected to public office by patriotic, America-loving citizens" (78), he also says "Christians seriously err when they insist that a candidate be a committed Christian before he is worthy of Christian support. We must learn that Christians are not the only ones with strong moral convictions. We need politicians sincerely committed to moral principles, with the character to stand up for them" (232). Jerry Falwell says that the Moral Majority believes in the separation of church and state; that it has no theological premise other than a concern for biblical morality; that it is committed to religious pluralism, and thus is not trying to elect "born-again" candidates, and that it is not trying to control the government but is mightily trying to influence the government. Jerry Falwell, *The Fundamentalist Phenomenon: The Resurgence of Conservative Christianity* (Garden City NY: Doubleday and Co., 1981) 189, 191.

as much as secular bodies and private citizens have that right." . . . In short, government may not as a goal promote "safe-thinking" with respect to religion and fence out from political participation those, such as ministers, whom it regards as overinvolved in religion. Religionists no less than members of any other group enjoy the full measure of protection afforded speech, association and political activity generally. The Establishment Clause, properly understood, is a shield against any attempt by government to inhibit religion. . . . It may not be used as a sword to justify repression of religion or its adherents from any aspect of public life.

Our decisions under the Establishment Clause prevent government from supporting or involving itself in religion or from becoming drawn into ecclesiastical disputes. These prohibitions naturally tend, as they were designed to, to avoid channelling political activity along religious lines and to reduce any tendency toward religious divisiveness in society. Beyond enforcing these prohibitions, however, government may not go. The antidote the Constitution provides against zealots who would inject sectarianism into the political process is to subject their ideas to refutation in the marketplace of ideas and their platforms to rejection at the polls. With these safeguards, it is unlikely that they will succeed in inducing government to act along religiously divisive lines, and, with judicial enforcement of the Establishment Clause, any measure of success they achieve must be short-lived, at best.[83]

In short, religious groups of all types should try to influence the government, but they should not try to make it over in their own image.

Because morality is at its core, the religion of the Republic has the potential to be prophetic.

Man, says Whitehead, is the animal that can cherish aspirations, which is to be religious, to be committed to an ideal world beyond the present world and to the incarnating of that world in actuality. The religion of this, our Republic, is of that nature. Therefore to be committed to that religion is not to be committed to this world as it is, but to a world as yet above and beyond it to which this world ought to be conformed. . . . Seen thus the religion of the Republic is essentially prophetic, which is to say that its ideals and aspirations stand in constant judgment over the passing shenanigans of the people, reminding them of the standards by which their current practices and those of their nation are ever being judged and found wanting.[84]

---

[83]Concurring in *McDaniel* v. *Paty* 435 U.S. sec. 618, 640 (1978). The quote is from *Walz* v. *Tax Commission* 397 U.S. sec. 664, 670 (1970).

[84]Mead, *Nation with the Soul of a Church*, 64-65.

The nation has the capacity to be self-correcting. Its built-in moral precepts—which are not the same as the theological morality of any religious group or coalition thereof, but not incompatible with any of them related to the Judeo-Christian tradition[85]—can be the standards by which a moral society can be maintained. The role of religious institutions is to challenge the nation (including the Supreme Court) to be true to what it was created to be.

> Sectarianism, religious or national, is a greater threat than secularism or outright atheism, because, as the story of religious persecutions reminds us, when it comes in the guise of "the faith once delivered to the saints" it may legitimate terrible tyrannies. The primary religious concern in our nation must be to guard against national idolatry; against the state becoming God; against the Republic assuming a heteronomous stance vis-à-vis other nations. The founders sought to incarnate such a guard in the legal system of the new nation, the spiritual core of which is a theonomous cosmopolitanism. The constitutional structure was designed eventually to deny the traditional resort to coercive power to every religious sect, while protecting the right of each freely to compete openly with all the others. In this situation the sects "correct one another" for the civil authority by curbing all of them, encourage each to tell "the other that he is not God." And under constitutional protection each individually, or all with one voice, have the right and ought constantly to remind all civil servants of this salutary principle.[86]

Amen and amen.

---

[85]The religion of the Republic is compatible with the Judeo-Christian tradition, not with non-Western religious traditions, many of which are also found in America. Those traditions, of course, also have the right to address the nation and to enjoy religious freedom; the First Amendment guarantees them that freedom. Furthermore, the Judeo-Christian tradition advocates it, since it recognizes that not even God has forced all humans into one religious view, but has allowed us to respond to what we perceive as the divine according to our best light. Cf. James E. Wood, Jr., "Christian Reconciliation and Religious Freedom: A Theological Inquiry," *Journal of Church and State* 12 (Spring 1970): 273-87.

[86]Mead, *Nation with the Soul of a Church,* 76-77. The quotations are from Albert Camus, *The Rebel: An Essay on Man in Revolt,* trans. Anthony Bower (New York: Vintage Books, 1958) 305-306. *Heteronomous* means a law imposed on one from beyond oneself and thus a law one would not accept if one were free. Heteronomy usually justifies itself by claiming to speak for God. *Theonomous* refers to a law, rooted in God, which is in harmony with the essential nature of humanity and thus is not destructive to persons. It calls persons to be what they are meant to be. Cf. Van Harvey, *A Handbook of Theological Terms* (New York: Macmillan Co., 1964) 118 and William E. Hordern, *A Layman's Guide to Protestant Theology,* rev. ed. (New York: Macmillan Co., 1968) 173-74.

·●9●·

An Emendation of the Church-State Problematic: The French Connection

Jo Ann Manfra

Ever since Constantine, Christianity's existence had involved political repression of individual consciences in the name of orthodoxy. European ecclesiastical institutions therefore found themselves bound to the tradition of a unitary society with its one Church. As a matter of course, virtually all early American religious groups also held to this Christian model. As Sidney Mead demonstrates, countervailing pressures for religious toleration came primarily from the fact of religious variety in the colonies and from British imperial policy—pressures exerted not for the sake of some abstract notion of freedom of worship, but against the potential political domination of any one group.[1] After 1789, in mandating religious neutrality by the state, the United States Constitution offered organized Christianity a compelling opportunity to pursue a purely spiritual mission, reminiscent of the early ministry of the apostles. America's Catholic prelates of the early national period (1789-1851) embraced that opportunity, as reflected in their collective view of papal authority.

Unquestionably the bishops remained unswerving in their devotion and loyalty to Rome. Their fidelity, however, was of a distinctive character.

---

[1]Sidney E. Mead, *The Lively Experiment: The Shaping of Christianity in America* (New York: Harper & Row, 1963) ch. 2.

They maintained that their allegiance belonged exclusively to the pope, but that in both belief and practice such fealty was properly confined to spiritual matters and excluded politics. These men did not question the Catholic understanding that the spiritual embraced the ecclesiastical, yet collectively they maintained that civil allegiance, as Archbishop Francis Kenrick put it, "is a duty independent of all ecclesiastical sanction." In American thought at large, however, the spiritual and ecclesiastical tended to be viewed as hostile, the former associated primarily with the subjective (and hence invisible) and the latter with the civil. As Elwyn A. Smith aptly observes, "The persistent misunderstanding between Catholics and Protestants in America on the meaning of these terms has exacerbated friction. So long as Catholics owned property and exercised political power, Protestants regarded the claim to 'spiritual' independence as a screen for sinister political designs."[2] In asserting that church should remain separate from state, the American bishops committed themselves to a theory of church-state relations that Roman Catholicism would not—until the second half of the twentieth century—officially acknowledge as any more than tolerable.[3]

---

[2]Francis Patrick Kenrick, *A Vindication of the Catholic Church in a Series of Letters Addressed to the Rt. Rev. John Henry Hopkins, Protestant Episcopal Bishop of Vermont* (Baltimore, 1855) 227; Elwyn A. Smith, "The Fundamental Church-State Tradition of the Catholic Church in the United States," *Church History* 38 (December 1969): 488, 491.

[3]James Hennesey deserves the credit for originally positing this argument in 1963 in writing about the American bishops at the First Vatican Council (1869-1870). Three years later he briefly suggested that the uniquely American attitude toward the papacy expressed at the end of the 1860s may have had its origin in the beginnings of American Catholic development. Subsequently, I addressed that very issue in a collective biographical study of the men who governed the Catholic Church in the United States from the appointment of the first bishop in 1789 through the eve of the First Plenary Council in 1852. Hennesey, *The First Council of the Vatican: The American Experience* (New York: Herder and Herder, 1963); idem, "Papacy and Episcopacy in Eighteenth- and Nineteenth-Century American Catholic Thought," *Records of the American Catholic Historical Society of Philadelphia* 77 (September 1966): 175-89; Jo Ann Manfra, "The Catholic Episcopacy in America, 1789-1852" (Ph.D. dissertation, University of Iowa, 1975) ch. 3. For a synopsis of that study, which is in the process of revision and enlargement, see idem, "The Politics of Ultimate Ends: The American Catholic Episcopacy, 1789-1852," in *An American Church*, ed. David J. Alvarez (Moraga CA, 1979) 43-52. See also Hennesey, "First Vatican Council: Views of the American Bishops," *Historical Records and Studies* 50 (1964): 27-39; idem, "National Traditions and the First Vatican Council," *Archivum Historiae Pontificiae* 7 (1969): 491-512. The Church did not accept this position until the Second Vatican Council, which opened in 1962. Donald E. Pelotte, *John Courtney Murray: Theologian in Conflict* (New York: Paulist Press, 1976) 74-100.

Certainly political and social pressures from Protestant America helped impel the prelates to embrace this position. Their liberalism clearly reflected a keen understanding of what was necessary in order to subsist institutionally in the United States: separation of church and state would prove as good, if not better, for the Catholic Church in America as the Reverend Lyman Beecher believed it to be for Congregationalism in Connecticut. On the other hand, some of the prelates clearly reached this conclusion of their own accord, claiming to know as a matter of faith what only bitter experience had taught other American religious groups such as the New England Puritans. When the bishops, then, urged a liberal church-state theory, thereby making an extraordinary break with the Western Christian tradition, they did so not simply as an expedient but also because they spoke out of as deeply felt a Catholic faith as any in the Old World. Although certainly not indifferent to humans' secular estate, America's prelates would separate church from state to protect and elevate the spiritual dimension. And they were free to do so because "separation of church and state" was a rough description of constitutional polity, acceptable at least in practice to almost all Catholics, and because the entire issue had not yet become directly entangled with European events and Roman responses to them.[4]

---

[4]Taking form in the Leonine Corpus, the Church's official position respecting the relationship of church to state was not clearly defined during the period under consideration. Much has been said about whether those American prelates who maintained a liberal perspective on the church-state issue did so as a matter of principle or of expediency. This debate, which came to be expressed in the terms *thesis* and *hypothesis,* revolved around the so-called Americanist controversy of the 1880s and 1890s. Foreshadowing this later phenomenon was the European reaction to the American bishops' distinctive contribution to the church-state problematic at Vatican I. As James Hennesey writes: "European theorists might dismiss their effort as sheer pragmatism. It seems instead to have been prompted by a keen pastoral awareness and the desire to seek out the best way of carrying on their apostolic mission in the modern world. As such, it merited at least as much consideration as shopworn formulas which in many cases were themselves only the relics of practical adaptations which had been achieved in the past centuries and in other political and cultural climates." Undoubtedly, pastoral concerns also prompted the liberal ecclesiology espoused by the nation's first bishops. But the evidence suggests that at least some of them "accepted," as Margaret M. Reher says their counterparts in the 1880s and 1890s did, "the situation of the American Church as the future model for the Church universal." They tended, that is, to support America's religious condition *in thesi*, not simply *in hypothesi*. Hennesey, *First Council of the Vatican*, 141-42; Reher, "The Church and the Kingdom of God in America: The Ecclesiology of the Americanists" (Ph.D. dissertation, Fordham University, 1972) 92; Manfra, "Catholic Episcopacy," 69-82, 86-87, 97-106. See also Reher, "Pope Leo XIII and Americanism," *Theological Studies* 34 (1973): 679-89; Thomas T. Love, *John Courtney Murray: Contemporary Church-State Theory* (Garden City NY: Doubleday,

Recent historiography has tended to ignore the contribution of the French-born bishops to this process. Indeed, the dialogue between bishops Simon Bruté, John David, and Benedict Flaget highlighted some of the issues confronting the hierarchy in defining a proper theoretical relationship between American pluralism and Roman Catholicism. The three men, ardent followers of events in their native France, maintained a special concern for recent European religious developments. Before coming to America all had known the brilliant French theologian Hugues-Félicité Robert de La Mennais, usually referred to simply as Lamennais, and thus were peculiarly attuned to news of the intellectual thunderheads that would gather about that internationally important figure.[5]

Lamennais, according to Alec Vidler, "was the founder, if anyone was, of modern ultramontanism, and of liberal catholicism, and perhaps of christian socialism, while he was pronounced to be an heresiarch and apostate by a church that has since appeared to adopt many of his ideas."[6] Lamennais spent nearly thirty years (1809-1836) developing the so-called "mennaisian" body of ideas. These embraced (1) a "common consent" philosophy positing that religious certitude is grounded in the general reason of the human race, in contrast to the then-favored Cartesian rationalism; (2) the ecclesiology of "ultramontanism"—enhancement of the power and authority of the papacy, in contrast to "gallicanism"—administrative independence from papal control of churches in each nation; and (3) the politics of Catholic liberalism, especially the doctrine of separation of church and state, in contrast to the assumption of their divinely ordained union or alliance.

Those three doctrines are by no means necessarily interdependent. Lamennais himself did not combine traditionalism and ultramontanism with liberalism until 1829. And Rome, while condemning mennaisian liberalism in 1832 and common-consent philosophy in 1834, ultimately canon-

---

1965) 9-31, 97; Alec R. Vidler, *Prophecy and Papacy: A Study of Lamennais, the Church, and the Revolution* (New York: Charles Scribner's Sons, 1954) 164n; Pelotte, *Murray,* 79, 141-85. Other studies of the Americanist controversy include Thomas T. McAvoy, *Great Crisis in American Catholic History* (Chicago: H. Regnery, 1957); Robert D. Cross, *The Emergence of Liberal Catholicism* (Cambridge: Harvard University Press, 1958); Gerald P. Fogarty, *The Vatican and the Americanist Crisis* (Rome: Università Gregoriana, 1974).

[5]Thomas W. Spalding, *Martin John Spalding: American Churchman* (Washington: Catholic University of America Press, 1973) 7.

[6]Vidler, *Prophecy and Papacy,* 13.

ized the ecclesiology of ultramontanism.[7] Mennaisianism, then, is as complicated as it is fascinating; for our purposes, however, we need only outline the evolution of Lamennais's ecclesiology of ultramontanism and his theory of church-state relationships.

From publication in 1809 of *Réflexions sur l'état de l'Église en France pendant le xviiie siècle, et sur sa situation actuelle* to publication in 1825-1826 of *De la religion considérée dans ses rapports avec l'ordre politique et civil*, Lamennais's dream of a great European social revival through a renaissance of Catholicism rested on the substitution of an ultramontane for a gallican doctrine of the relation between spiritual and temporal powers. According to Lamennais, gallican maxims, especially the doctrine that temporal sovereignty is completely independent of spiritual authority, had subjected the church in France to the bondage of a "democratic" state that was actually bent upon de-Christianizing and laicizing that country. Lamennais adhered to the traditional Christian assumption that temporal power is ultimately subordinate to spiritual authority. Confronted with the problem of how to make the spiritual power effective, Lamennais set forth what Vidler labels the distinctive notion of modern ultramontanism when he located divine authority, or the rule of God, in the Holy See. According to Lamennais only a Church that relied on the supernational authority of the papacy could prevent civil government, royal as well as democratic (Vidler argues persuasively that Lamennais never was a truly committed royalist), from "crushing all freedom, both in church and in state."[8]

A thoroughgoing ultramontanist, Lamennais nevertheless rejected, as early as 1814, the notion that the pope had a divinely ordained authority, direct or indirect, over kings in temporal matters. And in 1826 he actually anticipated his own eventual acceptance of a separation between church and state, which he was then in the process of censuring. Lamennais finally realized that something other than the ultramontane church-state doctrine would be required to guarantee the church the freedom necessary for the accomplishment of its mission, since ultramontanism stood scant chance of gaining dominance in France.[9]

---

[7]Ibid., 68-69, 184-253.

[8]Ibid., 44-59, 82-84, 101, 105-14, 118.

[9]In *Tradition de l'Église sur l'institution des évêques* (1814), maintains Vidler, Lamennais was saying that "if either the prince or the pope should be found to encroach on the other's

At this juncture Lamennais discovered the apparent compatibility of political liberalism and ultramontanism in other European countries, especially Belgium. He associated this compatibility with the common-consent philosophy, and was deeply dismayed by Rome's failure to support the Catholics of France in their opposition to governmental ordinances establishing state control of secondary education. Against this background, Lamennais published *Des Progrès de la révolution et de la guerre contre l'Église* (1829), in which he argued strongly for a combination of ultramontanism and liberalism as the only means of freeing the Church to bear effective witness to the universality of Christ's kingdom.[10] In short, he accepted the separation of religious and political spheres while yet maintaining that within the religious realm the locus of spiritual and moral authority resides in the Holy See.

As hostile as ever to conventional liberalism and gallicanism, he now differentiated these positions from those held by the "true" liberal and gallican. The liberal camp, he concluded, sheltered a nefarious remnant of French Jacobinism, which to him represented anarchy and de-Christianization, in addition to men who broadmindedly supported complete liberty for Catholics even though they had little sympathy with Catholicism. Respecting gallicanism, Lamennais continued to believe that in the name of a national church that movement had propped the altar against the throne and therefore represented despotism. "True" gallicans, however, would separate church from state in order to protect and elevate the Church.[11] La-

---

authority and sphere of responsibility or if either should plainly offend against the natural or divine law, he must expect to forfeit Lamennais's support." In *De la religion considérée dans ses rapports avec l'ordre politique et civil* (1826), Lamennais emphasizes that "the true dignity, the real strength, of bishops as of priests depends today on their detachment from public affairs; there is enough for them in the work of the church. The future of religion is assured; it will not perish, its foundations are unshakable. Separate it then from what is collapsing [that is, the political order]. Why try to combine things that do not belong together?" Vidler, *Prophecy and Papacy*, 44, 57, 113-15.

[10]Ibid., 114, 119-39. According to Harold J. Laski, the philosophy of common consent "left open the road to liberalism," since Lamennais "had only to convince himself that the majority of men disbelieved in ecclesiastical conservatism to be able to urge its untruth." Laski, *Authority in the Modern State* (New Haven, 1919) 213.

[11]Vidler distinguishes the meanings that the terms *liberal* and *liberalism* had in France in 1826. As for Lamennais's belief that France was becoming de-Christianized and laicized, Vidler reminds us that liberal democracy in that nation did "eventually and overtly issue in the *état laïque*." John Courtney Murray points out that the Jacobins used the term *laicization,* and that *the people* meant the sect of Jacobins, the political heirs of the philosophes. The French Rev-

mennais, although seemingly advocating a "christian retreat from politics," concludes Vidler, was "preparing the ground for the new christian political initiative—the liberal catholic initiative," which he knew would mean another revolution. In 1830 the theologian joined like-minded men in launching a daily newspaper, *L'Avenir*, dedicated to the promotion of liberal Catholicism as a fundamental element of the Catholic faith, not just a strategy for any particular age.[12]

In America, meanwhile, often expressing to one another their mutual concern about social disorder and "irreligion" in France, Bruté and David closely followed Lamennais's career. Before being recruited for the American mission by Flaget, Bruté had played an influential role in the publication of Lamennais's first book, and had been one of several churchmen important in the young intellectual's decision to enter the priesthood. He, as well as Flaget and David, maintained written contact with the increasingly eminent theologian. Moreover, in their correspondence with one another, they often made mention of "our dear friend Lamennais." In return, the Frenchman maintained a deferential concern for American church affairs. According to David, Lamennais expressed himself always "greatly interested in the Kentucky missions," where Flaget and David presided, and he sent them copies of all his new books as well as a subscription to the mennaisian monthly journal—*Le Mémorial catholique*, the predecessor of *L'Avenir*. At one point the theologian even suggested that Bruté, who had once nourished hopes of a literary career, write a history emphasizing the unique character of the church in the United States—a notion that flattered but unfortunately failed to move Bruté to sustained action.[13]

---

olution was, in effect, "Jacobin Sectarianism, as a set of ideas and as a sociological force." This laic state, which Murray refers to as "totalitarian democracy," destroyed the dyarchy of the individual and thus his or her freedom. Christopher Dawson observes that "the new [French] Republic as conceived by Robespierre and St. Just and by their master Rousseau before them was a spiritual community, based on definite moral doctrines and finding direct religious expression in an official civic cult. . . . Thus, the democratic community became a counter-church of which Robespierre was at once the high priest and the Grand Inquisitor, while Catholicism and atheism alike were ruthlessly proscribed." Vidler, *Prophecy and Papacy,* 108-10, 115, 137; Murray, "Leo XIII on Church and State: The General Structure of the Controversy," *Theological Studies* 14 (March 1953): 530; Christopher Dawson, *Beyond Politics* (New York: Sheed and Ward, 1939) 71.

[12]Vidler, *Prophecy and Papacy,* 136-37, 152-83.

[13]Ibid., 44, 49, 55, 61, 64, 70, 85, 265; Mary Salesia Godecker, *Simon Bruté de Rémur:*

The three émigrés also, of course, read the theologian's works. They were "almost the only books," Flaget once confessed, that he "read from the beginning to the end," since they were to him "sugar and honey."[14] Bruté even talked of preparing an English translation of one of them—the four-volume *Défense de l'essai sur l'indifférence en matière de religion.* Early in 1818 Lamennais sent three copies of that work to Bruté, adding that he was "preparing a second [volume] and if you persevere in your intention of translating it, you had better follow this new edition." Bruté, however, lacked the temperament for such a prolonged undertaking. Instead—and certainly as a more emphatic means of bringing the theologian's ideas to the United States—he invited Lamennais to join the American mission, an offer that was graciously declined.[15] As for David, the *Essai,* which he read in 1825, convinced him that "our logical ideas

---

First Bishop of Vincennes (St. Meinrad IN, 1931) 31-34, 41-42, 45, 68, 74, 80, 91-92, 119, 263, 359, 372; David to Bruté, 13 November 1826, 28 February 1832, Mount Saint Mary's Papers, Archives of the Sisters of Nazareth (ASN), Nazareth, Kentucky. Paul Leo Gregoire offers a terse and somewhat superficial treatment of the relationship between Lamennais and Bruté. Admittedly unconcerned with "any specific doctrine of Lamennais," and believing that Vidler's work is "more of an apology than a study of the man," Gregoire attempts "to evaluate the intimacy of the friendship, discover if possible the definite role Bruté played in Lamennais's ordination, and finally witness the final and irreconciled break in relations which occurred in 1836." In that year Bruté visited Lamennais, who by then was an apostate. At Lamennais's urging, Bruté, who was always making jottings, did collect notes for a history of American Catholicism, but the nearest he came to producing a book was a series of sketches on his boyhood during the French Revolution. Gregoire, "The Relations between Félicité de Lamennais and Simon Bruté" (M.A. thesis, University of Notre Dame, 1961) ii, iv, 1-80; Theodore Maynard, *The Reed and the Rock: Portrait of Simon Bruté* (New York: Green, 1942) 116-17; *Memoirs of the Right Reverend Simon Wm. Gabriel Bruté, D.D., First Bishop of Vincennes, with Sketches Describing His Recollections of Scenes Connected with the French Revolution, and Extracts from His Journal,* ed. James Roosevelt Bayley (New York, 1860) 93-183.

[14]Benedict Flaget to Bruté, 1 May 1830, Mount St. Mary's Papers, ASN.

[15]Maynard, *Reed and Rock,* 116-17. The first volume of the *Essai* was published in 1817, the second in 1820, and the third and fourth volumes in 1823. It is possible that as early as 1818 Bruté's ardor respecting Lamennais's work had begun to cool. Obviously smarting from Sulpician criticism of his apologetics, Félicité in May 1824 informed his brother that Bruté "is a fine soul, has a good mind, vivid imagination, but poor judgment. His adoration of the Sulpicians debases him to their level and one can hardly go lower than that. They do a lot of harm without knowing it." According to Theodore Maynard, Bruté was a "free lance"; although "he greatly admired and loved the Sulpicians, he was perhaps never really a Sulpician, except in name." Vidler, *Prophecy and Papacy,* 68-70; Gregoire, "Relations," 50-52; Maynard, *Reed and Rock,* 55.

on the principles of instinctive evidence'' as the source of religious certitude had been ''somewhat disturbed'' by common-consent philosophy.[16]

The American bishop here displayed a gift for understatement. In
France at that very moment, numerous dioceses were tearing themselves
apart over the respective merits of the Cartesian and common-consent phi-
losophies. This was dramatized in a virulent pamphlet war. And as early
as 1820 many members of the Society of Saint Sulpice had withdrawn their
initial support of Lamennais, in good part because he had broken from
Cartesian rationalism, of which the society's seminary was the long-standing guardian within the French church.[17] Yet David, a Sulpician along with
Bruté and Flaget, not only embraced the ''new'' philosophy—which had
made him ''clearly see now that each man, isolated from the rest of men,
that is, each particular reason isolated from other reasons, remains subject
to error''—but also informed Flaget that he wanted to have mennaisian logic
taught in the Bardstown, Kentucky, seminary by none other than its creator. In the interim, he thought, they might employ a newly published
mennaisian catechism—''the very idea'' proposed earlier by Flaget, he
noted—especially ''if it were translated into English.'' In reply, Flaget en-
thusiastically assured David that he had already written Lamennais and invited the scholar to accept an appointment at Bardstown. How Lamennais
couched his second declination we do not know.[18]

---

[16]David to Bruté, 23 December 1825, Mount St. Mary's Papers, ASN; J. Herman
Schauinger, *Cathedrals in the Wilderness* (Milwaukee: Bruce, 1952) 208. Unknown are
the exact number of the *Essai* volumes that David had read.

[17]It could be said that Rome gave some encouragement to the theological rectitude of the
philosophy of common consent by permitting the appearance of an Italian translation of *Défense de l'essai sur l'indifférence en matière de religion,* which Lamennais published in 1821—
that is, between the second and third volumes of the *Essai.* Vidler, *Prophecy and Papacy,* 70-
94.

[18]David to Bruté, 23 December 1825, Mount Saint Mary's Papers, ASN. Schauinger's discussion of this issue appears colored by the papal condemnation of common-consent philosophy. He tends to portray David's and Flaget's acceptance of this notion as more a matter of
heart than of head. The same is true of Thomas W. Spalding. Writing as late as 1973, Spalding
dismisses, or at least fails to take seriously, David's acceptance of Lamennais's ideas. ''Normally conservative in his theology,'' says Spalding, David ''was at this period [1826] *under
the spell* [italics mine] of Abbé Félicité De Lamennais.'' Vidler says nothing about a mennaisian catechism, but does tell us that an English translation of the *Essai* was indeed published,
though not until 1895. Schauinger, *Cathedrals,* 208-209; Spalding, *Martin John Spalding,*
7; Vidler, *Prophecy and Papacy,* 70.

In 1832, six months before Rome's first condemnation of various aspects of mennaisianism, David was still reading Lamennais's books "with singular pleasure." He also "read from time to time several articles of his new MISCELLANY" (most likely *L'Avenir*). Admittedly David had to struggle to grasp some of Lamennais's arguments, since "exposition of these fundamental doctrines does not always appear to me very clear. There is a subtly [*sic*], at least for me, which my old head has much trouble penetrating, because it is necessary for me several times to reread the same phrase."[19] David expressed such sympathetic thoughts despite the powerful hostility mennaisians had already aroused in France, especially among members of that nation's hierarchy, this time as a result of their writings in *L'Avenir*. "Instead of trying," as Vidler puts it, "to woo possible supporters gradually and tactfully" toward what most Frenchmen understandably viewed as an "unnatural union" between liberals and Catholics, *L'Avenir* employed "shock-tactics." In the midst of this turmoil Lamennais and his close associates suspended publication of the paper in November 1831 and voluntarily traveled to Rome to seek approval of their efforts.[20]

Unquestionably aware of both the escalation of the controversy and Lamennais's appeal to Rome, David remained calmly unimpressed by the negative reactions of the French bishops. He thought it "not surprising" that "they pursue at every opportunity the writer who has refuted them so well." He refused to condemn Lamennais's ideas out-of-hand, but said he would accept the eventual decision of the Holy See—the position of Lamennais himself.[21] Here David clearly articulated a deep commitment to the spiritual authority of the papacy shared by his fellow American bishops.

Lamennais's sensational appeal to Rome, buttressed by a memorandum in which he and other leading mennaisians informed the Holy See that a papal pronouncement on the issue was indispensable, may have been a

---

[19]David to Bruté, 28 February 1832, Mount Saint Mary's Papers, ASN. Schauinger's insistence that David "had not then [1832] seen any of the numbers of De Lamennais's paper *L'Avenir*" is questionable, since this journal was the "new" organ of mennaisianism, published from 16 October 1830 to 15 November 1831. Schauinger, *Cathedrals*, 209; Vidler, *Prophecy and Papacy*, 162. See also n. 24 below.

[20]Vidler, *Prophecy and Papacy*, 184-89.

[21]David to Bruté, 28 February 1832, Mount Saint Mary's Papers, ASN. Schauinger incorrectly dates Lamennais's appeal to Rome "within a year or so" after David's letter of 28 February 1832. Schauinger, *Cathedrals*, 209.

colossal strategic error: it is very possible that Rome would otherwise have remained silent. Pressed, however, by both the mennaisians and the French hierarchy, the recently appointed Gregory XVI issued the encyclical *Mirari vos*. Although not as thoroughly antimennaisian as sometimes inferred, the encyclical did condemn various mennaisian positions, particularly liberalism.[22] That, however, was not the end of it. During the first half of 1833 Lamennais interpreted the encyclical as a political act without any doctrinal authority and became increasingly radicalized, as reflected in his correspondence. His hope for the recovery of the Universal Church came to rest in God, not in the pope, and a deepening apocalyptic element infected his outlook. A letter clearly advocating principles that had been condemned in *Mirari vos*, and assumed to have been written by Lamennais following his submission, appeared in a Dutch newspaper, strongly suggesting that the theologian remained in a state of intellectual rebellion.[23]

In far-off America Bruté seems to have expressed irritation over Lamennais's apparent defiance of papal authority. In response, David assured Bruté that he himself was "attached [neither] to the person of Mr. De Lamennais" nor to the ideas that that scholar had espoused—apparently referring to two highly provocative *L'Avenir* pieces on the issue of episcopal nominations by the French government. Not yet having seen the essays, David had read only the mennaisians' defense of their position presented at the French government's trial of Lamennais and other authors of the articles in question. David found "much exaggeration and enthusiasm" in the mennaisian defense, but nevertheless reiterated his belief that Lamennais's adversaries had overre-

---

[22]The memorandum to the pope was dated 3 February 1832. *Mirari vos*, dated 15 August 1832, was issued fifteen days later. Vidler, *Prophecy and Papacy*, 194, 206-15.

[23]According to Vidler, before 1833 Lamennais "had assumed that the church would be preserved intact throughout" the time of upheaval, and that "the pope would be God's vice-regent in bringing about the fulfillment of his glorious promises." In the first six months of 1833, however, Lamennais came to the conclusion that "the church itself and the papacy, as at present constituted, belong to what is going to be condemned and destroyed." Until 1933, when M. Gustave Charlier proved that the Lamennais letter, printed in the Dutch paper on 22 February 1833, had been written on 1 July 1832—that is, before the encyclical *Mirari vos* had appeared—Lamennais's biographers assumed the letter had been written after Lamennais's submission of 10 September 1832. Vidler believes Rome knew the letter had indeed been written before the promulgation of *Mirari vos*. Vidler, *Prophecy and Papacy*, 221-34.

acted. In all of this the one thing David remained "absolutely in favor of" was "complete submission to the judgment of the Holy See."[24]

That proved to be Lamennais's course. In December 1833 he made a second and this time unqualified act of submission to *Mirari vos*. In return, Pope Gregory sent Lamennais a message applauding his act.[25] News of this so pleased David that he urged Flaget to follow the pope's example and "write a letter of congratulations to [Lamennais] and to adjoin to it my name." The letter would also serve another purpose—"a kind of recommendation" to the theologian, as erratic as he was energetic, "to be more on his guard in the future." Understanding the nature of this second submission, David thought the congratulatory note might also politely suggest that he and Flaget had "not approved" what Lamennais "has been obliged to retract." David said he had not yet seen those writings of Lamennais "where errors Bruté was angry about are found." But "excesses" were not entirely surprising, since he considered Lamennais a genius, and "all the great geniuses, who are commonly so enamored of their systems, [invariably] end up pushing their ideas to the most extreme consequences." Besides, Lamennais had made "a humble submission to authority." Finally, as David confided to Bruté, "between us, let it be said, I believe that his adversaries are [themselves] not exempt from prejudice and perhaps from passion."[26]

---

[24]David to Bruté, 4 May 1833, Mount Saint Mary's Papers, ASN. Schauinger cites in full an undated letter from David to Bruté, which he supposes was written following the second and final condemnation of mennaisianism in 1834. In substance and many particulars the letter is identical to that of 4 May 1833, although Schauinger's reading of some particulars does differ. He fails to set the letter within the context of French events, not explaining, for example, the "trial" to which David was referring. In dating the letter 1834, Schauinger assumes that its contents express David's and Bruté's shock over Lamennais's post-1833 activities. He also apparently relies on the supposed 1834 letter in reaching the conclusion that in 1832 David had not seen, let alone read, any issues of *L'Avenir* (see n. 19). Taken together, David's 28 February 1832 and 4 May 1833 letters strongly suggest that while he had not read those *L'Avenir* pieces published in November 1830 that resulted in the French government's trial of Lamennais and others, he had indeed seen some issues of that paper. (See Vidler for details respecting developments before, during, and after the trial.) Schauinger, *Cathedrals*, 209-10; Vidler, *Prophecy and Papacy,* 170-72.

[25]Ibid., 237-41.

[26]David to Bruté, 11 May 1834, Mount Saint Mary's Papers, ASN. Schauinger fails to mention this letter. And David fails to identify those writings of Lamennais in which Bruté discovered "errors." We do know that from 1831 through 1833 Bruté warned Lamennais against denying—through word or act—papal authority. Also, in mid-May 1833, a French translation

Two months later the ideas Lamennais had been expressing in his private correspondence during the first half of 1833 appeared in print with publication of *Paroles d'un Croyant*. There followed a second and final condemnation of mennaisian doctrines: on 15 July 1834 Gregory XVI issued the encyclical *Singulari nos* condemning both the book and the philosophy of common consent.[27]

Unquestionably, Lamennais's "excesses" had disturbed David as well as Bruté and Flaget, especially the theologian's virtual denial of even the spiritual authority of the pope. And all three readily accepted the ultimate papal condemnation.[28] Yet the fact remains that mennaisianism intellectually animated these French-born bishops, at least as much as the friendship they felt toward the great theologian. As David told Bruté in May 1834: "I am not able to disabuse myself of the feelings of esteem and friendship for the good Lamennais."[29]

This brings us to the last and most interesting dimension of the Lamennaisian connection. David, Flaget, and Bruté brought both French and American sensibilities to their reading of Lamennais's works. They understood the vast difference between church-state relations in France—in-

---

of *Le livre des pèlerins polonais* by Adam Mickiewicz appeared. An apocalyptic encouragement to Polish exiles, the book resembles and to a certain extent influenced Lamennais's later *Paroles d'un Croyant*. The epilogue features some verses addressed to Poland that Lamennais composed in 1832. Bruté was aware of this development. Jean Lamennais, brother of the theologian, had written him that, in a brief to the Bishop of Rennes dated 5 October 1833, the pope complained that the publication of this book and the letter in the Dutch paper were public evidences that Lamennais refused to accept the judgment of the Holy See. Jean interpreted the brief as a papal order for Félicité's second, or complete, submission to the doctrine of *Mirari vos* and said that Rennes was divided on the issue. Bruté requested that Bishop John Purcell ask Flaget to write Félicité about the matter. Schauinger, *Cathedrals*, 206-10; Gregoire, "Relations," 58-60; Vidler, *Prophecy and Papacy*, 228-35, 238; Bruté to Purcell, 20 January 1834, Cincinnati Collection, Archives of the University of Notre Dame (AUND), Notre Dame IN.

[27]The book was published on 30 April 1834. Vidler, *Prophecy and Papacy*, 227, 242-53.

[28]With the exception of Lamennais himself, all leading members of the mennaisian school in France made complete submissions to the doctrine of *Singulari nos*. Ibid., 254.

[29]David to Bruté, 11 May 1834, Mount Saint Mary's Papers, ASN. In 1836, shortly after having failed to persuade Lamennais to submit to both papal encyclicals, Bruté wrote his "Dear Friend" Félicité, beseeching him to return to "the sole faith of the Catholic Church." Bruté also wrote Pope Gregory XVI and informed him that Lamennais "seemed to deny entirely the authority of the Church as infallible judge of doctrine. . . . The consensus . . . is that he has lost his faith. I would like to think otherwise . . . to continue to hope that [he] will return to the Church and be converted." Gregoire, "Relations," 61-72.

deed, in all of Europe—and in the United States. For example, in the same passage in which David embraced Lamennais as the foremost defender of traditional church-state doctrine against laicization, he also acknowledged the compatibility of that scholar's liberalism with fundamental American political precepts. "God breathed on him," wrote David of Lamennais, "in order to maintain His church and the defense of the Catholic state." At the same time, he added, "I see a great enthusiasm for liberty, which is very suitable for our United States but which scarcely appears to be proper and suitable for France—that is, not in accordance with the situation in France."[30] Certainly David, Flaget, and Bruté had not entirely transcended their French experience, but the American circumstance was indeed freeing them from thinking in strictly Old World terms about the relationship between political and religious authority.

Particularly illustrative of this were the sentiments of Bruté, Lamennais's friend, confidant, and critical admirer, and probably the most scholarly and skeptical of these three French-born members of the American hierarchy. In a remarkable three-cornered correspondence between himself, Bishop John England, and Judge William Gaston of North Carolina (a prominent Catholic layman) that had been prompted by postrevolutionary French developments, Bruté explored the subject of "holy alliance & republican alliance."[31] An admirer of Bruté's theological acumen, England yet thought Bruté possessed an imperfect understanding of American freedom and a residual respect for pre-1830, or even pre-1789, France. Denying that he himself was an ultrademocrat, England attempted to diagnose Bruté's set of mind in a letter to his friend. "You appear to make great mistakes of my sentiments," he said, "when you imagine me favorable to the infidel school of France & [its] revolutionary projects—you do not condemn them more than I do.—But you run, and I can not blame you for it, to the extreme of attachment to all the ancient regimé.—I respect those who do—but I differ from their views & opinions—though I unsparingly condemn their raucous and irreligious enemies." Having disavowed any enthusiasm for the "July Revolution" that in 1830 overthrew the reactionary Bourbon restoration and replaced it with a constitutional

[30]David to Bruté, 28 February 1832, Mount Saint Mary's Papers, ASN.

[31]Bruté to William Gaston, 30 December 1823, Charleston, South Carolina, Papers, 1814-1839, AUND; Maynard, *Reed and Rock,* 154.

monarchy, England then proceeded to contrast what he interpreted as
Bruté's unenlightened political ideals to his own conservative republicanism.
"I am attached to the American Constitution," he insisted, "but I am not blind
to its great imperfections, nor am I reckless of the inordinate ambition & gross
corruption which I fear will at an early period produce its ruin.—I do not think
our confederation is likely to last a great many centuries.—But my duty is
whilst I live under it to live according to its principles."[32]

This appears to be an unfair contrast, failing as it does to recognize the
complexity of Bruté's thought. Indeed, the Frenchman shared with England and Gaston an admiration for the American system, thinking highly
of it as "such a practical case of sincere choice."[33] Unlike England, however, Bruté—always the intellectual—did not hesitate to go beyond mere
acknowledgment of those imperfections and corruptions that might result
in the failure of the Great Experiment. Acutely aware of the distance between liberal theory and practice, he offered specific criticisms. Inevitably
"in favor of religious liberty," he noted that as president of Saint Mary's
College in Baltimore, for example, he had made "a few little changes in
the prospectus" in the direction of "openness and frank discussions about
religion." This was in pointed contrast to the alleged disallowance of such
freedoms in England's own educational institution.[34] But "polemic an-
ecdote[s]" against Catholicism made Bruté question whether or not Americans actually practiced what they preached. He found it disheartening to
"see how far this country, where good sense and faith are so much in theoretical esteem and daily set up in declamatory pieces as the pride of sober

[32]John England to Bruté, 31 October 1831, Mount Saint Mary's Papers, ASN. In his dissertation, Patrick Carey accepts and then applies to most members of the hierarchy England's
interpretation of Bruté's state of mind, a position he subsequently modified in his book on England. Carey, "John England and Irish-American Catholicism, 1815-1842: A Study of Conflict" (Ph.D. dissertation, Fordham University, 1975) 217, 265-67, 314-15; idem, *An Immigrant
Bishop: John England's Adaptation of Irish Catholicism to American Republicanism* (Yon-
kers, 1982). In 1822 England founded the *United States Catholic Miscellany* and was always
begging Bruté—once described by England as "one of the best of men"—to send him articles.
Believing, however, that his friend was too scholarly and eccentric, England opposed Bruté's
nomination to the hierarchy. England to Paul Cullen, rector, 16 December 1833, Irish College,
Rome: American Papers, 1828-1849, no. 12; Maynard, *Reed and Rock,* 152-54.

[33]Bruté to Gaston, 28 August 1828, Charleston, South Carolina, Papers, 1814-1839, AUND.

[34]Bruté considered England to be one of "our most respected . . . & loved" bishops.
Bruté also claimed he was as "eager as Gaston to see [England] become your own [John]
Carroll." Bruté to Gaston, 4 January, 14 August 1823, ibid.

people, does however in reality and practice neglect to judge assertions by their grounds.'' Bruté also sadly considered the limitations of other American freedoms. Reading ''those strange & humbling bills of Maryland and Virginia,'' mandating forced removal to Africa of all freed slaves, Bruté asked: ''What now of all those principles assumed for the main ground of merit of the great liberators & Vindicators of the first & inalienable right of men, *Liberty!*'' For millions of black Americans, personal freedom remained an ''undefined and ineffective'' concept.[35]

Nevertheless, once he had become a bishop, Bruté strongly urged the compatibility of Catholicism and republicanism. His pastoral of August 1835, for example, emphasized that here in America there flourished a ''new'' (or strictly spiritual) ''carrying out of the original Divine Commission given to the Church by her Lord: 'Go and teach all nations.' '' And he had come to share his confreres' confidence that Catholicism could and would prosper within the American social and political environment.[36]

When discussion turned to France, however, Bruté's concern over the ''excess of modern liberalism'' darkened his perspective. Back in 1793, as a badly frightened fourteen-year-old, he had witnessed trials of priests conducted by the regular criminal court of Rennes, ''one of the three Tribunals,'' he recalled, ''which supplied the Guillotine with victims.'' For a time, another of those tribunals actually met in a room over his family's apartment, where the Brutés once had concealed two priests in ''all that awful and anxious privacy,'' he remembered, ''which their own safety and our own prescribed.'' Not surprisingly, he declared himself profoundly skeptical of supposed similarities between the French and the American

---

[35]Bruté to Gaston, n.d., and 29 February 1831, ibid.

[36]*Memoirs of Bruté*, 68; Maynard, *Reed and Rock*, 214-15; *Selected Writings of Simon Gabriel Bruté*, ed. Thomas G. Smith (Emmitsburg, 1977) 33-35. Bruté's enthusiasm about Catholicism's future prospects is plainly evident in a series of sketches he wrote for the Cincinnati *Catholic Telegraph* and the Vincennes *Western Sun* depicting conditions in his diocese (which encompassed a 55,000-mile area). He reported that ''all seem to welcome the establishment of this new Catholic diocese [Vincennes], all view the settlement of the bishop [Bruté] among us as a thing no less favourable to society than to religion.'' His diocese was fortunate, he said, in that it was ''universally on the liberal side.'' It ''had never blue laws [nor] blue habits. . . . All honors, all trusts, legislative, municipal and financial lay open to all; our assembly has Catholics amidst its members both in the House of Representatives and the Senate; society numbers them in all its lines of best usefulness and highest respectability, this is no ground for tracts and trash, fair play for religion, peace and prosperity for our country, is the only spirit and motto.'' *Selected Writings of Bruté*, 21-23.

revolutionary experiences.³⁷ Likewise, he doubted Lamennais's conten-
tion that the liberals of the 1830 Revolution were any "truer" than their
1789 predecessors. The July Revolution had seen the "overthrow of [a
monarchy] not for the principle substitution of any given system, but merely
as in 1789 an overthrow of what existed to begin experiment & a trial of
strength . . . amidst quite different parties!" In any event, he convinced
himself that Frenchmen who now talked of "imitating the system in America" actually knew nothing of the United States Constitution. A *"french
United States"* was only a fantasy, in part because France lacked that key
ingredient of American federalism: the important political subdivision
known as the state. The eighty-six departments of France lacked even a
"shadow of resemblance with [America's] 24 States."³⁸

Besides contrasting the political systems of France and America, criticizing the effectiveness of the latter, and fearing that the excesses of modern liberalism might destroy religion and therefore civilization, Bruté
ultimately questioned the efficacy of universal popular sovereignty, strongly
doubting that humans could truly govern themselves until the "real corruption of mankind is mended."³⁹ Skeptical and critical of modern liberalism Bruté indeed remained. But by no means did he qualify as an
unreflective reactionary; his pessimism about democracy, for example,
differed from John England's more in degree than in kind. He simply could
not bring himself to share the kind of naive admiration of American and
post-1830 French republicanism that characterized some American prelates of French background. A few years after the second condemnation of
mennaisianism, for example, Bishop Mathias Loras confided to his ecclesiastical colleague Anthony Blanc that he was himself a "bit of a Republican."⁴⁰ When the Bishop of Mobile, Michael Portier, visited France, he

³⁷Bruté to Gaston, 7 June 1829, Charleston, South Carolina, Papers, 1814-1839, AUND;
Memoirs of Bruté, 93-100, 179-80. Simon's father served as superintendent of the royal do-
mains in Brittany until his death in 1786, following which Madame Bruté operated a printing
business and was allowed to continue to reside in the Parliament House. From Bruté's vantage
point Thomas Jefferson was a "fanatical philosopher" for holding that "rivers of blood & years
[of] desolation may be necessary for France to have [the] liberty of America." *Memoirs of
Bruté*, 9-10, 26; Bruté to Gaston, 1 October 1830, Charleston, South Carolina, Papers, 1814-
1839, AUND.

³⁸Bruté to Gaston, 29 September 1830, Charleston, South Carolina, Papers, 1814-1839,
AUND.

³⁹Bruté to Gaston, 1 October 1830, ibid.

⁴⁰Mathias Loras to A. Blanc, 27 December 1838, New Orleans Collection, AUND.

discussed American and French republicanism with Blanc's brother, and was "glad to see that the Archbishops of Lyons and Paris have . . . shown themselves as good Republicans."[41] Such sentimental Gallic attitudes ultimately provoked American-born Bishop John Chanche's annoyance. Writing to Bishop Blanc, Chanche dryly noted that, although he was naturally happy to learn that the prelates of France were staunchly republican, "it is droll to see them writing about the happy government of the United States and lauding the labouring classes."[42]

Certainly it was the developing convictions of articulate native-born and Irish-born, rather than French-born, bishops that contributed a special impetus to the systematic and distinctively American church-state perspective. Yet the pervasive gallicanism of the period clearly influenced their arguments. Theoretically supporting papal spiritual jurisdiction, gallicans practiced a national church-state unification as well as national autonomy. America's prelates, as Lamennais had done, embraced the latter and rejected the former, in large part, it seems, because of what Sidney Mead once referred to as "the peculiar experience of the old Christianity in the New World." In short, their nationalism remained strongly influenced by the United States Constitution, which precludes the union of church and state at the same time that it elevates and protects the consciences of the nation's citizens.[43]

---

[41]Michael Portier to A. Blanc, 1848, ibid. Anthony Blanc's brother reported from France that he also had "faith in Republican government" (14 August 1849, ibid.).

[42]John Chanche to A. Blanc, 15 April 1848, ibid.

[43]Sidney E. Mead, "Religion of (or and) the Republic" (paper delivered at the Johns Hopkins Religious Studies Conference, Harwichport MA, 23-25 August 1973) 21; Manfra, "Catholic Episcopacy," 97-106; idem, "Politics of Ultimate Ends," 47. Vidler reminds us that the Declaration of 1682 contains the so-called gallican liberties or four articles: "(i) that the pope's jurisdiction is in things spiritual and not in things temporal, and therefore kings are not subject to ecclesiastical authority in such matters; (ii) that the authority of a general council is superior to that of the holy see; (iii) that the pope's authority is limited by the rules, customs and institutions of the universal church, and therefore the institutions of the Church of France remain inviolable; and (iv) that the judgment of the pope in matters of faith is not irreversible until it has been confirmed by the consent of the church." The American hierarchy collectively maintained some of those very positions. Vidler also tells us that Lamennais "would have been well advised to make the best, instead of the worst, of the gallican liberties." Actually, while in the midst of breaking with Catholicism, Lamennais admits in Troisièmes Mélanges (1835) that the gallicans "stood for safeguards against the abuse of papal power, which the history of the church had shown to be necessary." Vidler, Prophecy and Papacy, 109-10n, 257-58, 282.

———— ·● 10 ●· ————

The "Lively Experiment" in Canada

Robert T. Handy

Early in his book, *The Lively Experiment: The Shaping of Christianity in America,* Sidney E. Mead observes that "it is not too much to say that in America space has played the part that time has played in the older cultures of the world."[1] In this and in other comments, he does what many historians of religion in America have done: points to significant contrasts between American and other (especially European) cultures. While historical comparisons of European and American religious life have often been attempted, there has been little thorough work by scholars of religion comparing Canadian and American scenes. The Canadian experience of religion remains too little known in the United States, yet there is much that can be learned from it. The developments of religion in the two nations have sufficient similarities that comparisons can be effective, but they also have certain differences so that informative contrasts can be drawn.

General treatments that deal with the United States of America and the Dominion of Canada usually refer at least briefly to religion, suggesting the need for increased attention to these matters.[2] The completion in 1972

---

[1](New York: Harper & Row, 1936) 6.

[2]E.g., cf. Gerald M. Craig, *The United States and Canada* (Cambridge: Harvard University Press, 1968) 35; Seymour Martin Lipset, "Revolution and Counter-Revolution—The United States and Canada," in Thomas R. Ford, ed., *The Revolutionary Theme in*

of the three-volume work, *A History of the Christian Church in Canada,* with its excellent bibliographical aids, marks a new stage in the church historiography of the younger and numerically much smaller nation, and can contribute to some fruitful comparative studies of the religious histories of these North American neighbors.[3] The early 1970s also saw the appearance of some specialized studies of aspects of Canadian history that are related in significant ways to American religious life.[4]

One way to advance the comparative effort now is to make use of interpretations developed from one historical setting to probe the other, with the expectation that significant similarities and differences will be highlighted. Though Mead has not touched on the Canadian scene in his writings, his work has been familiar to Canadian religious historians. In several instances one or another of his interpretative themes has been cited to point out certain contrasts and congruences. This suggests that a careful look at the Canadian scene from the vantage point of his concepts could be fruitful.

The very title of Mead's book of interpretative essays, *The Lively Experiment,* immediately discloses an important difference between the two contexts, for it is not the title that would be chosen for a similar book on Canadian religion. Those British North American provinces that did not support the American Revolution and were then the recipients of Loyalist migrations clung more firmly to European religious traditions than did the American states. Efforts to combine in appropriate ways traditional and indigenous influences have been much more characteristic of Canadian history than the yearning for fresh starts and new departures that marked the *novus ordo seclorum* to the south. As Goldwin French has put it, ''In this light the destiny of Canada was not to figure as a great experiment, cut off from the history of its peoples, but to prolong and blend its traditions in a

---

Contemporary America (Lexington: University of Kentucky Press, 1967) 44-49; Dennis H. Wrong, *American and Canadian Viewpoints* (Washington: American Council on Education, 1955) 13-17.

[3]Vol. 1: H. H. Walsh, *The Church in the French Era: From Colonization to the British Conquest* (Toronto: Ryerson Press, 1966); vol. 2: John S. Moir, *The Church in the British Era: From the British Conquest to Confederation* (Toronto: McGraw-Hill Ryerson, 1972); vol. 3: John Webster Grant, *The Church in the Canadian Era: The First Century of Confederation* (Toronto: McGraw-Hill Ryerson, 1972). Grant is the general editor of the series.

[4]E.g., see Richard Allen, *The Social Passion: Religion and Social Reform in Canada, 1914-1928* (Toronto: University of Toronto Press, 1971); Robin W. Winks, *The Blacks in Canada: A History* (New Haven: Yale University Press, 1971).

new context."[5] In an important summary, John Webster Grant has stressed the Canadian religious commitment to the basic values of Christendom, stressing that

> a corollary to this constant reference to an existing Christendom was the virtual lack of any suggestion that the task of the churches in Canada might be to institute a new Christian society that would be an alternative to older ones and perhaps even render them obsolete. The recurrent theme of the new Christendom led in the United States to almost endless experimentation. In Canada, by comparison, church life was strikingly devoid of the bizarre or even the novel.[6]

Grant illustrates the lack of innovativeness by noting that Canadian religious controversies were usually reflections from the outside, and that suspected heretics were popularizers of critical ideas imported from Europe. Of course, his point must not be pressed too far. There has been much traditionalism in American religious life, and considerable boldness and daring in Canada, yet one would still not choose the image of experiment for a book of essays on Canadian religion.

A closely related difference between the two histories is revealed by Mead's discussions of the historylessness of American Protestantism, in which he traces the antihistorical bias that has long characterized much American religious life. Denominations, especially those of left-wing sectarian background, have appealed "over all churches and historical traditions to the authority of the beliefs and practices of primitive Christianity as pictured in the New Testament." This perspective became widely current in a formative period in American church history. According to Mead, "The constellation of ideas prevailing during the Revolutionary epoch in which the denominations began to take shape were: the idea of pure and normative beginnings to which return was possible; the idea that the intervening history was largely that of aberrations and corruptions which was better ignored; and the idea of building anew in the American wilderness on the true and ancient foundations."[7] Such interpreters of the Canadian church scene as Neil Gregor Smith and Goldwin French have directly re-

---

[5]"The Evangelical Creed in Canada," in W. L. Morton, ed., *The Shield of Achilles: Aspects of Canada in the Victorian Age* (Toronto: McClelland and Stewart, 1968) 29.

[6]Grant, *The Church in the Canadian Era*, 214.

[7]Mead, *The Lively Experiment*, 109, 111.

ferred to Mead's analysis at this point and insisted that it does not fit their Northern dominion. While admitting that the ties of Canadian churches with Britain and America have led to some irrelevant controversies and to doctrinal conservatism, French finds that nevertheless such links had the "positive merit" of inhibiting "the emergence of that sense of history-lessness so characteristic of nineteenth century American Protestantism." Quoting from *The Lively Experiment,* he reports that few Canadian preachers would have argued, as did John Cotton, "that any church was a near replica of what would be established 'if the Lord Jesus were here himself in person.' Significantly, too, no major Canadian denomination would claim with the Disciples of Christ that it was 'picking up' the 'lost threads of primitive Christianity.' "[8] Mead's concentration on Protestantism, especially evangelical and left-wing Protestantism, has enabled him to stress as heavily as he has the theme of historylessness; greater attention to Anglican, Roman Catholic, and Eastern Orthodox histories might show greater similarities to the Canadian scene.

David W. Lotz, however, has shown that the concept of historyless-ness can also apply to churches of conservative, right-wing, Reformation background. He illustrates how the Lutheran Church-Missouri Synod had a dynamic of return to "normative beginnings" (to the biblical teachings of Luther and the Lutheran Confessions) and harbored "the idea that the intervening history was largely that of aberrations and corruptions"—in this case the intervening history was that of the "decline and fall" of "true Lutheranism" in the eighteenth and nineteenth centuries.[9] Thus Mead's thesis may apply to a wider range of churches than he had originally suspected, and Canadian church historians may have to take a second look at several of their smaller, more conservative denominations with this in mind.

One of the strengths of Mead's interpretative efforts is that he keeps in his purview both intellectual and institutional factors and their interrelationships. Though he searches for the ideas out of which institutions grow and the meanings that organizational configurations reveal, he has dealt

---

[8]"The Impact of Christianity on Canadian Culture and Society before 1867," *Theological Bulletin, McMaster Divinity College,* no. 3 (January 1968): 19. The quotations are from Mead, *The Lively Experiment,* 110-11. See also Neil Gregor Smith, "Nationalism and the Canadian Churches," *Canadian Journal of Theology* 9 (1963): 116.

[9]"The Sense of Church History in Representative Missouri Synod Theology," *Concordia Theological Monthly* 42 (1971): 597-619; see esp. 602.

responsibly with the institutional structures of religious life as they have been. Many years ago the late H. H. Walsh, referring appreciatively to Mead's discussion of the way that denominationalism combines features of both church and sect, stressed that the theme of organization is important to both American and Canadian church history.[10] Mead's description of the denomination as "a voluntary association of like-hearted and like-minded individuals, who are united on the basis of common beliefs for the purpose of accomplishing tangible and defined objectives" has been much debated.[11] It fits best for the early nineteenth century, the period he had especially in view when he framed that generalization. It has also been useful in Canada; Goldwin French has observed that "in British North America as in the United States, a number of denominations developed—religious communities whose members were held together in each case by their pursuit of a common objective."[12]

Mead's definition of denominationalism may actually be valid for a longer period of time for the Canadian than for the American churches. In part because of denominational divisions concerning such issues as revivalism and slavery, combined with the varied and voluminous currents of immigration in the nineteenth century, the American scene early became considerably more complex than the Canadian. The tendency for the rapidly increasing diversity of American religious life to become considerably internalized in the denominations, especially the larger ones, soon appeared—a pattern intensified by the intense competitiveness of the time. In Canada, however, the nineteenth-century trend was toward the consolidation of denominational families, and the "like-hearted and like-minded" characteristics persisted longer. And though American Protestants saw the Roman Catholic church as a menace, they did not have to confront any such reality as the consolidated power of the Catholic Church in French-speaking Quebec. This tended further to prolong the cohesiveness and purposiveness of the other Canadian churches. That Mead's basic insight can apply to both situations suggests that despite the traditionalism of Canadian religion and the historylessness of much American Protestantism, there

---

[10]"The Challenge of Canadian Church History to Its Historians," *Canadian Journal of Theology* 5 (1959): 167.

[11]Mead, *The Lively Experiment*, 104.

[12]French, "The Evangelical Creed in Canada," 17.

are some important functional similarities in the way denominations operate. This may be one of the reasons why ministers and members have been able to move back and forth between Canadian and American churches in most periods without great apparent difficulty.

The rise of religious liberty is an important aspect of the histories of both countries. There are many parallels in the two stories; in both, the facts of religious multiplicity, the separation of church and state, and the victory of voluntaryism in religion are central. The patterns and chronologies are different, however. In the United States important turning points were the First Amendment and the disestablishment of religion in the states, completed by legislation in Massachusetts in 1833. In Canada the most dramatic struggle erupted regarding the lands (the vast Clergy Reserves) set aside for the support primarily of the Church of England. The great majority of this land was located in Upper Canada. It took many years before the resourceful resistance to the secularization of these lands was finally overcome in 1854. The law that settled the issue stated that ''it is desirable to remove all semblance of connexion between Church and State.''[13] Nevertheless, by providing for the continuation of lifelong stipends to the clergy then receiving them, and allowing them to give their churches the estimated total lump sum due them, the principle was compromised. This is one illustration of a point often made: that religious freedom and the separation of church and state mean somewhat different things in the two contexts. John Moir puts it in these words: ''Canada has rejected the European tradition of church establishment without adopting the American ideal of complete separation. Here no established church exists, yet neither is there an unscalable wall between religion and politics if for no other reason than that much of the Canadian Constitution is unwritten.''

Canadians ''assume the presence of an unwritten separation of church and state,'' he adds, in an ''ill-defined—and difficult to define—relationship'' that is peculiarly Canadian.[14] Gerald M. Craig makes a similar point with specific application to education: ''It is official doctrine in the United States that there is a 'wall of separation' between church and state, but this view has never prevailed in Canada, particularly in the school system.''[15]

---

[13] 18 Victoria Cap. 2 (1854), as cited in John S. Moir, ed., *Church and State in Canada, 1627-1867: Basic Documents* (Toronto: McClelland & Stewart, 1967) 244.

[14] Ibid., xiii.

[15] Craig, *United States and Canada*, 35.

Noting that there is much more religious instruction in publicly financed schools than in the United States, he shows how varied the educational picture is in the Canadian provinces. The range goes from Newfoundland, where the schools are denominationally controlled, through the dual school system of Quebec to British Columbia, where the public educational system is much like that of the United States.

It is instructive to appreciate the lack of any "wall of separation" (Thomas Jefferson's image) between church and state in Canada, for Mead has regretted its role in American church-state relations. He believes that Madison's concept of a "line of separation between the rights of religion and the Civil authority" is much better—more descriptive, fluid, and forward looking.[16] This image of a line of separation might well be pursued in comparative study of the churches and the civil authorities in the two nations. Such an effort would perhaps show greater similarities in church-state patterns than have been suspected, in part because of the overuse of Jefferson's image of the wall.

Granted that religious freedom has somewhat different meanings in the two countries, how do we account for it? In his complex analysis of the rise of religious liberty in America, Mead emphasizes the importance of Enlightenment thought and its application. In part because others had neglected it somewhat, he has stressed the role of the rationalists in the achievement of religious liberty in the United States, noting that they especially were interested in giving it theoretical justification. "Most of the effectively powerful intellectual, social, and political leaders were rationalists," he writes, "and these men made sense theoretically out of the actual, practical situation which demanded religious freedom." The sons of the Enlightenment consistently labeled the various religious bodies as "sects" and insisted that their role was "to define, articulate, disseminate, and inculcate the basic religious belief essential for the existence and well-being of the society." In this view, the distinctive tenets of the religious bodies were quite secondary. Often unthinkingly, the churches "accepted by implication the typically rationalist view that only what the churches held and taught in common . . . was really relevant for the well-

---

[16]"Neither Church nor State: Reflections on James Madison's 'Line of Separation,' " *Journal of Church and State* 10 (1968): 349-51. Along with half a dozen other essays Mead published since *The Lively Experiment,* this is reprinted in *The Nation with the Soul of a Church* (New York: Harper & Row, 1975).

being of the society and the state."[17] In Canada, however, the Enlightenment spirit in religion and in politics was largely suppressed. Both the American and the French Revolutions were generally rejected. And, as H. H. Walsh once put it: "Perhaps even more significant in creating a basis for a common Canadianism was a third rejection, that of the Enlightenment. The closest either of the Canadas came to the Enlightenment, which has played such a prominent role in shaping reform movements in the rest of the new world, was during the rebellious era of the 1930's."[18] The rebellions failed; and the element that Mead sees as so important to the American story of religious freedom is largely missing from the Canadian.

Other factors must also be considered in an effort to clarify more fully the differences between American and Canadian patterns of religious freedom. The Churches of England and Scotland had many loyal supporters in Canada, and as those churches continued to be established by law back home, why shouldn't their offspring have privileged status in the provinces? Moreover, the profoundly different Roman Catholic histories of the two lands must especially be stressed. Catholicism has been a minority church in America since the earliest beginnings of European settlement, but the Roman Catholic Church dominated the long French period of Canadian history, and in Quebec has remained the church of the overwhelming majority. Characterized by strong ultramontane tendencies, French-Canadian Catholicism was conspicuously anti-Enlightenment at a formative time.

At the same time that Mead emphasizes the importance of the Enlightenment tradition in the rise of religious liberty in the United States, he attributes the evasion of its challenges by the evangelical denominations as a principal cause of nineteenth-century Protestantism's greatest failure— theological structure. Here there are some very interesting parallels between American and Canadian religious histories. Scholars of religion in Canada have been much aware of the limitations of the theological life of Protestantism, usually attributing them to the domination of British scholarship. Gerald R. Cragg has remarked that "Anglo-Canadian theology has been painfully diffident, content to repeat what others have formulated, and

---

[17]Mead, *The Lively Experiment*, 36, 65.

[18]"A Canadian Christian Tradition," in John Webster Grant, ed., *The Churches and the Canadian Experience* (Toronto: Ryerson Press, 1963) 146.

hesitant to write anything at all. To Edinburgh and to Glasgow, as to Oxford and Cambridge, we are immeasurably indebted. It is unfortunate our gratitude has so effectively stultified our originality."[19] John Webster Grant has emphasized the same point: "Many writers have called attention to the scarcity in the Canadian church of intellectual originality and mystical imagination, although learning and piety were always highly valued."[20] Some of the same factors were at work in weakening the theological life of Protestantism in both nations. The interplay of what Mead has called traditionalism, sectarian-pietism, and rationalism has been different in the two contexts, but in Canada as well as in the United States churches of both established and free-church backgrounds went along with the general rejection of rationalism. Moir has explained that "the very victory of Reason in the American and French revolutions produced a political and religious reaction among the churches in the remaining British colonies in America that fostered a return to orthodox Christian beliefs."[21] The continuing anti-Americanism, especially following the War of 1812, further diminished possibilities of an increase of Enlightenment influence in Canada. Jerald C. Brauer has suggested that Mead's basic generalization about the relation of Christianity to the Enlightenment needs to be tested;[22] its testing by comparative study of both Canadian and American scenes might prove to be most fruitful.

As part of a wide-ranging debate about the nature of civil religion in the United States, Mead has argued that the Republic, as it emerged, offered a cosmopolitan, universal theology. In his article, "The Nation with the Soul of a Church," he declares that the theology of the synergistic and theonomous religion of the Republic stands up against idolatrous tendencies equally with Christianity, and perhaps more effectively. He contends that "the Christian sects carried the universal vision until it was, largely

[19]"The European Wellsprings of Canadian Christianity," *Theological Bulletin, McMaster Divinity College*, no. 3 (January 1968): 9.

[20]Grant, *The Church in the Canadian Era*, 13.

[21]Moir, *The Church in the British Era*, 2.

[22]"Changing Perspectives on Religion," in Jerald Brauer, ed., *Reinterpretation in American Church History* (Chicago: University of Chicago Press, 1968) 15. Mead's belief in the weakness of Protestant theology has not gone unchallenged; see Sydney E. Ahlstrom, ed., *Theology in America: The Major Protestant Voices from Puritanism to Neo-Orthodoxy* (Indianapolis: Bobbs-Merrill, 1967) esp. 12.

in spite of them, incarnated in a religious pluralistic commonwealth.''[23] Aware of those in past and present who have been much less inhibited than he in speaking of the religious character of the American nation, Mead writes with a care that many of his critics have missed.

There has, however, been little talk in Canada about civil religion. Canadians have not often interpreted their nation in religious terms. Central among the reasons for this is the historic tension between the two major cultural inheritances, French Catholic and British Protestant, which has inhibited both from explicit overall religious interpretation of the nation. In a book written in 1906 and republished sixty years later, *The Race Question in Canada*, André Seigfried said, "If Catholicism is one of the essential factors of the French Canadians, Protestantism does not count for less in that of the English race in the Dominion.''[24] In the United States the cultural domination of white Protestantism that had divided and redivided encouraged the transference of the hope for the unity and destiny of the whole people under God to the nation. The voices of blacks, Roman Catholics, and others who questioned this common Protestant interpretation of the nation were angrily shouted down by the majority, until in the twentieth century the various minorities have matured and developed firm bases for pressing their own interpretations of America. But in the dual Canadian situation, neither side has ever been able convincingly to offer an overall religious interpretation of the Dominion. The Confederation of 1867 was primarily a political and economic matter. Grant declared that "Canadians have always recognized the secular origins of their nation.''[25] Keith Clifford has traced nineteenth-century Protestant efforts to present a vision of Canada as "His Dominion," but they failed because the churches were unable to articulate an ideology of Canadianism acceptable to those of other backgrounds.[26] In Goldwin French's summary, "Lacking a generally acceptable religious interpretation of national purpose, we were unable to

---

[23]*Church History* 36 (1967): 283. The article is reprinted in Mead's *The Nation with the Soul of a Church.*

[24]As quoted by Ramsay Cook, "Protestant Lion, Catholic Lamb," in Philip LeBlanc and Arnold Edinborough, eds., *One Church, Two Nations* (Don Mills, Ontario: Longmans, 1968) 4.

[25]Grant, *The Church in the Canadian Era,* 24.

[26]N. K. Clifford, "His Dominion: A Vision in Crisis," *Sciences Religieuses/Studies in Religion* 2 (1973): 315-26.

generate in our society the dynamic egoism, so deeply embedded in American nationalism."[27] Mead's insight that it was largely Enlightenment influence that provided the framework for a broadly acceptable "religion of the Republic"—an emphasis underlined in his collection of essays, *The Nation with the Soul of a Church*—would seem to find some negative confirmation from the Canadian experience.

In a Canada where religious freedom does not have a strict separationist corollary and where no overall religious interpretation of the nation has held broad consensus, the several major churches tend to fulfill some of the functions of national churches. How the Roman Catholic Church in Quebec has historically played this role for French Canadians has been often described.[28] For a Protestant example, the preamble to the Basis of Union for the United Church of Canada, drafted early in this century, affirmed that "it shall be the policy of The United Church to foster the spirit of unity in the hope that this sentiment of unity may in due time, so far as Canada is concerned, take shape in a Church which may fittingly be described as national."[29] Actually the phrase *national church,* which recurred frequently in Canadian church-union literature in the first quarter of the century, came from the title of a book by an American Episcopal clergyman, William Reed Huntington. The idea the book advocated had no real chance in the United States since the religious situation was far too diversified, and federation rather than union was followed as the more appropriate line of advance. But the phrase *national church* was a spectacular success to the north and seemed thoroughly Canadian.[30] Hence it was the churches, and not the Dominion itself, that have carried some of the religious overtones that in the United States have been transferred to the Republic, whether in Mead's terms or in those of others.[31] Moir has expressed the

---

[27]French, "The Impact of Christianity," 34.

[28]E.g., see Mason Wade, *The French Canadians, 1760-1967,* 2 vols. (Toronto: Macmillan, 1968).

[29]As cited by John Webster Grant, *The Canadian Experience of Church Union* (London: Lutterworth Press, 1967) 29.

[30]Ibid., 28-29. The book was *A National Church* (New York: Scribners, 1898).

[31]For another view of the transfer of certain religious overtones from church to nation, see my *A Christian America: Protestant Hopes and Historical Realities* (New York: Oxford University Press, 1971).

point in essentially political terms in declaring that Canada "has preserved churchism to preserve itself. Whenever military, economic, political or cultural absorption by the United States threatened, as in 1776, 1812, 1837, 1911 or even 1957, Canada has turned to its counter-revolutionary tradition for inspiration. And ecclesiasticism is a traditional part of that tradition."[32] It is doubtful if a Canadian Robert Bellah could produce anything like that scholar's famous article, "Civil Religion in America," but it would be informative for someone to try.[33]

In his essay on "The Fact of Pluralism and the Persistence of Sectarianism," Mead has realistically analyzed some of the difficulties of trying to effect church union on the American scene. He finds that while there is "much grand talk of ecumenism and church unity, when representatives of two or more religious groups meet eyeball-to-eyeball on the ecumenical or merger line they often exhibit an extreme sectarianism."[34] The difficulties encountered by the Consultation on Church Union provide some illustrations of Mead's point. There have been some significant occasions of church union, both within and across denominational lines, yet the hope for a major denominational merger has been frustrated a number of times. Church union, however, is one thing Canadians point to as distinctive about their religious history. After many unions within denominational families, the union of 1925 that created the United Church of Canada brought together Methodists, Presbyterians (who divided over the issue), and Congregationalists. Grant writes that in almost every case,

> unions between comparable groups have been achieved in Canada earlier than in any other Western nation, and the union that brought The United Church of Canada into being almost fifty years ago has not yet been duplicated in Britain, the United States or any other British dominion. This apparently inexorable trend has clearly been a major motif of Canadian church history, although its effects thus far have clearly been limited to the middle range of the ecclesiastical spectrum.[35]

---

[32]"Sectarian Tradition in Canada," in Grant, *The Churches and the Canadian Experience,* 132.

[33]Bellah's article was originally published in *Daedalus* 96 (Winter 1967): 1-21; it has been reprinted in several places, notably in Russell E. Richey and Donald G. Jones, eds., *American Civil Religion* (New York: Harper & Row, 1974).

[34]In Elwyn A. Smith, ed., *The Religion of the Republic* (Philadelphia: Fortress Press, 1971) 263-64; reprinted in *The Nation with the Soul of a Church.*

[35]Grant, *The Church in the Canadian Era,* 211.

These achievements have been significant enough in Canada to show that denominational loyalties can be focused on larger wholes.

The Canadian religious scene, however, though also diversified, is much less complex than that of the larger nation, for there are only three major denominational giants claiming an inclusive membership of nearly a million or more. Mead's analysis of the American situation suggests that freedom, experimentalism, and the "historical flood of religious pluralism" have eroded the concepts and premises of voluntary Christendom, and that without such common ground the denominations react defensively to union moves. All this invites comparative investigation, which would seem to be especially timely, for the Canadian ecumenical situation may soon be more like what the United States has had for a long time. Some of the conversations about further union are facing difficulties, and the time may have passed for another major union. "Realization that Christendom was dead, even in Canada," observes Grant, "dawned with surprising suddenness in the 1960s—at some time during 1965, for many people."[36] Significantly, in 1965 Pierre Berton's critique of Canadian Christianity, *The Comfortable Pew*, appeared and sold more copies than any book that had been published in Canada.

One of the striking parallels in the religious history of the two nations was the emergence of the social gospel to a conspicuous but controversial place in the late nineteenth and early twentieth centuries. In Mead's view, "the social-gospel movement must be seen within the context of the widespread feeling that planned social and economic controls in the interests of justice were becoming necessary, and that this would be contingent upon a revolution in thinking and attitudes as well as in practice." Calling attention to the work of Walter Rauschenbusch, Mead finds that in the United States "the social gospel became the church party platform of all theological progressives, liberals, or modernists—of all those movements that represented attempts to come to terms with the ideas and spirit of modern civilization while maintaining continuity with the Christian tradition."[37] These generalizations also fit the Canadian scene; not only were there many similar urban and labor problems, but American social Christianity was well known in Canada. In John Grant's judgment,

[36]Ibid., 216.

[37]Mead, *The Lively Experiment*, 177, 179.

Protestant social concern represented in the main an overflow of the "social gospel" that had come to maturity in the United States about 1895, although there was a constant fertilization of British ideas as well. Social radicalism gained a foothold during the depression years of the early 1890's, but it was stimulated even more by Canada's later crisis of growth. Canadians continued to respond to developments elsewhere, and such American books as Walter Rauschenbusch's *Christianity and the Social Crisis* (1907) and *The Social Creed of the Churches* issued by the Federal Council of Churches (1908) were equally influential on both sides of the border.[38]

The Canadian version of the social gospel had some distinctive features, and its influence on Protestantism was probably relatively stronger than in the United States. In Richard Allen's words, "No major Protestant denomination in the nation escaped the impact of the social gospel, and few did not contribute some major figure to the movement."[39]

The high point of the social gospel in America, Mead explains, was the Men and Religion Forward Movement of 1911-1912[40]; in Canada the peak was the Social Service Congress at Ottawa in 1914.[41] In both lands the social gospel encountered inner divisions, crisis, and decline following World War I. And for both countries Mead's analysis of the one-sidedness of the social gospel seems appropriate.

Keeping in mind that central to the social-gospel movement was reaction against the individualism of pietistic revivalism, the identification of Protestant Christianity with economic *laissez faire* and the exploitation of natural and human resources characteristic of industrial capitalism, we can understand why the movement tended to swing to the opposite extremes of substituting social concern for individual Christian experience; of identifying the gospel with current schemes for reconstructing society; of judging the work of the church on the basis of its effectiveness in furthering social reform; of substituting sociology for theology.[42]

In view of some of the conspicuous differences between Canadian and

---

[38]Grant, *The Church in the Canadian Era*, 101.

[39]Allen, *The Social Passion*, 15.

[40]Mead, *The Lively Experiment*, 182, following C. Howard Hopkins, *The Rise of the Social Gospel in American Protestantism, 1865–1915* (New Haven: Yale University Press, 1940) 296-98.

[41]Allen, *The Social Passion*, 19ff.

[42]Mead, *The Lively Experiment*, 182-83.

American religious histories, the similarities in movements that reached their peak early in the present century may suggest the operation of certain trends toward uniformity in recent North American history.

This preliminary look at the Canadian religious scene through some of the concepts Mead developed out of the study of American religion has highlighted both important differences and some striking similarities. In one of his most imaginative pieces, Mead declared:

> He who would understand America must understand that through all the formative years, space has overshadowed time—has taken precedence over time in the formation of all the ideals most cherished by the American mind and spirit.
>
> Among these ideals, none is more dear than "freedom," and the simple fact is that this concept has always had for Americans a primary dimension of space.[43]

As if in echo, Walsh observed that "there can be little question that the most dynamic aspect of the Canadian way of life is this feeling for space: space to roam in, space in which men of all nationalities, creeds, and traditions may settle down alongside one another and do and believe as they please."[44] The natural environment of the vast northern country has a harshness that has meant a much slower growth of population and economic resources than has been true of the United States. The concept of freedom has perhaps not been so closely tied to space as in the United States, for much of it has been formidable and threatening. Freedom has been defined more in terms of utilizing wisely and self-consciously the space one has. Vast spaces are still there, however, providing opportunities for fresh starts. Technology now makes possible the possession of much of the remaining space—and in an age of "outer space," earthly space seems more limited. As for the United States, Mead reminds us that already "Americans [are becoming] increasingly aware that their space is almost filled up and hence that their predominant conception of freedom is somehow askew and inadequate."[45] Canada and the United States share the bulk of this shrinking continent, and need to take the time now to understand each

---

[43]Ibid., 11-12.

[44]Walsh, "A Canadian Christian Tradition," 147.

[45]Mead, *The Lively Experiment*, 15.

other better, to redefine their concepts of religious and other freedoms in view of current situations, lest the liberties both prize be jeopardized.

Mead's characteristic emphases on such matters as the roles of space and time in religion, the consequences of historylessness, the impact of the Enlightenment, the rise of religious liberty, the nature of denominationalism, the erosion of theological integrity, the tension between unitive and divisive tendencies of religion in a nation's life, and the emergence and decline of the social gospel are helpful in the effort to understand religion in North America. His approach has its limitations, for Mead has focused on certain problems that emerged primarily in eighteenth- and nineteenth-century Protestant history, and has not devoted major attention in his published writings to Roman Catholicism, the black experience, the impact of immigration on religion, or ecumenical history. Still, the fact that his generalizations, formed without reference to the Canadian situation, prove to be illuminating in examining that scene is impressive tribute to their over-all usefulness. It is characteristic of him to welcome the testing and improvement of his interpretative themes, since he views his essays as "interim reports that were issued periodically by one devoted to the exploration of the complex terrain of American church history."[46] That his "interim reports" have become indispensable tools for the understanding of modern religious history is a tribute to him.

---

[46]Ibid., ix.

Reinterpretation in American Church History

Sidney E. Mead

Because the word *reinterpretation* in the title suggests the propounding either of a new interpretation or of a new manner of interpreting American church history, I hasten to say flatly that I make no such claim, and that I am somewhat weary of hearing others make such claims. An epidemic seems to be raging in our seminaries that perhaps descended to them from ancient Athens where, Scripture tells us in parentheses, all "spent their time in nothing else, but either to tell, or to hear some new thing" (Acts 17:21). Fads follow one another in rapid succession. One week it is *Honest to God*, the next, *The Secular City*, and the third, the "death of God" and *The Gospel of Christian Atheism*. *Life*, *Look*, and *Playboy* supplant the staid old theological journals, and being sandwiched in between bunnies is the puberty rite of the avant-garde. Meanwhile, concentration on these waves on the surface of the vast ocean of civilization distracts attention from the cultural winds that create them and the massive human continuities in the unfathomed depths beneath them. Defenders of the faith seem rapidly to be beating their battleships into surfboards and their submarines into waterskis.

In our old academic world the claim to have a "new" approach usually reveals the parochial orientation of its author. I remember the day in 1940 or 1941 when Professor K. S. Latourette came riding out of the East like a misdirected Lochinvar to tell those of the "Chicago school" about his

"New Perspectives in Church History."[1] His "new perspective," he said, resulted in "a transition from the history of the Christian church to the history of Christianity." Concentration on the former, he argued, tended to separate the institution "from its environment," while his "new" approach would emphasize the effect of the environment upon Christianity and "the effect of Christianity upon its environment." The trouble was that he expounded this to a group of Chicagoans who, with what they called their "social-historical methodology," had been writing the history of Christianity in that fashion for a quarter of a century, and had just published an inclusive example of their views in a symposium entitled *Environmental Factors in Christian History*.[2] After the first flurry of dialogue Professor Latourette was candid enough to confess that his perspective was not new after all. I have never forgotten that lesson, or my youthful amazement that one who seemed to know so much about what was and had been going on all over the world apparently did not know what was and had been going on in Yale's backyard west of the Hudson River. I am almost persuaded that "The Preacher" was right so far as "new" interpretations are concerned:

> The thing that hath been it is that which shall be;
> and that which is done is that which shall be done:
> and there is no new thing under the sun.   Ecclesiastes 1:9

In this perspective my more modest claim is only to have pulled together some observations on interpreting, on interpretations, and on the interpreters.

I suppose that "to interpret" means to explain rationally or to represent artfully the meaning[3] of something. It is implied that three elements are always necessarily present if interpretation is to take place: an interpreter, a reasonably receptive audience, and something of common inter-

---

[1]Published in *Journal of Religion* 21 (October 1941): 432-43.

[2](Chicago: University of Chicago Press, 1939). Edited by John T. McNeill et al., the work contained twenty-one essays in honor of Dean Emeritus Shirley Jackson Case, and was collectively "designed to illustrate an approach to the history of Christianity" that takes into account "the impact of non-Christian and non-religious elements in culture and society upon the historical development of Christian thought, life, and institutions."

[3]Of course, "the meaning of meaning" is no simple matter. See e.g., C. K. Ogden and I. A. Richards, *The Meaning of Meaning* (New York: Harcourt, Brace & World, 1923).

est to be interpreted. To "reinterpret" means, literally, merely to interpret again—the thing we teaching professors do year after year for the benefit of the hopeful neophytes in our introductory survey courses. More commonly in academic circles the word suggests a new and different explanation or representation of known "facts"—the communication of how this particular constellation of "facts" looks from a perspective other than the one commonly held. I have placed "facts" in quotation marks to indicate that of course an observed or experienced event looked at from different perspectives does not "mean" quite the same thing in each of the possible conceptual contexts in which it may be placed. This, for example, is why I have often advised students to study their teachers as well as the subject content of their courses. For one cannot understand a person's interpretation of a subject until and unless one understands the perspective from which he views it.[4]

In other words, a thinker must be grasped as a whole before his arguments and the details of his system can be seen to make consistent sense. It is certainly possible in our pluralistic culture that a theologian's or historian's perspective cannot be grasped as a whole because there is no wholeness there to be grasped. And there is no wholeness in the man because his mind, thanks largely to our modes of education, is cluttered up with unorganized snippets of accumulated information, and the only thing the snippets have in common is that they are all entertained in the same head. From such a mind a man's pronouncements and writings will be little more than the premature regurgitation of identifiable lumps of the intellectual food he has ingested. Technically the lumps are commonly known as "footnotes." Usually, I suppose, we teachers, even in what is called "higher education," communicate what we have learned with the hope that it will be digested. But many things in our multiversity systems militate against this hope—for some of which we teachers are responsible.

Of course we are not primarily responsible for what has been called the "knowledge explosion." But we are partly responsible for overpublication and for the fact that much of what is published can hardly be considered a contribution to the explosion of knowledge. And we are most responsible for drenching our students with too much information until some of them experience "a total communications overload" and blow their

---

[4] I think I learned this from Horace Bushnell.

intellectual fuses. I, like A. N. Whitehead, "In my own work at universities . . . have been much struck by the paralysis of thought induced in pupils by the aimless accumulation of precise knowledge, inert and unutilized."[5] By clogging his system, the sheer amount of material the student is sometimes required to ingest under the pressures of time makes digestion almost impossible. At best he ends up knowing practically everything about a subject and understanding nothing. At worst he ends up under the expert custodial care of the men and women in white. And probably somewhere in between are those who drop out after their wrestle with the angels of higher education, thereafter to be marked by a limping conception of what the intellectual life is all about.

Perhaps even more insidious in our era of specialists is the exposure of a student simultaneously to the conflicting perspectives of a number of experts without any serious attempt to help him to see the pattern of coherence and integrity in the whole program. Seminaries seem to me especially culpable in this respect. For a seminary is a university in microcosm, its four to seven or more "fields" analogous to the university's schools and departments. But there is one big difference between the seminary and the university, namely, the seminary commonly labors under the illusion that its degree program is a unit. Therefore, while in the university the graduate student may usually concentrate in the work of one discipline, in the theological school the preliminary or comprehensive examinations are usually compounded of the several fields. It is as if the graduate student in history were required to take preliminary examinations, not only in history but also in anthropology, psychology, sociology, philosophy, and perhaps law, medicine, and astronomy.

Commonly, also, the seminary student is exposed each term simultaneously to professors in several different fields, no two of whom may be operating on the same set of premises or viewing the overall purpose of the school in the same way. The professors are also likely to be competing, each trying to convince the students that his perspective is the only up-to-date and therefore viable one. Indeed, a professor who is not doing this is by implication hiding behind a misconception of "objectivity" while really teaching that what one believes and how one thinks do not make any difference.

In this situation, which is not entirely unknown today, one would suppose that a consuming passion of faculty members would be to explore their

---

[5]A. N. Whitehead, *The Aims of Education* (New York: New American Library, 1949) 48.

conglomeration of outlooks to ascertain if perchance it might be possible to come to some common understanding of their joint enterprise and develop a common language with which to articulate it. But seminary faculty members, as I have known them, have usually exhibited a strong resistance to this venture. I have been told by a most able theologian, who professionally was busily engaged with proclaiming how Christianity ought to be understood and unified, that "we cannot discuss that! It would disrupt the faculty." The result is that a faculty often appears to be merely a gathering of highly independent entrepreneurs, each paid to operate his own private concession stand in a "plant" maintained by a board of trustees with funds the president can persuade or coerce "the constituency" to contribute. Each belongs to his own national association of the manufacturers of knowledge in his specialty, in whose meetings he finds consolation with those who speak his dialect and refuge from his immediate colleagues who do not. Meanwhile the student is largely left on his own intellectually and emotionally to integrate as well as possible what the faculty members cannot or will not integrate.

Here may lie one explanation of the appeal of a philosophy of "the absurd" to many seminary students. For while the professors may be claiming that Christianity is a—or the—unifying force in their society, their inability to come up with even the appearance of agreement among themselves makes their claim absurd.[6]

Such a concept has meaning only in relation to its opposite.[7] I suppose that the opposite of "the absurd" is "the reasonable" or rational. In our culture, then, "the absurd" would not make sense to intellectuals today unless they were nourished in the long tradition of believing that an inherent rationality characterizes their universe.[8] This, I think, is ploughed into

---

[6]From the perspective of those concerned with preserving social order, "religion" as exemplified and defended by the churches has, for almost 500 years, been primarily divisive.

[7]"To itself, no life lacks meaning, even if, like some professors and poets, it cultivates its own meaning by charging everybody else's life with lacking any" (Horace M. Kallen, "How I Bet My Life," *Saturday Review*, 1 October 1966, 80).

[8]For example: "And yet the one insistence that rings through history, the one plain platitude on which angry and arrogant philosophers instantly agree, is that in all of this festering turmoil, this implacable tragedy, this cynical comedy of clinging indecency, we are in the constant presence of order. From Plato to T. S. Eliot the refrain varies little. Plato, never quite certain whether he trusted artists or not, was nevertheless willing to explain that 'we

their conceptual order and dominates what they expect of all aspects of their experienced and observed order.[9] Therefore, they tend to confront the task of trying to understand any one of their inherited institutions with the assumptive premise that it is a rational structure.

What happens? Interpretation begins at home, and the seminary is the primary actual household in which the theologue and his professor live. If in trying to understand *its* institutionalized structure one begins with the premise that he is dealing with a rational structure, he is likely to be frustrated because there is little in his experience and observed order to bear out any such supposition.

Suppose, for example, we observe a faculty meeting called to discuss what is to go into the general curriculum, or into the requirements for a degree. The meeting is more likely to resemble a clash of interest groups, each bargaining to get the most, than it is a dialogue between rational scholars, each concerned, first, to be sure that he understands the common enterprise, and second, to understand how what he has to offer may be fitted into it. Naturally the outcome is seldom a rationally coherent and understandable program. Rather, from the viewpoint of each participant, it is a compromise of his ideal forced by the actualities of the possible rooted in the obtuseness of his colleagues.

If now the faculty members persist in trying to convince the students, the constituency, and perhaps themselves that the program is a rational structure—as they seem to do in announcements, catalogues, and other promotional literature—the recognized gap between what is observed and experienced and what is claimed is likely to lead to the conclusion that the claim is absurd. This conclusion, the result of observation and experience

---

are endowed by the Gods with vision and hearing, and harmony was given by the Muses to him that can use them intellectually' in order to 'assist the soul's interior revolution, to restore it to order and concord with itself.' T. S. Eliot, wanderer of the wasteland, remains certain that 'it is ultimately the function of art, in imposing a credible order upon ordinary reality, and thereby eliciting some perception of an order *in* reality, to bring us to a condition of serenity, stillness, and reconciliation.' '' Walter Kerr, *The Decline of Pleasure* (New York: Time Inc., 1966) 155. See also Michael Polanyi, *Science, Faith and Society* (Chicago: University of Chicago Press, 1964).

[9]I am invoking here A. N. Whitehead's concept of "the meeting of two orders of experience. One order is constituted by the direct, immediate discrimination of particular observations. The other order is constituted by our general way of conceiving the Universe. They will be called, the Observational Order, and the Conceptual Order" (*Adventures of Ideas* [New York: New American Library, 1933] 158).

at home, then tends to be generalized and projected as the primary premise to be invoked for an understanding of all institutions—churches included—past and present.

I suppose that through most of Christian history one primary and perennial task of the theologian was to examine, explain, and defend the premises of the intellectual structure explanatory of the modes of thinking and acting that characterized the church community of which he was an actively participating and responsible member. In this situation the nature of his responsibilities and the purpose of his school were reasonably clear. But few theologians today are practicing and responsible churchmen. Most appear to belong to the highly abstract and conveniently "invisible" church whose fulfillments are "beyond history" and not of this world. Hence, they tend to be at best tolerant, at worst contemptuous of the actual institutional incarnations of this church in our denominations and congregations. Therefore, much of their written work is addressed only to their fellow denizens of the self-made ghetto in which they live, and is almost totally unrelated to the experienced order of the mill run of pastors and church members. Chicago's ubiquitous, prolific, and penultimately infallible Marty noted that one might "attend a discussion of theological educators talking about improving the ministry" and discover that "they can talk for a week and not mention preaching and parish routine." And Fairchild and Wynn, delving into the understanding of *Families in the Church*, concluded that theologians who write books about "the church" seem to be talking about something that even better-than-average members of the congregations simply do not recognize as part of their experience.[10]

But if the theologian today seldom lives responsibly in the church as institutionally incarnated and therefore can hardly be expected to understand it existentially, he does live in and with the actualities of the seminary as institution—in fact, he runs it. One would expect him to be quite self-conscious and realistic about the presuppositional premises on which *his* institution actually operates. But is he? What are these premises?

One seems to be the principle of "automatic harmony": the idea that each professor may go his own highly individualistic way because the "in-

---

[10]Roy W. Fairchild and John Charles Wynn, *Families in the Church: A Protestant Survey* (New York: Association Press, 1961) 174: "Theologians who write books about Christian doctrine have one type of definition of the church; but parents, we were to learn, have quite another."

visible hand'' postulated by Adam Smith sees to it that '' 'the private interests and passions of men' are led in the direction 'which is most agreeable to the interest of the whole society.' '''[11] It follows that collectively, in concocting programs, they may concentrate on technical means and gimmicks, for there is a destiny that shapes their ends—and one cannot do anything about destiny. They may be exquisitely critical of laissez-faire as a philosophy to guide the social, economic, and political affairs of their ''secular'' community, while implicitly defending it for the guidance of their own institution, usually under the aegis of academic freedom covertly understood to mean theoretical anarchy.

Meanwhile, the palpable inconsistency of their dichotomous stance probably leaves a deep impression on students that ought to be examined by those interested in finding out what students are actually being taught in the school. For what they are actually being taught will determine how they will interpret and reinterpret not only American church history but everything else.

I think they must be learning that at least the institution that most directly impinges upon their lives at the moment is not subject to rational understanding, and that there is not necessarily any relation between the ideas academics expound and the institutions academics run. To be sure, administrators and professors may be always ready ''to give a reason'' for everything in the program. But the reasons given, and the way they are given, are apt only to convey an impression of the truth of Benjamin Franklin's dictum that it is a wonderful thing to be a rational creature, for it enables one to make or find a reason for everything he is inclined to or has to do.

From one perspective the students' conclusion is essentially correct. But this does not mean that the institution is necessarily absurd in the sense that it cannot be rationally understood. For it can be, provided one begins not with the premise that one is dealing with a rational structure, but with the premise that one is dealing with a historical structure. The Ford Motor Company, at least in origin, was a rationally structured institution. Its purpose, conceived largely in a single mind, was to turn out Model T Fords, and all its structure, from mines to the rattles built into the finished product, was rationally built to order means to this end.

---

[11]Robert L. Heilbroner, *The Worldly Philosophers: The Lives, Times, and Ideas of the Great Economic Thinkers* (New York: Time Inc., 1962) 47.

A seminary, on the other hand, is not today a rationally structured institution in this sense, but a historical structure. By this I mean that for about three-quarters of a century in the United States most seminaries have just "growed" like Topsy, without any clear purpose or commonly held conception of the end for which they existed. The Niebuhr, Williams, Gustafson three-volume study of *Theological Education in the U.S. and Canada* fairly well documented this. The net results of that extensive study on the thinking of the conductors of seminaries are fairly well summarized in Alice's exchange with the Cheshire Cat:

> "Cheshire Puss," she began, rather timidly. . . . "Would you tell me, please, which way I ought to walk from here?"
> "That depends a good deal on where you want to get to," said the Cat.
> "I don't much care where—" said Alice.
> "Then it doesn't matter which way you walk," said the Cat.
> "—so long as I get *somewhere*," Alice added as an explanation.
> "Oh, you're sure to do that," said the Cat, "if you only walk long enough."
> Alice felt that this could not be denied, so she tried another question. "What sort of people live about here?"

Because few seminaries have an idea of where they want to get to, they cannot be understood in terms of the rational ordering of means to an end. Nor can it be supposed that there is a rational coherence of the diverse parts.

Students should be helped to understand this intellectually and accept it emotionally. First, for the simple and immediate reason that if they begin with the premise that the program is a rational structure, they may waste a great deal of time and energy butting their inherently rational heads against its obvious irrationalities. But second, and much more important, because this is the immediately perceptible prototype of all institutionalizations of religion—especially in our democratic setting where government is projected on the principle of consent, and society is organized in purposeful voluntary associations—including, of course, the religious groups.

From the perspective of the discipline of history, such associations are institutionalized attempts to incarnate in actuality some ideal conceptualized in the mind—what Whitehead called a "great idea." But religious ideals are of necessity on the level of very high generality—ideas "expressing conceptions of the nature of things, of the possibilities of human society, of the final aim which should guide the conduct of individual men."[12] As such, they "rarely receive any accurate verbal expression. They are hinted at through their special forms appropriate to the age in question."[13] Therefore, the purpose of a religious institution can never be as clear, definite, and tangible as that of the institution designed for the production of Model T Fords. To argue, as did H. Richard Niebuhr in *The Purpose of the Church and Its Ministry*,[14] that the goal of the church is "the increase among men of the love of God and neighbor" is to suggest an extremely broad generalization under which innumerable specific notions respecting its abstract meaning and its implications for practice may legitimately be entertained. No one could rationally entertain all these specific notions, for some pairs of them are mutually exclusive. So from the perspective of any one person among those who readily accept the high generalization, some of the specific notions respecting its meaning and practical implications will be extremely repulsive.

This, I suppose, is what A. N. Whitehead had in mind when he wrote that "great ideas enter into reality with evil associates and with disgusting alliances."[15] As the author of *The Last Temptation of Christ* (Nikos Kazantzakis) reminded me, a truly human body will smell of the flesh even though the one who is truly God dwells in it. Almost all of the divisions among Christians, often devastating and bloody, have been created by conflicting specific notions respecting the meaning and practical implications of the high generalities held and professed by all. What Thomas Jefferson said of the political conflicts that attended his election to the presidency could as well be applied to religious controversy between Christians; they are rooted in a confusion of principles with opinions.[16] It is difficult even for perceptive intellectuals to recognize the ideas for which they are contending when they are expressed by another person in somewhat different terminology.

---

[12]Whitehead, *Adventures of Ideas*, 19.

[13]Ibid., 13.

[14](New York: Harper & Brothers, 1956) 31.

[15]Whitehead, *Adventures of Ideas*, 26.

[16]Jefferson said in his First Inaugural address, "But every difference of opinion is not a difference of principle. We have called by different names brethren of the same principle. We are all Republicans, we are all Federalists."

Man—who is fearfully and wonderfully made, whatever else he may be—is the animal that entertains high ideals, on the basis of which he adumbrates aspirations respecting his ultimate goals and devises, as best he can from the materials that Providence provides him in his generation, the means for their attainment.[17] His basic drive is to incarnate his image of the ideal situation—the world he sees beyond this world—that can now only be hoped for.[18] His assurance that the ideal hoped for, his conviction that the things not seen will be "tangibilicated" (to use Father Divine's wonderful word) is called faith. Anyone who has ever tried to make anything is aware of the painful gap between the ideal conceived in the mind of the maker and the actual finished product—between, for example, the ideally conceived purpose of an institution and its tangible results as seen in its everyday practices. But in faith man asserts that those who cherish the ideal "shall overcome."

It is not, therefore, legitimate to judge a religious institution solely on the basis of the shapes it assumes in its everyday practices with its "evil associates and . . . disgusting alliances." These are unavoidable and, like the poor (at least until we win the War against Poverty), will be ever with us. Nor is it legitimate, on the other hand, to judge it solely on the basis of the great ideas and aspirations it cherishes and perpetuates in our culture— as many pious people are inclined to judge their churches. This would be to judge it solely by its good intentions, and among us it is axiomatic that good intentions without works pave the road to hell. Such people in discussing Christianity and democracy often judge the former by its great ideas and the latter by the smelly shenanigans that characterize its current political operations.

Rather, an institution is to be judged by the amount and quality of the awareness of the tension between its ideal and its actuality that its members

---

[17]Compare Whitehead's, "And yet the life of a human being receives its worth, its importance, from the way in which unrealized ideals shape its purposes and tinge its actions" (*Modes of Thought* [New York: Capricorn Books, 1938] 37-38).

[18]Compare Tillich's "The form of religion is culture. This is especially obvious in the language used by religion. Every language, including that of the Bible, is the result of innumerable acts of cultural creativity. All functions of man's spiritual life are based on man's power to speak vocally or silently. Language is the expression of man's freedom from the given situation and its concrete demands. It gives him universals in whose power he can create worlds above the given world of technical civilization and spiritual content" (*Theology of Culture*, ed. Robert C. Kimbal [New York: Oxford University Press, 1964] 47).

exhibit, and by the realism of the efforts they are making to reduce the gap. This "critical discontent, which is the gadfly of civilization"[19] and of all the religious denominations, is the hallmark of the prophetic posture and the source of the perennial renewal of the life of institutions.

So in judging our religious and democratic institutions (and I cannot separate the two), we note first that "the ultimate ideals, of which they profess themselves the guardians, are a standing criticism of current practices"[20]; and second, that in this perspective no matter how disgusting and evil some of their earthly associates and alliances may now be, nevertheless, of the aspirations that they perpetuate it may still be said that their "greatness remains, nerving the race in its slow ascent."

This is what I mean by historical understanding. It is an attempt to understand when and where and how great ideals enter into the minds of men with such compulsive motivational power that they are often called "revelations," and gradually through the years and the centuries they get incarnated in the social arrangements of a people goaded by that "critical discontent" that results from man's gift to be self-consciously aware of the discrepancy between what is and what he thinks ought to be. All religious activity is devoted to reducing the distance between the actuality and the ideal, and an essential purpose of all preaching is to keep alive the sense of tension between the "ultimate ideals" and the "current practices."[21]

This is the foundation, compounded of images and ideas, upon which I would attempt to build an interpretation of American denominations and their place in our society. It leads me to suppose that one loves an institution both *as it is* and for what it could be. This, I think, is the way we love people; certainly it is the only way we can love students. From this stance it is highly irrational to suppose that a person or an institution must be rational in our way, and to judge him or it solely on that basis. Yet this expectation seems often to form the premise of critics of our congregations and denominations.

So, for example, a bit of an earthquake was created five years ago on the tight little island inhabited by the seminaries' elite, by the noise of a solemn Berger who crashed in from the hills of New England to tell the

[19]Whitehead, *Adventures of Ideas*, 19.

[20]Ibid., 26.

[21]Ibid., 18-19.

American religious "Establishment" that "I take no delight in your solemn assemblies." Proclaiming in a gross understatement that he was "not concerned . . . with historical explanations,"[22] and in the context of a grotesque caricature of what the discipline of history is all about for which I would flunk an undergraduate, this self-chosen assumer of the mantle of Amos candidly detailed what was left out of his analysis. The list is so revealing that I quote it at length.

> We have left out a complex intellectual development among the best minds of American Protestantism, a development which represents a steady advance towards greater realism concerning the nature of society. The name of Reinhold Niebuhr may serve as a symbol for this development. We have also left out the frequent attempts of denominational and interdenominational bodies to speak relevantly on specific social issues. These attempts may often have been naive, but they have almost always been well-intentioned. We have left out the courageous attempts of Protestant ministers and laymen to witness to the social implications of their faith in local situations of crisis or conflict. Finally, we have left out completely the question of what the churches have meant to many individuals in their search for religious truth, beyond and even within the functionalities that we have analyzed.[23]

In other words, left out of consideration was the work of the "best minds" (except perhaps his own), the relevant pronouncements on social issues, the instances of courageous witness to the social implications of the faith, and consideration of the "religious truth" many individuals found in their churches. In brief, he built his case against the "Establishment" by refusing to consider the evidence of intelligence, of the judgment of the actual by the ideal, of courageous witness in practice, and of the religious commitment of many of its members. From my perspective this was to leave out all possibility of understanding either the institutions or one's self as a historical being shaped by the constellation of ideas and standards—with their consequent customs—that give his culture and himself a distin-

---

[22]Peter L. Berger, *The Noise of Solemn Assemblies: Christian Commitment and the Religious Establishment in America* (Garden City NY: Doubleday & Company, Inc., 1961) 60.

[23]Ibid., 106.

guishable identity.[24] The result seems to me to have been a loud and fantastically individualistic burp, reminding one of Henry David Thoreau's cynical suspicion that what really bugs every reformer is the pain in his own digestive tract.[25]

The obvious question left unanswered by this approach is: if the Establishment is as stupid, defensive, and worthless[26] as pictured, how is it that it has not only nourished but also supports, listens to, and rewards such sharp critics? In other words, how do you account for your origins; how do you think you were shaped to such acute insights, except by, and in the context of, the Establishment in which intellectually and sociologically you always have and do still live, move, and have your being? That is the historian's question, namely, what is it in the institutionalized church that perennially produces these prophets afflicted with such "critical discontent" with its current practices as to bring about continuous evolutionary change and periodically to create constructive revolutions in its life?

In its more general form, the question is the relationship between ideas and institutions—between the pregnant ideals adumbrated in the high myths of a culture ("expressions of the ultimate meaning of man's existence,"

---

[24]Ruth Benedict, *Patterns of Culture* (Boston: Houghton Mifflin, 1959) 2-3: "No man ever looks at the world with pristine eyes. He sees it edited by a definite set of customs and institutions and ways of thinking. Even in his philosophical probings he cannot go behind these stereotypes. . . . The life-history of the individual is first and foremost an accommodation to the patterns and standards traditionally handed down in his community. From the moment of his birth the customs into which he is born shape his experience and behaviour. By the time he can talk, he is the little creature of his culture, and by the time he is grown and able to take part in its activities, its habits are his habits, its beliefs his beliefs, its impossibilities his impossibilities."

[25]"I believe that what so saddens the reformer is not his sympathy with his fellows in distress, but though he be the holiest son of God, is his private ail. Let this be righted, let the spring come to him, the morning rise over his couch, and he will forsake his generous companions without apology" (in *Walden*, 3d from the last paragraph of ch. 1).

[26]"The sharp edge of the Christian engagement with the modern world is not likely to be in the parish. We might possibly make some hopeful concessions about the potentialities of the local congregation in the task of personal conversion and of the accustomed church institutions in the task of theological construction. But even this becomes hard to do when we think about the task of social engagement, especially in the active varieties that we discussed. . . . We would contend that these will have to occur in 'supraparochial' settings, some of them to be created as new forms of the Church in the modern world" (Berger, *The Noise of Solemn Assemblies*, 167).

as Paul Tillich called them[27]) and the intricate complex of customs, habits, and organizational forms developed by its people.[28] In this context, and from this perspective, the history of religion has to do primarily with the motivations of men.[29] It follows that we do not interpret the nature and place of religion in our culture merely by writing stories about the development of religious institutions whereas "secular" historians write similar stories of voluntary associations, and of political, economic, or military institutions, but by assessing the place religious beliefs and convictions played in affecting what men did in all their societies, and in their political, economic, and military activities.[30]

There is suggested here an approach to what in the seminaries has commonly been called "American Church History" that has far-reaching implications. I would not claim that it is "new"—and below I shall note that in the context of this outlook a reinterpretation of religion in American history has been going on among the "secular" historians of the United States for more than a generation.

In this approach, the guiding motif is the incarnation of ideals in practices; institutions are seen as the shape given the ideals in the history-that-happens. The shape that any incarnation of an ideal takes in any particular place and era is determined first by the specific notions respecting its meaning that dominate the thinking of the period. H. Richard Niebuhr ex-

---

[27]*Christianity and the Encounter of the World Religions* (New York: Columbia University Press, 1963) 97.

[28]Compare Tillich's observation that "religion as ultimate concern is the meaning-giving substance of culture, and culture is the totality of forms in which the basic concern of religion expresses itself. In abbreviation: religion is the substance of culture, culture is the form of religion. Such a consideration definitely prevents the establishment of a dualism of religion and culture. Every religious act, not only in organized religion, but also in the most intimate movement of the soul, is culturally formed" (*Theology of Culture*, 42).

[29]Cf. "You cannot write the history of religious development without estimate of the motive-power of religious belief. The history of the papacy is not a mere sequence of behaviours. It illustrates a mode of causation, which is derived from a mode of thought" (A. N. Whitehead, *Modes of Thought*, 25).

[30]This statement is a paraphrase of a statement by my colleague, Professor Stow Persons: "A convincing demonstration of the pervasive effects of religion in its peculiar American forms will be made not by stressing formal religious history where secular historians talk about politics or economics, but by showing how religious convictions have had their effects upon politics and economics." *William & Mary Quarterly*, 3d series, 9 (October 1952): 558-61.

emplified this in his book, *The Kingdom of God in America,* in which he argued that the kingdom of God had indeed been the dominant ideal throughout the history, but that it had not always meant the same thing.

> In the early period of American life, when foundations were laid on which we have all had to build, "kingdom of God" meant "sovereignty of God"; in the creative period of awakening and revival it meant "reign of Christ"; and only in the most recent period had it come to mean "kingdom on earth." Yet it became equally apparent that these were not simply three divergent ideas, but that they were intimately related to one another, and that the idea of the kingdom of God could not be expressed in terms of one of them alone.[31]

In the second place, the shape is determined by the finite number of practical possibilities that the people of an era and place have at hand, and in the third place, by the ingenuity they can muster in manipulating these possibilities into furthering the attainment of the ideal.

On each level, the essential quality determining achievement is imagination. In this context, imagination means the complex ability intellectually to conceive and emotionally to entertain the possibility of what A. N. Whitehead called the "vast alternatives"[32] to one's cultural and hence personal ideals, and to the current specific notions about the limits of what is possible, and the means available. Hence the perennial enemy of achievement is a hardened orthodoxy that maintains conformity to accepted ways of thinking and acting by overt coercive power or through social and economic pressures. Such orthodoxy is the last refuge of the unimaginative, who fear nothing more than the "critical discontent, which is the gadfly of civilization," and of religious institutions.

Guided by this motif, two opinions form the premises on which I would rest an interpretation of the significance, nature, and place of religion in the United States. The first is that this "critical discontent" with things as they are, which motivated the launching of our Republic and still keeps it alive, is not only rooted in the Judeo-Christian tradition derivatively but is therein and thereby given elemental religious and metaphysical sanctions of tremendous motivational power. The second is that the forms of our democratic government that were delineated and put into practice during

---

[31]*The Kingdom of God in America* (Chicago: Willett, Clark & Co., 1937) x.

[32]*Modes of Thought,* 62-63.

the eighteenth century were deliberately shaped to prevent any unimaginative orthodoxy from ever again gaining control over the society. So long as the system is working, heteronomy is prohibited. In this sense, the civil authority guards institutionalized religion against its traditionally most common temptation and tendency.

That is what the Bill of Rights and the elaborate legal structure that protects the free expression of all minorities are all about. It is this that has kept our social, religious, and civil institutions fluid enough to adjust to the changing contours of the history-that-happens. And upon such fluidity the continuous renewal and maintenance of their lives depends. In defending the right of all minorities to be heard, the civil authority protects that gadfly of its civilization—that imaginative grasp of possible viable alternatives to current patterns of thinking and acting. For the critical discontent that provides the motivational impetus necessary for developmental change always sprouts in a minority. The prophet is always a lonely figure.

In this perspective the relationship between the religious groups that continually nourish and provide divine sanctions for "critical discontent" with things as they are, and the civil authority that protects the right of the discontented to be heard, is of tremendous importance. The two are inseparable aspects of our system—of our "American way of life," if you please. But the understanding of the relationship is commonly confused and the discussion of it obfuscated by insisting upon it under the traditional but obsolete and inapplicable categories of "Church" and "State."[33] "The difficulty in the use of church-style terminology" was clearly stated by Paul G. Kauper in his book, *Religion and the Constitution*. It "is that it at once creates a picture of two competing power structures and suggests a clear line that marks their separate functions." This made sense in the England

---

[33]See, e.g., Paul G. Kauper, in his *Religion and the Constitution* (Baton Rouge: Louisiana State University Press, 1964) 3-4: "Although this terminology has its usefulness as a shortcut and as a symbol of current problems, it suffers from weaknesses and inadequacies. Church-state terminology comes to us from Europe and recalls a background which is quite unlike the American scene. It has its origin in a time when the church was indeed a single monolithic Church and governmental power was centered in a single ruler. It is inadequate to describe the American situation because of both the multitude of churches in this country and the dispersion of governmental power among the federal government, the states, and the local communities.

"In our situation, it is more illuminating to call them problems of the interrelationship of the civil and religious communities. This phrase at least makes clear that we are discussing communities that embrace in part a common membership."

of Henry VIII, but it has made no sense in the United States of George Washington to Lyndon B. Johnson. Adherence to the church-state terminology suggests a paralysis in the conceptual order that prevents understanding of the actual experienced order in which we live and the history behind it.

Closely related is my long-standing critical discontent with the phrase "American Church History" to designate the hunting grounds allotted to our discipline. For if the words "Church history" are understood to mean, as they appear to, the history of "*the* Church" in the United States, then— at least so far as Protestants are concerned—its subject content is ambiguous to a point of being undefinable. For, granted the facts of religious freedom and its consequent pluralism, the words "the Church" do not point in our society to any tangible historical entity but, at best, to a highly abstract theological assertion better dealt with in histories of Christian thought—at worst, to a verbal tranquilizer used to assure undisturbed dogmatic sectarian slumber in the midst of the clanging symbols of the high clerical-sounding brass of the competing denominations. The once-popular slogan, "Let the church be the church," provided for some a way of deadening "the sense of vast alternatives, magnificent or hateful, lurking in the background, and awaiting to overwhelm our safe little traditions."[34] The Psalmist walked through the valley of the shadow of death, and the Christian "looked for a city which hath foundations, whose builder and maker is God" (Hebrews 11:10). Both saw, and stood with fear and trembling before "vast alternatives" to their "safe little traditions." Bunyan's Pilgrim was never closer to hell than when he finally touched the gate of the celestial city. But Whitehead was not just being petulant when he complained that most of "the liberal theology of the last two hundred years . . . has confined itself to the suggestion of minor, vapid reasons why people should continue to go to church in the traditional way."[35]

I would, then, drop the confusing phrase "American Church History" in favor of "The History of Christianity in the United States," or "Religion in American History." These titles have the immediate virtue of suggesting awareness of the continuity of developments in this country with those of the whole Christian past. America, said Philip Schaff, presents "a

---

[34]Whitehead, *Modes of Thought*, 62-63.

[35]Whitehead, *Adventures of Ideas*, 174.

motley sampler of all church history, and the results it has thus far attained.'' But, he added, these results ''must be regarded on the whole as unsatisfactory, and as only a state of transition to something higher and better''—thus exhibiting that ''critical discontent'' with things as they are in the light of the ideal nourished in and by the institutions.[36]

This is in keeping with the overall interpretive motif noted above, namely, the incarnation of ideals and aspirations nourished in and by the religious tradition of the culture. In this context, the history has to do with the relation between the activities of people and the ideals that motivated them. If, then, we are dealing with the history of Christianity in this country, the attempt is to delineate the place Christian beliefs and convictions played in affecting what men thought and did in *all* areas of their lives, not just in their ecclesiastical organizations. This approach enables one to distinguish between conceptions of the ideal character of Christianity and of the particular shapes it has assumed in theological structures and institutions in our society. Ability to make this distinction provides a guard against judging it solely on the basis of its current institutionalized forms. To be sure, there is a sense in which an institution is what it does. But religious and democratic institutions do more than can be ascertained by mere observation of the everyday shenanigans of their members. For these institutions are the vehicles through which the ideals of the culture are carried to the people of each successive generation, creating in them that ''critical discontent'' with things as they are that sparks all change. The egregious blunder of Will Herberg in his *Protestant-Catholic-Jew* was to equate the American faith or ''common religion'' with the outward manifestations of ''the American Way of Life,'' and to confuse specific notions with high generalities.[37] He and that other academic burgher noted earlier fail to give due credit to the institutions in which their prophetic posture is rooted. Both present a view of institutions comparable to a paper-doll cut out of a newspaper—it is flat, has no depth, and they read only what happens to be written on the surface.

The approach I have suggested also enables us to understand the emergence of our democratic ideals and institutions out of the complex of the

---

[36]*America: A Sketch of Its Political, Social and Religious Character,* ed. Perry Miller (Cambridge: Harvard University Press, 1961) 80.

[37]*Protestant-Catholic-Jew: An Essay in American Religious Sociology* (Garden City NY: Doubleday & Co., 1955) 88-91.

culture of Christendom, and thus stimulates study of the continuity of democratic ideas and ideals with those of the Jewish-Christian traditions. But more important, it enables us to see how our American conception of the relation between the civil authority and religious institutions was deliberately intended and has effectively worked to prevent any religious group, or any combination of religious groups, from becoming heteronomous in our society. In this context we can understand that the neutral civil authority is not antireligious, but must be antisectarian—neither favoring nor hindering any religious group. It seems to be antireligious only to those who cannot distinguish between the "religious," or generic Christianity, and the particular theological and institutional shapes of their sect. Perhaps this might be designated as a confusion of ultimate with penultimate things.

I had fun above in describing the collection of entrepreneurial specialists who commonly constitute a seminary faculty. But I was serious in suggesting that while the situation they represent has no rational order, it can be understood historically. Now I would add that the general approach I have adumbrated could provide, if not a basis for unifying the enterprise, at least a context in which the situation might be understood and hence discussed to some purpose. My criticism of the seminaries is not that the professors are at present woefully divided as specialists, but that so many of them are apparently content to have it so. They have anesthetized the gadfly of their own institution while often presuming—in the ecumenical and civil rights movements—to be the gadflies of "the Church" and the social order. This is why some professorial ecumenical leaders are much more honored when far away from home than they are in their own seminary-country.

Finally, I emphasized above[38] that the approach of which I have spoken is neither new nor original to me. There would be something wrong with a historian who supposed he had originated a new approach to his subject. He appears original only to those ignorant of his history—as Horace Bushnell intimated.

It is not easy for one to delineate the men and movements that have influenced his thinking. Surely having passed through the Divinity School of this university during the twilight years of the "Chicago school" with its social-historical methodology, I had the intended thrust of the movement

---

[38]See 219-20.

indelibly impressed upon me. I remember especially the freedom I felt in the presence of such men as Shirley Jackson Case and William Clayton Bower—men who demonstrated a willingness to shed all defensiveness in examining the record. It was, of course, their general intention and stance that impressed me, more than the specific notions they espoused. It was from the Chicago group, and not from Professor Latourette's "New Perspectives in Church History," that I learned that the subject was the history of Christianity, not the history of "the Church." This view, of course, was exemplified in the work of my special mentor, William Warren Sweet.

Much later, after a reviewer of my work said that I had been greatly influenced by A. N. Whitehead, I began seriously to read Whitehead's works and found—especially in *Adventures of Ideas*—an overall view of historical development that greatly enlightened my understanding of what I was trying to do. A concurrent influence was R. G. Collingwood's *The Idea of History,* which idea I found most congenial.

But the context in which I have primarily operated is that delineated by Henry F. May in his article, "The Recovery of American Religious History," published in *The American Historical Review* of October 1964. May argues that "for the study and understanding of American culture, the recovery of American religious history may well be the most important achievement of the last thirty years," because this "has restored a knowledge of the mode, even the language, in which most Americans, during most of American history, did their thinking about human nature and destiny."

The recovery came about as the subject matter of the history was broadened to include what is variously called cultural, social, or intellectual history. Analysis of intellectual developments tends to push one to awareness of the common presuppositions upon which the intellectual structures of an era are built—and to the realization that the presuppositions that undergird American thinking have been largely derived from the Judeo-Christian tradition. Hence May's second point, that American religious history provides about the only way fully to understand the continuity of American with European thought. These historians are, of course, little concerned with the abstract truth of the ideas held by the people they are studying, but they are greatly concerned with trying to understand how the ideas motivated them. Hence May's third point is that religious history provides a readily available way of studying the relation between ideas and institutions.

These "secular" historians during the past generation have been, from their perspective, reinterpreting what in the seminaries is commonly called "American Church History." During that period, almost two hundred articles on religious developments in the United States have been published in *American Historical Review* and *Mississippi Valley Historical Review* (now *Journal of American History*) alone. This means that because of the sheer number of studies published by the "secular" historians, the locus of the reinterpretation of "American Church History" has shifted out of the seminaries and into the history departments of the private and state universities. I will not attempt a comparison of the relative quality of the studies emanating from seminary and "secular" sources—although I have my impressionistic opinion. But the shift does suggest that the church historians have lost the initiative in communicating an understanding of religious developments in the United States to the coming generations, and perhaps they are becoming relatively irrelevant so far as directing the mainstream of the historical discussion of matters pertaining to religion in the United States.

I am tempted to advise the able young student of what is called "American Church History" to take a long look at the work these "secular" historians are and have been doing. A basic dictum of the discipline of history is: if you can't lick 'em you have to join 'em—or become a candidate for academic oblivion.

Index

Idealism, 227-30
Identity, in history, 33, 55. *See also* Self
Ideology, 74
Imagination, 46, 234
Immigration, 218
Imperialism, U.S., 107, 109, 131
Incarnation, 228
Incorporation, judicial concept of, 167-70, 173-75
Indians, American, xvi; denationalization of, 128-29, 130; Jefferson on, 95-97. *See also* Cherokee Nation
Infidelity, 92
Institutions: Mead on, 39-43, 229-30
Intellectual life, Mead on, 222
Intentions: of Constitutional founders, 170-74, 175n, 176-77
Intermarriage, racial: Jefferson on, 96-97, 99-100
Interpretation, 220-21, 224. *See also* Methodology, historical
Irish Catholics, 202

Jackson, Andrew, 73; and American Indians, 121, 127, 130
Jacobinism, 190
Jefferson, Thomas: and American Indians, 95-97, 115-16, 117, 119, 120, 127; Bill for Establishing Religious Freedom, 90-91; and blacks, 98-101; on church and state, 209; Declaration of Independence, 87; on First Amendment, 164-65; as libertarian, 85; Mead on, 228; *Notes on the State of Virginia*, 91-92; and political liberty, 86-89; and Priestley, 172; and religion of the Republic, 85; and religious liberty, xv-xvi; and U.S. Constitution, 92-94; and Virginia, 89-90; and women, 97-98
Jehovah's Witnesses, 168
Jernegan, Marcus, 16
Jesus Christ, 58-59
Johnson, Franklin, 7-8
Judeo-Christian tradition. *See* Christianity, American
Judson, Henry Pratt, 11

Kauper, Paul G., 235
Kazantzakis, Nikos, 228
Kenrick, Abp. Francis, 186
Kentucky, 110, 193

Kerr, Clark, 41
Kirtland, Ohio: Mormon Declaration at, 156-57
Knowledge explosion, 221-22
Knox, Henry, 110, 111
LaHaye, Tim, 182n
Laicization, 189, 198
Laissez-faire, 226
Lamennais, Félicité de, xvii; on church and state, 188-91; condemned by Rome, 195; influence in America, 191-98; *Paroles d'un Croyant*, 197. See also *L'Avenir*
Lamennais, Jean, 197n
Land, and American Indians, 106, 114, 128
Larkin, George, 79
Laski, Harold J., 190n
Latin America, 130-31
Latourette, Kenneth S., 219-20, 239
L'Avenir, 191, 194, 195
Law, English common, 75-79, 90, 171
Law of nature, 77
Levy, Leonard, 172-73
Liberalism, Catholic: and America, 198; and church and state, 187; condemned by Gregory XVI, 195; of Lamennais, 188-91
Liberalism, political, 190; Bruté on, 200
Liberalism, theological, 236
Liberty, academic: Jefferson on, 101-104; Mead on, 226
Liberty, individual, 57-58, 217
Liberty, religious, 64; and American Christianity, x; and American Revolution, 80-84; Bruté on, 199; in Canada, 204, 208-209; and Catholic Church, xvii; and First Amendment, 167-68; Jefferson on, 89-95; Mormons on, 140, 156-59; and persuasion, 180; product of American circumstances, xii, 236; rhetoric of, xv. *See also* Church and state; First Amendment
Lincoln, Abraham, 65, 74; and Mead, 36-37; as "spiritual center of American history," 60-61, 85
Literalism, 149, 164, 173
Lively Experiment, The. See Mead, Sidney E.
Locke, John, 75, 77, 82, 95
Loras, Bp. Matthias, 201
Loyalists, in American Revolution, 87, 204
Lutheran Church-Missouri Synod, 206

Lutheranism, xii
Lyttle, Charles, 15
McGiffert, Arthur Cushman, Jr., 17, 18-19
McIntosh, William, 124
McKenney, Thomas L., 124
McLaughlin, Andrew C., 7, 10, 11-12
McLoughlin, William G., xvi
McMinn, James, 125
McNeill, John T., 15
Madison, James: and First Amendment, 164-65, 209; and Jefferson, 90; and U.S. Constitution, 91, 171
Magna Charta, 76, 176
Manfra, Jo Ann, xvii
Manifest destiny, 106
Market economy, 108, 116
Marriage, celestial: Mormon, 155
Marshall, John, 102, 130, 167
Marty, Martin E., xiv, 50, 225
Mason, George, 90
Massachusetts, 75, 79, 88; religious liberty in, 81-84
Mather, Cotton, 25
May, Henry F., 239
Mayhew Jonathan, 71-72
Mead, Sidney E.: and the academy, 15-16, 39-44; and American Protestantism, 205; assumptions of, viii-ix, xvii-xviii, 22-23, 51; bibliography of works by, xivn; and Canada, 204; collegiality and, 44; critiques of, 63-67, 218; and denominations, xii; on Disciples of Christ, 137; and Enlightenment, 181, 209; and frontier thesis, xi; and historical methodology, xiii, 6, 21, 22, 37, 105-106, 206; on human nature, 56-57, 181; idealism of, 54, 239; influences on, 22, 33-34, 62-63, 229; and Jefferson, 85; and Lincoln, 85; *The Lively Experiment*, vii, xiii, 44, 66-67, 135, 203; major contributions of, vii-xiii, 218; and morality, 179-81, 183-84; and nationalism, 59, 184; *The Nation with the Soul of a Church*, 56, 63; *The Old World Religion in the Brave New World*, 55; predecessors, 43; and reading public, 28; and religion of the Republic, xi, 49-51, 161-62; and religious liberty, 185; and the sixties, 28; on the Social Gospel, 215-17; and students, 22, 28, 30, 42-43, 45; and

Sweet, 20-21; as teacher, xiv-xv, 26; and tendencies of history, 36-38; and tragedy, 51, 52-53, 57, 58; universalism of, 34, 55, 57, 211; and University of Chicago, 21-22, 219. *See also* Christianity, American; Denominations; Enlightenment; Liberty, religious; Methodology, historical; Pluralism, religious; Rationalism; Religion of the Republic
Meadville Theological School, 12
Meese, Edwin, 169-70, 175-76
Meigs, Col. Return J., 115, 117, 118-19
Merk, Frederick, 107
Methodists, 214
Methodology, historical, viii; comparative, 203-204; defined by Mead, 37-38; and Mead, 22, 35, 54, 105, 206; Mead on, 219-22, 230; self in, 26, 33; and social history, 220; and theology, 51; trends and significance of, 36. *See also* Discontent, critical; Historians; Self
Mickiewicz, Adam, 197n
Military, U.S.: and American Indians, 107, 113-18, 123-26
Millennialism: Campbell on, 136; Mormon view of, 148, 151, 152-53, 157-58
Miller, Perry, 19
Ministry, Christian, 225, 228
Minorities, 235
Missionaries, Christian, 107, 112-13, 126-28; and Mormons, 143
Mode, Peter G., 6, 7, 9, 11-12, 13; dismissal from University of Chicago, 16; *The Frontier Spirit in American Christianity*, 13-14; *Source Book and Bibliographical Guide in American Church History*, 13-14
Moir, John, 208, 211
Monroe, James, 130
Montgomery, Hugh, 129
Morality: and education, 177-78; and Mead, 179; Neuhaus on, 178; and religion of the Republic, 180-84
Moral Majority. *See* Conservatism, religious
Morgan Park Baptist Union Theological Seminary, 6
Mormonism/Mormons. *See* Church of Jesus Christ of Latter-Day Saints